Women Ministers

According to Scripture

Judy L. Brown

Distributed by
Judy L. Brown
3000 North Grant
Springfield, MO 65803
(417) 833-2551

Brown, Judy L.
  Women Ministers According to Scripture / Judy L. Brown
  Includes bibliographical references and index.
  1. Women in the Bible
  2. Women in Christianity—Biblical Teaching
  3. Ordination of Women—Biblical Teaching
  4. Women Clergy
  I. Brown, Judy L.   II. Title
LC Call Number BS680.W7B7 1996
Dewey Call Number 261.8'344

Printed in the USA by

MORRIS
PUBLISHING

3212 E. Hwy 30
Kearney, NE 68847
800-650-7888

To the
students
whose
questions and concerns
prompted
the writing of this book

Contents

Introduction

I have but one cause in life, and that is the cause of Jesus Christ. I neither seek nor desire any other crusade. In fact, throughout my years of ministry I have deliberately avoided the one additional cause that might seem rather natural—defending the "rights" of women ministers. I have declined from speaking or writing on the topic. I wince any time someone asks about it. This particular battlefield does not attract me in the least.

It's not that I have not been given good reason to "fight for my rights." Even though I have enjoyed wonderful treatment by most people, I have probably been wronged as much as any woman minister. If I were to compose a list of those experiences, it would crisscross my entire life and would involve countless denominational officials, fellow ministers, and local churches. I have noticed that having my calling questioned is one of the things that happens just as often and hurts just as much no matter how seasoned or positioned I become. Despite all of this, my reaction has never been animosity or anger. The notion of responding by waging a campaign for women's rights has never been a temptation.

Two things, however, have grieved my heart to the point of feeling as if this issue has been thrust upon me. First, I have had numbers of ministerial training students, male and female, stateside and abroad, literally beg me to tackle the issue for their sake. They ask for a book thorough enough to withstand the rigors of expert scrutiny yet simple enough in its presentation to be understandable to a college freshman or a local church lay person. Learning that these young people, the church of the future, are noticing the wrongs against women has proven to be more pressing than experiencing those wrongs myself.

Second, I am becoming more conscious as time goes by of the enormous damage that is being inflicted upon the church and upon the world by banning or limiting the ministry of God-called, God-anointed women. There are local congregations going without pastors, and I can name women willing to shepherd those flocks. Why are we not allowing and encouraging them to do so? There are people groups around the world not yet aware of Jesus Christ, and I can name women willing to go and share the good news with them. Why are we not sending them? Instead, are we hindering virtually half of God's labor force from entering the harvest in various capacities at the very point in time when the fields are the most ready for reaping? What would these last days be like if the other half of God's mighty army were suddenly unleashed to do what God desires to accomplish through them?

This is not a one-denomination issue; it is a whole-church issue. Many denominations, evangelical and non-evangelical, are feeling the need to rethink their historical position on women ministers to be sure it is a biblical position. Even the denominations that are known for an official policy favoring women are sensing the need to practice their policy more faithfully. Much of Christendom is at a decisive juncture regarding this issue. It is not an overstatement to say that the church of the twenty-first century will be greatly affected by the outcome.

But even recognizing the need for this book to be written, I dread the misunderstandings that may result. The accusations that whirl around the issue of women in ministry are more threatening than fiery darts or poisonous arrows. Advocating full ministry opportunities for women does not mean I align myself with any of the other causes or attitudes that have attached themselves to the subject. I will not be sidetracked by efforts that focus on changing society rather than on changing souls and impacting eternity. I would do nothing to undermine God's design for the family or His regard for the role of wife-mother. I am not in agreement with the beliefs or practices of radical, secular feminism. I am not sympathetic to a non-biblical view of homosexuality and lesbianism. I do not think that women ministers have to be non-feminine or, worse yet, masculine in any way, nor do I think that abrasiveness or bitterness or rebelliousness should characterize their spirit.

Ironically, the individual criticized for leaving us with the most difficult passages regarding women in ministry, Paul, is the one New Testament minister who spent his life defending his existence as a minister. Women can receive direction and instruction from him. God's calling drove him, and God's anointing enabled him. With or without credibility, credentials, compensation, or credit, he found people needing Jesus. Whether he went through front doors or back doors, whether he had it easier or harder than the other apostles, he was consumed not by his *right* to minister but by his *need* to minister. May women not wait for *positions* of ministry to open but allow their *passion* for ministry to propel them toward lost souls. Paul did not have to be one of the twelve, and I have not had to be one of the boys to have a ministry rich in God's grace and power.

Though the arguments that fill this book may be firm and forceful, this lady's spirit is sweet with joy over the great privilege of being a servant of Jesus Christ. *He* has been faithful to me. *He* has given to me a fruitful, fulfilling ministry. I share Paul's testimony that God's grace is sufficient for me, that God's power is made perfect in weakness. Though my struggles do not compare with Paul's, I can join him in viewing weaknesses, insults, hardships, persecutions, and difficulties as opportunities for God's grace and power to demonstrate themselves (2 Corinthians 12:9–10). And I, like Paul, could include, in any document that I write, the names of *many* brothers and sisters in Christ who have been supportive of my ministry without qualification.

Again I proclaim, I have but one cause—the gospel of Jesus Christ. If I become identified with any other cause, I will be sorely disappointed and will do everything in my power to correct the misunderstanding. I am simply trying to answer some of the questions that honest hearts and open minds have asked me to address. And this I do solely for the cause of Christ Jesus, my Savior and Lord.

1

The Debate and Damage Continue

Contrary to Scripture! Contrary to the will of God! Capable of throwing family, church, and society into anarchy! Nothing but a concession to the demands of contemporary culture! Nothing but a scheme of Satan!

Such accusations leveled against the beliefs of a sincere Christian would have to be heard and felt. Such accusations, hurled forcefully enough, could result in considerable discouragement and even doubt. But could the accusers be wrong?

They were wrong in the past. The very accusations that are commonly directed against today's proponents of women ministers are the same weapons that were used by yesterday's advocates of human slavery. Some of the most impressive biblical scholars and some of the most prestigious church officials of past centuries were the accusers. But as tenacious and intimidating as they were, they were wrong. Though they said God and Scripture stood behind them, they were wrong. And unfortunately, the slavery that was protected and promoted by these individuals was some of the most despicable in human history. If "experts" were wrong in the past, they could be wrong today.

Inconsistent Practices

Evidence of error may be found in the inconsistent practices of those who oppose women in ministry. What they allow and disallow does not ring with the harmony and unity that results from rightly interpreting and applying God's Word. It seems, instead, to result from a patchwork of personal biases, convenient accommodations, and favoring of two or three passages of Scripture over the whole. The ever-changing array of tedious allowances and disallowances is so complex and confusing that there are probably no two local churches that draw the same lines.

Some churches will not let a woman speak on Sunday because that would be a sermon, but the same message may be given during a mid-week service because it would be called "sharing" or something else other than preaching. Or the message that cannot be given in the sanctuary can be given in a classroom or in a home because the one setting is church and the other settings, though just as much gatherings of believers, are not church. Still other congregations will allow a woman to speak at any time and in any place if, and only if, her message is given the spoken benediction or the unspoken approval of a man, perhaps her husband or a church official who is in position over her.

Many churches will not let women teach men but will let them teach women, youth, and children. If, as it is claimed, women are more easily deceived than men, it is curious that the supposedly more impressionable minds of these three groups are left to the supposedly more easily deceived female teacher. Surely their souls do not matter less than the souls of men. Churches that do not permit any type of preaching or teaching will usually let a woman pray, or testify, or sing. They contend that these activities do not contain any doctrinal or instructional content; but, of course, that claim is far from true. All of these practices are surprisingly elastic applications of the "Be silent!" passages quoted as proof of their rightness. It is possible that these churches could not even function without their convenient "exceptions to the rule" that make many of their ministries viable.

Most evangelical churches would encourage women to evangelize people which requires a considerable amount of instruction, indeed, even authoritative instruction. If a woman were to evangelize a man, perhaps even her husband, she would be exercising authoritative instruction over that individual, but somehow this would be all right. Many of the same churches, however, would not let a woman baptize this very convert because doing so would be too authoritative, especially if the convert were a man.

The inconsistencies extend into many phases of local church activity. It is frequently permissible for a woman to prepare communion, but it is probably not permissible for her to serve it. The women of the church may be depended upon to be the congregation's "prayer warriors" in their homes and in various types of prayer meetings; but if special individuals are called forward during a service to pray for the sick, women may be excluded altogether or included only alongside their husbands. A woman may count, record, and deposit an offering; but collecting it is likely to be reserved for men.

Still other churches differentiate between carrying out a task and holding a position. They draw a fine line between letting women teach and preach versus letting them "hold the office" of teacher or preacher. In this way, they may deny women ministerial credentials and/or pastoral office. In some circles, then, a woman could be responsible for planting a church but not be welcome to become its official pastor. Indeed, there are entire denominations that were very supportive of women ministers in their early days when ministry was mostly thankless, servant-like work; but as success brought position and prestige into the picture and as organization brought administration and authority into the picture, the encouragement of women diminished.

Women have also been moved aside by the belief that God is willing to use them if and only if men are not available. So, if a woman is willing to step into a particularly challenging ministry situation, she is allowed to do so. Conveniently, however, after the "hard, dirty" work has been done, a man becomes available to oversee the end result.

Yet another version of "first class versus second class" biases may be found in the fact that some churches view women as desirable for children's pastors but as undesirable for youth pastors, unless, of course, no man is willing to take the youth pastorate. Some churches think women make acceptable ministers of music or ministers of education, but would not consider a woman as a senior pastor.

An interesting contradiction is likely in local churches that practice congregational government.[1] It is not unusual for a church to have more female members than male members; consequently, the vote of women could control the church and be responsible for "hiring" and "firing" a pastor, certainly an exercise of authority over him. However, a woman could not serve that church as pastor because that would be exercising authority.

Several evangelical denominations permit a woman to do things on foreign soil, including authoritative leadership responsibilities over men, that the same woman is not allowed to do on home soil. Indeed, in some cases, even though she has the denomination's full blessing to serve as a missionary, she cannot stand in an American pulpit and tell what she did in a foreign country. She may have compromised her health or jeopardized her life to accomplish the task, but telling about it might be misconstrued as preaching. Preaching would be particularly problematic if men were in the audience, though men were very much in her audience on the mission field, including Christian men.

A woman is capable of earning a doctoral degree in nuclear physics or biochemistry or philosophy at the most rigorous universities in the world, but she is not permitted to earn a degree in theology from certain seminaries because Eve is permanent proof of her inferior mind. It frequently goes without notice that women are permitted to write the curriculum from which the men teach either at the local church or at the seminary level. So a woman could write a seminary textbook, but learning from it or teaching from it might be reserved for men.

It is difficult for many women to comprehend how such insistence upon inferior status does not imply inferior being. If someone limits their opportunities, that someone seems to be questioning their abilities. If all women are unfit to hold certain positions, that seems to equate with being unfit in their person. The dichotomy that this thinking proposes is reminiscent of Black-White race relations in America and in other parts of the world. A white person may see the sense in "separate but equal," but a black person may not see the sense or the equality. A white person holding position over *a* black person is one thing, but positioning *all* white people over *all* black people is clearly a claim to a superior race. Similarly, putting all women under the authority of any and all men is most certainly indicative of perceiving the female gender as inferior in some way.

There seems to be particular confusion and contradiction regarding the positioning of a woman under her husband versus under all men. The man who believes his wife is to be under his husbandly authority and leadership rarely agrees that she is equally under the purview of all other men in the church and in the community. Yet this is precisely the basis for denying her ministry opportunities; she would be in authority and leadership "over" men who evidently should be over her.

One of the most frustrating inconsistencies of all is experienced in organizations or with individuals professing to welcome women ministers but failing to practice their profession. A woman may be accepted into a training institution and enrolled into ministerial training courses in which she periodically hears the notion of women ministers mocked, questioned, or totally rejected. Before leaving for school and upon returning home for visits, she may not receive the encouragement from her pastor that an equally promising young man would be given. Perhaps a quick look at the composition of the school's leadership would produce further discouragement. There may be many female professors but only male professors in Bible/Theology or Church Ministries courses; there may be female staff and faculty but only male department chairs, administrators, and members of the board of directors. Upon completion of her training, she may be given credentials; but there may be few local congregations that would welcome her services. After all, a quick look across the denomination's directory might show that only very few and very selective positions of leadership, if any, are held by women; therefore, nothing is signaling the constituency to operate any differently.

Such a maze of permissible loopholes and selective restrictions is foreign to New Testament Christianity. Its arbitrary and contradictory rules seem to be man-made rather than God-made. In fact, the host of rules is so intricate and at times bizarre that a lay person would not be able to decipher them directly from Scripture; they would have to be dictated by the organization, a further sign of their man-made origin. Perhaps the only religious maze that was more absurd was that devised by the Jewish rabbis. In their efforts to interpret and apply Old Testament Scripture, they produced a vast array of concessions and commandments which Jesus called the rules of men rather than the rules of God (Mark 7:6–8). Though the rabbis were trying to teach the truths of Scripture, their vision was blinded by their arrogance, by their hypocrisy, and by their own self-serving agendas. May God free men and women alike of all such hindrances so that His Word is able to resound with the consistency for which it is known.

If the church is praying as Jesus taught, that the Lord of the harvest would send forth workers, then is the church receiving and encouraging the workers that Christ is sending? It may not be enough to *believe* the right things about women; are the right things also being *done*? Are pastors inviting women to discover and fully cultivate their spiritual gifts? Are women being asked to participate in church services and in other responsible activities? Are women being positioned on committees and boards and being welcomed to podiums and pulpits as much as men? Especially in light of the fact that women outnumber men in most congregations and denominations, ministers who fail to offer this encouragement are missing opportunities to be part of the solution.

Those who favor women ministers must not only act on their convictions, they must also challenge and correct those who discriminate against women. Of course, this must be done thoughtfully and wisely; but if it is not done at all, then the wrongdoing will continue. While it is true that a qualified woman is not always available to fill a position of ministry, the dearth of women has much to do with the treatment that capable women repeatedly receive. Until women can see other women not just tolerated but truly welcomed into positions of spiritual leadership, many will not realize that they can even enter the ministry. Generation after generation of women will fail to hear and heed God's call into service, thus ensuring that the cycle continues. May the church not experience this great tragedy.

All of the accusations that are leveled against the advocates of women ministers are oftentimes rallied into one particularly taunting charge: "Feminist!" The allegation is that those who favor the entry of women into ministry are simply bending to the latest whim of society and are buying into a full agenda of radical, secular ideology. How interesting that advocating women ministers is supposedly reflective of contemporary feminism, but opposing women ministers is somehow not reflective of centuries of chauvinism. Unfortunately, the world had to awaken the church to the ills of slavery rather than the reverse, and history may be repeating itself regarding the proper view of women. The church must never attempt to change or ignore Scripture, but it must not fear the rereading and restudying of Scripture lest yesterday's errors continue into today and tomorrow.

Inconsistent Interpretations

Many well-meaning individuals and some not-so-well-meaning ones will protest, "I am simply insisting that we obey 1 Corinthians 14:34–35 and 1 Timothy 2:11–12." Fortunately or unfortunately, the solution is not quite that easy. The Bible has far more to say about women in ministry than is found in the four verses of these two passages. Both the Old Testament and New Testament depict women in a most favorable light who did not comply with a simplistic, superficial reading of these two sections of Paul's letters. In fact, the number of Bible passages that favor the leadership and ministry capacities of women far outnumber the passages that seem to limit or deny such activities. Paul, himself, wrote tedious instructions in 1 Corinthians 11 as to how women should go about prophesying in church services in a way that would be culturally acceptable in first-century Corinth. Doing so would not obey an absolute "be silent" rendering of the other two portions of Scripture. Those who oppose women ministers must address all of God's Word, not just certain selections, so that the resulting interpretation and application of any one passage is harmonious with the whole, not contradictory. Select passages must be interpreted according to the whole of Scripture rather than interpreting the whole of Scripture according to select passages.

If an absolutely literal and universal reading of 1 Corinthians 14:34–35 and 1 Timothy 2:11–12 is mandatory in order to be true to Scripture, then the same type of reading would have to be given to other passages, including other verses in 1 Corinthians and in 1 Timothy. 1 Corinthians 7:8 states that single people ("virgins" in the Greek text not specifying either gender) should remain single, and verse 29 adds that a married man should live as if he did not have a wife. 1 Timothy 2:9–10 forbids women from braiding their hair and from wearing pearls, and 5:9–10 indicates that no widow should be treated in an especially supportive manner unless she is over the age of 60 and is well known for washing the feet of the saints. According to 1 Timothy 5:23, young ministers are commanded to drink wine instead of water (NIV word "only" not appearing in the Greek text). According to 1 Corinthians 16:20, believers are commanded to greet each other with a holy kiss. If two passages in Paul's letters must be read absolutely literally and universally, then it is curious that others are not read in the same way.

The portion of Scripture in 1 Timothy that is used to claim that deacons must be men (3:8, NIV) dictates just as specifically that they must be married and have children (3:12). Identical requirements are set for the bishop/overseer (3:2,4) which would disqualify Paul as a candidate for either position. Much is made about the fact that male dominance and female subordination are supposedly creation-based and therefore unchangeable (1 Timothy 2:13), but most of the individuals who push this point fail to keep a seventh-day Sabbath which is equally creation-based (Exodus 20:8–11; Hebrews 4:4).[2] Some contend that according to Paul, all women are permanently disqualified from leadership and ministry because Eve's deception resulted in sin (1 Timothy 2:11–14). Little is said, however, about Paul's contention that Adam sinned knowingly (1 Timothy 2:14), which could be construed as more serious, and that it is Adam who is responsible for sin and death entering the world (Romans 5:12; 1 Corinthians 15:21–22). It is interesting that such willful wrongdoing did not disqualify all men for all time. Interesting, as well, is the fact that a man may attempt to lessen the effects of Adam's sin (Genesis 3:17–19) by using weed killer on his land or antiperspirants on his body; he may ride his fields in the cool cab of a John Deere tractor or choose not to farm at all and still eat quite well. A woman, however, is said to be unscriptural if she desires to lessen the subordinate position society dictates to her.

Proper Hermeneutics

Both inconsistent interpretations and inconsistent practices are avoided with sound hermeneutics, the proper handling of God's Word. How one determines the true meaning of Scripture is particularly crucial in dealing with difficult passages and controversial issues. If hermeneutical principles are correct, then accurate interpretation and accurate application/practice are the result.

It is naive to claim that the passages regarding women require no use of hermeneutics. Even the "simplest" passages that young children recite are only understood through the exercise of sound hermeneutical principles, unconscious as the use of those principles may be. For example, John 3:16 is only understood with the proper interpretation of several key words. Even Satan believes in Jesus, so what does it mean that we must believe? All of us will live eternally, so what is meant by eternal life? Without even realizing it, we use our knowledge of other passages to help us understand this passage. In other words, we use a fundamental principle of hermeneutics—Scripture interprets Scripture. The very same principle must be used with passages regarding women; the whole of Scripture must be used to interpret any one part of Scripture. Without this principle, the Bible is left with countless contradictions. And this principle is particularly critical in trying to understand uncertain passages, because the more clear passages must interpret the less clear passages.

God's clothing of Adam and Eve in animal skins (Genesis 3:21) does not mean that we are to dress in sheep pelts or goat hides. Yes, a universal truth is being taught by the passage—as a result of the presence of sin in our world, we must cover our nakedness modestly and appropriately. This truth was applied to Adam and Eve in one way; however, we practice it rather differently, with cotton underclothes and polyester outerwear. After all, the skin of an ox would not seem modest or appropriate in most societies today. A second hermeneutical principle is at work in this example which affects the proper interpretation of many other passages as well—universal truths are sometimes "wrapped" in details that pertain only to certain circumstances and/or certain cultures.

Whenever this occurs, we must avoid several mistakes. We must not view the passage as irrelevant, totally without meaning for our lives today. No passage of Scripture is irrelevant. But few passages are completely untouched by their setting. We must avoid viewing both the truth of a passage and the cultural/ circumstantial details within which it is wrapped as having equal value. The truth is changeless, but the situational details, like the animal skins, may be quite changeable. Certainly, we must avoid missing the truth altogether and becoming obsessed with its wrapping. Instead, we must ask ourselves, "What was being taught to the original audience, and what was clearly understood by them?" That is the lasting truth which transcends all circumstances and all cultures. That truth should be taught to all peoples, today and always. It is not undermining the authority of Scripture, nor is it leaving God's Word overly relative and flexible, nor is it "explaining away" the Bible to use this hermeneutical principle. It is simply acknowledging the fact that the Bible addresses real people in real situations; consequently, it contains some details of those real situations, details which may be different or nonexistent across time and space. It is simply acknowledging the possibility of a distinction between a universal principle and a particular application of that principle.

A third practice of sound hermeneutics begins to surface at this point. In understanding a passage of Scripture, particularly one that seems to contain details foreign to our day and way of life, it is helpful to apply as much knowledge of the historical setting as possible. When and to whom was the material written? Who is thought to be the human author? Was there a special reason for the writing, a certain problem or event or purpose associated with the writing? Many such details are provided by the verses and chapters surrounding the passage. Other details may be gleaned from historical sources. For example, the reason for the first-century Jews' extreme hatred of tax collectors is only hinted at in Luke 3:13 but not fully explained; secular documents from Jesus' day provide additional helpful information.

Not only should a passage be understood in light of its cultural and historical settings but also in light of various literary details. This fourth hermeneutical principle is rather general and fans out in many directions. The following represents just five examples. (1) Most books and letters have an overriding theme threading its way through the entire document and shedding light on each part of the whole. (2) Paragraphs or chapters may comprise a unit of thought so that an individual verse should be read against the backdrop of the surrounding verses. (3) Sentence structure may combine or separate certain words and phrases or force them into relationship with each other such as a cause-effect relationship. (4) A word may be known to have a certain meaning or range of meanings according to the time or place of the writing or according to the author's own peculiarities. (5) Subtleties and nuances may be available and present in the original language that do not translate into English.

It is not necessary for someone to earn a doctoral degree before being able to understand and obey the Bible. These hermeneutical principles are implemented by lay people every day in their personal devotions and in their preparations for teaching Sunday School lessons. Both the lay person and the scholar, however, are capable of resisting the legitimacy of one of the principles if its use threatens to undermine a preexisting conclusion they have drawn. This is particularly likely to occur if the issue is a sensitive one such as women in ministry. A fifth absolutely imperative principle, then, is that the student of God's Word must not impose his (or her) personal bias upon the reading of a passage. Those who conclude that Scripture permits and even encourages women ministers are, for some reason, more frequently accused of basing their interpretations on hidden agendas than those who conclude that Scripture prohibits women from entering the ministry. Actually, both camps are equally susceptible to the danger of obscuring objectivity unless minds and hearts are kept open to hear only what God is saying, nothing more and nothing less.

Of course, personal preferences and societal pressures should not determine the teachings of Christianity. Instead, the sixth and most important hermeneutical principle must be followed. Scripture must be allowed to be what it is—the inspired, infallible, and authoritative rule of belief and behavior. Because of what the Bible is, it should govern attitudes and behaviors rather than attitudes and behaviors governing it. Also because of what the Bible is, it does not contradict itself but contains a consistent, cohesive message. If two passages seemingly conflict, then one or both of the passages is not being understood correctly. A legitimate solution to a controversial issue such as women in ministry must address all passages of Scripture pertaining to the topic and any and all apparent discrepancies between those passages. Nonetheless, a solution is not welcome or legitimate if it in the least bit undermines the highest possible regard for the integrity and reliability of God's Word.

One last principle is worth noting—there is a progressiveness that characterizes scriptural revelation, and individual passages must be understood according to that progression. The unfolding of God's plan for humankind moves from creation, through the tragedy of the fall, through the period of the law, to redemption. Without having to be overly dispensational, it is necessary to interpret any one passage of Scripture according to its frame of reference, according to its place in the overall picture. Original creation was said by God to be "very good" (Genesis 1:31). However, its perfection was drastically altered by the invasion of sin at the point of the fall. The Old Testament law was given because of sin (Galatians 3:19), to curb and limit sin's effects, though the law was incomplete and imperfect (Romans 8:3; Hebrews 7:19). But, praise be to God, the ideal has been made available again through redemption (2 Corinthians 5:17).

The Old Testament stands between the fall and redemption. Understandably, then, its pages reflect a constant tension between the negative impacts of the fall and a positive anticipation of redemption,[3] between what was and what was meant to be. Many Old Testament passages describe man's reality but do not prescribe God's ideal. God's perfect plan for women cannot be derived from the imperfection of the fall or of the law, but must be drawn from what is set forth in creation and from what is available again through redemption. This is not to say that Old Testament passages are immaterial. In such a sin-sick society, it is all the more striking that several Old Testament women rose to positions of spiritual leadership. God's revelation reached its zenith, though, in the ministry of Jesus,[4] the one who treated women much more favorably than many churchmen are willing to treat them today.

2

The Creation Account

Genesis 1 records what can be called a general overview of God's creation of the entire universe, including the creation of Adam and Eve. Genesis 2 provides additional details about the pinnacle of God's work, the creation of Adam and Eve. The two accounts are not in any way contradictory. There is no need to emphasize one over the other. God's original and perfect design for a husband and wife to live in unity and equality is quite evident in both accounts.

The Hebrew Word "Adam"

The first reference to humanity is made in Genesis 1:26 with God saying, "Let us make man in our image, in our likeness." The word for "man" in this verse in the Hebrew text is "adam." The proper name "Adam" does not appear in the verse in English translations because the Hebrew word can be used as a collective, generic common noun referring to humanity in general or as a proper name, depending primarily upon how the word is intended in the original sentence. So, "man" in this verse and in several other verses of the creation account is intended by the translators to be understood as "mankind" or "humanity" which would include both the male and the female.

The English language allows the same flexibility with the use of the word "man." For example, John 3:3, "Unless a man is born again, he cannot see the kingdom of God," is automatically read as referring to all persons, both male and female. Therefore, Genesis 1:26 is not being wrongly translated in the King James Version (KJV) or New International Version (NIV) because "mankind" is one of the legitimate English meanings that is automatically understood anytime the word "man" is read, and the context indicates a collective, generic understanding.

The claim that Genesis 1:26 not only *can* be translated "humanity" but *should* be translated in this way is strengthened by the rest of the verse: "and let *them* rule over the fish of the sea and the birds of the air, over the livestock, over all the earth and over all the creatures that move along the ground." The plural "them" requires a reference to both Adam and Eve, not to just Adam. Genesis 1:27 strengthens the case even more: "So God created man ['adam'] in his own image, in the image of God he created him; male and female he created *them*." Grammatically, each of the three phrases must be read as referring to the same individuals, and the third phrase clarifies that those individuals include both male and female.

Genesis 5:2 should satisfy any doubt: "He created them male and female; at the time they were created, he blessed them and called them 'man.'" The word "man" in this verse is the Hebrew "adam," but it is obviously referring to both Adam and Eve. Interestingly, if the collective, generic understanding is not given to the wording of "man" ("adam") in Genesis 3:22–24 and in Genesis 6:5–7, then Eve would not have been put out of the Garden of Eden and women would not have been affected by the flood. Certainly, then, "humanity" is not only an optional translation for the Hebrew word "adam" but is sometimes the only accurate translation for the word.

The Image of God

Since Genesis 1:26–27 states that "humanity" was created in the image and likeness of God, then from its first reference to men and women, God's Word proclaims that they bear the image/likeness of God in exactly the same way and to exactly the same degree. The biblical account does not differentiate in any way; in whatever way Adam bore the image of God, Eve bore the image of God. Everything that scholars say about the specialness of man, his intellectual and spiritual capacities, the fact that he represents the crowning achievement of God's creative activities—all of it is equally applicable to woman. The biblical writer gives absolutely no reason to think otherwise. Male and female together constitute the "humanity" that was made in the image of God.

Those who oppose women ministers usually agree that Eve was created in God's image, but they frequently insinuate that she was somehow less in God's image. There are claims that she bore God's image in some secondary way or in some "via Adam" indirect fashion. Such arguments usually conclude that Eve was spiritually equal to Adam but was societally subordinate to him, meant to be personally and privately equal but publicly unequal.[1] The Bible fails to support any such ideas and, in fact, refutes them. Eve was not an afterthought, a last minute addition. The counsel that God took within Himself regarding the creation of Adam is found in Genesis 1:26, the passage that speaks of collective humankind. Eve was just as much in God's original plan as was Adam. Humanity, as God intended it, was incomplete with Adam alone. And if counsel within the triune God underscores the worth of humanity, as is typically taught in Christendom, then Eve's worth is even more solidly established in that God took counsel within Himself before creating Eve in particular (Genesis 2:18).[2]

The fact that Adam was made with dust from the ground and Eve was made with bone from Adam does not in any way support a claim that Adam was made primarily in God's image and that Eve was made primarily in Adam's image and only secondarily in God's image. The logic of the argument falls apart. If Eve was made in the image of Adam because of coming from his bone, then Adam was made in the image of the ground because of coming from its dust. If Adam is better than Eve by virtue of supplying a bone, then the ground is better than Adam by virtue of supplying the dust. The dust and bone were simply raw materials in the hands of the true source of life, the one from whom both Adam and Eve were given their existence.[3]

Whereas the rest of creation was spoken into being, God was directly and intimately involved in the forming of both Adam and Eve.[4] Nothing else in all of the universe is said to bear the image of that personal Creator except the man and woman. But both of them are said to bear it, so they bear it equally. There is no basis in Genesis 1 or 2 to conclude otherwise. The erroneous claim that Eve was inferior or less reflective of God's image than was Adam would have to be read *into* Scripture rather than read *out of* Scripture for it is contrary to the scriptural record. According to the Bible, a woman's participation in the image of God is not less than or different from that of a man.

Volumes have been written about the meaning of the "image of God." It is not essential to the study of women in ministry to exhaust all of the possible meanings of the expression, but one explanation is interesting enough to merit a moment of consideration. "Man" ("adam") is simultaneously singular and plural in Genesis 1:27: "humanity" is one, but "male and female" are two. One cannot read this verse without reflecting upon the preceding verse: "God [singular] said, 'Let *us* [plural] make humanity in *our* [plural] image.'" The God who is one speaks as if He is more than one. And then that triune God, author of Genesis 1:27, *follows the reference to making humanity in His image with the explanation that humanity was made male and female.* Is it possible that the "image of God" is fleshed out in humanity via maleness and femaleness? In other words, is it possible that the state of unity and fellowship and equality enjoyed by the persons of the trinity was meant to define male-female relationships? Is that what it means to be made in the image of God?

This would not mean that someone must be married to be fully human or fully in God's image. Though marriage is perhaps the most intimate of male-female involvement, it is not the most basic or even the most pervasive of male-female relationships.[5] Though every human being does not marry, every human being is either male or female and experiences male-female associations. Countless circumstances may change across an individual's life span, but he or she will always be male or female and will always encounter male-female contacts. Gender is probably the single most defining characteristic of someone's personhood. And male-female dynamics constitute the foundation upon which most other social interchange is built. Though it is true that various members of the animal kingdom experience considerable inter-relatedness in their male-female roles, nothing of the mutuality and fellowship available to men and women is known to exist outside of humanity.[6]

If it is true that the fellowship between Adam and Eve, consequently between men and women in general, is a primary or even a partial means through which God's image is to be visible in humanity, then several compelling ramifications must be noted. Human sexuality would be at the very center of the Christian doctrine of "man."[7] The differences between men and women are to reflect the distinctions between the persons of the trinity. The equality and dignity of each member of the triune God and the complementariness and unity within the Godhead are essential traits of God that are to be reflected in the male-female relationships of humankind. There should be no attempt to disregard one's sexuality or to devalue or degrade the other, not on the part of men or women. Such posturing would distort or pervert rather than reflect the image of God.

The seriousness of homosexuality and lesbianism becomes quite clear. Each is a blatant denial of the very means through which an individual is to rightly reflect God's image. The male chauvinism that has been a blight upon society since antiquity *and* the radical, secular feminism that answers back today with equal venom are *both* diametrically opposed to the will of God. Each so disrespects the opposite gender as to negate any possibility of men and women reflecting the harmony that exists within the Godhead.

Instead of participating in these antihuman, sinful aberrations, every effort should be made to affirm one's own sex and to affirm the other sex as well.[8] The more this affirmation is present in someone's attitude and behavior, the more that individual is capable of reflecting the image of God. The less this affirmation is present, the less reflective one is of God's image. Men and women are different from each other but equal to and essential to each other. Without this admission, our humanness and our godliness remain deficient, whether we are male or female.[9]

Some go so far as to propose that Adam alone would not have been capable of reflecting God's image, that male and female are necessary to reflect the interrelationship within the Godhead[10] and that the characteristics of both genders are necessary to depict the fullest possible representation of God's nature.[11] If this is true, then it is all the more important for the church to exemplify proper relationships between men and women, including welcoming both into ministry. With Paul's declaration in Galatians 3:28 that the barrier between male and female has been broken down, perhaps Christ's work on the cross restores more than is sometimes realized. Perhaps the *re*-creation that occurs at salvation gives the church what was originally made available at creation, namely, the capacity for men and women to reflect the harmonious relationship that exists within God.

This may be one aspect of the unity among believers that is requested in Jesus' pre-cross prayer (John 17:20-23). Its potential impact is most compelling: "to let the world know that you sent me." The church need not think long or hard to realize that the world does not yet know about the One who has been sent to inaugurate a new creation (2 Corinthians 5:17). One cannot help but wonder how much of this stems from a lack of re-creation unity between men and women within the body of believers.

If the preceding explanation of the image of God being manifest relationally between men and women is not acceptable, then the explanation must be that God's image is seen in individual persons. Evidence of this possibility is found in Genesis 9:6 in which the death penalty is enacted for anyone wrongfully taking an individual human life because "in the image of God has God made man." (In the Hebrew text the word "adam" stands behind the English translation "man" and should be rendered "mankind" or "humanity.") Suggestions for the meaning of this individual reflection usually have to do with humankind's intellectual, volitional, and spiritual capacities such as the ability to be reflective and self-determining and the ability to fellowship with God. If this explanation is valid, it is important to remember that, according to Genesis 1:27, Eve received whatever capacities were given to Adam.

Yet a third possibility would be that humanity is capable of reflecting the image of God in both ways, individually and relationally.[12] Of course, none of these three options suggests that men and women replicate God. There is only one God, and human beings are not in any way small duplicates. There is merely a correspondence made available between humanity's nature and God's nature, a mirroring, a reflecting. This hint of likeness is necessary for a finite person to catch even a glimpse of the infinite God. And after all attempts are made for a better understanding of the trinity, it still remains one of the greatest mysteries of all Christian doctrines.

Whichever explanation of the image of God is most desirable (individual, relational, or both), what matters most to the discussion of women in ministry is twofold. First, whatever image of God was given to Adam was given in equal measure to Eve. Eve was not created in any way inferior to Adam due to receiving God's image to some lesser or different degree. Whatever effect Eve's sin had upon God's image in her, Adam's sin, of equal or greater magnitude (Romans 5:12; 1 Corinthians 15:21–22), must have had the same effect upon God's image in him. It is interesting to note that most evangelical scholars agree that sin may have marred the image of God, but it could not abolish it. It is still present in Genesis 9:6, after a depth and a pervasiveness of sin that led to the purging of the world. This means that there is a capacity put within humanity by God; even though people can ignore it, violate it , and even desecrate it, they cannot destroy it.[13] It remains available, and Jesus

Christ gave His life to reactivate this image of God to its fullest potential for all of eternity.

Second, whatever the connection between the image of God and male-female relationships, human sexuality is presented by the creation account as positive and as fundamental to what it means to be human. The biblical account is without sexual stereotyping. Male and female were created by God as equally good and equally perfect. There is no hint of superiority or inferiority, no mention of domination or subordination.[14] According to creation, then, if men are called by God to serve as ministers, women should be expected to be called as well. The church should *expect* the calling of women, not reject it.

Responsibilities and Privileges

Adam and Eve, both of whom were made in the image of God, receive God's blessing in Genesis 1:28 and His pronouncement of "very good" in verse 31. The blessing either consisted of or was immediately followed by the establishing of responsibilities and privileges for the twosome (1:28–30). These assignments were given to both of them at the same time without any indication of differentiation.

With the opening words "God said to *them*" (1:28), five tasks are introduced: be fruitful, increase in number, fill the earth, subdue the earth, and rule over the creatures of the earth. Each of the five charges is written in the plural in the Hebrew text, addressing more than just one person. Characteristic of Hebrew parallelism, there is obvious repetition—the first three tasks are basically identical, and the last two lines describe a second task. Thus, Adam and Eve were told to fill the earth and to rule the earth. There is not the slightest suggestion that the woman was left more responsible for "filling" and the man was left more responsible for ruling; both were assigned the same two roles. Not only is there no hint of a division of duties, there is no suggestion of a distinction in rank.[15] The passage portrays an original creation that was characterized by partnership, not hierarchy, by a perfect equality of the sexes.

It is particularly noteworthy that Adam and Eve were both commissioned to have dominion over the earth, a most authoritative assignment. They were both empowered to act as God's viceroys over all of creation.[16] They shared equally in the dignity of being made in God's image; consequently, they shared equally in exercising leadership over God's handiwork. Eve's "proper place" was not restricted to the home but was extended to all of creation in a ruling capacity.

God had one original, perfect desire for the earth—that it would function, without sin, just as it is pictured in Genesis 1:28. In that plan Adam and Eve were equal in every way. Of course, their physical bodies were different and were thereby mutually complementary in the task of filling the earth. But the emphasis of this passage is upon sameness rather than upon differences. Adam and Eve shared the same God-given assignments and positions. Man did not have dominion over woman; instead, man and woman together and equally had dominion over the rest of creation.[17] In fact, this authoritative activity on Eve's part was a command of God; to function in less than this capacity would have been to disobey the command of the Creator.

It must not go without notice that from the first mention of humanity in Genesis 1:26 and continuing throughout this opening chapter of Scripture, the text is permeated with the concept of hierarchical order. But in no way is it expressed or implied that man is to rule over woman. If such an arrangement was originally intended by God, the omission of any reference to it is perplexing. Man and woman constitute the climactic creative achievement of God. Therefore, mentioning any positions of authority between them would be at least as important as establishing their authority over the animals.[18] But there is no hint of any arrangement other than complete equality.

Adam was First

There are some who contend that because man was made first, he forever holds a primary position over woman in God's societal order. Nothing in the text suggests this conclusion; it is arrived at as a result of exercising logic (or lack thereof) and of applying (or misapplying) other Old Testament texts.

The logic of the argument breaks down rather quickly because it is arbitrary and invented. How has it been decided that first is best? Is first always best? Christ's first coming was lowly; His second coming will be majestic and triumphant. The first Jerusalem will not compare with the second Jerusalem, and the same is true of the old earth and the new earth. The Genesis 1 account, in particular, moves from nothingness to inanimate creation to the animal kingdom to Adam and Eve. The progression is toward ever-increasing sophistication and worth. Accordingly, it is just as logical if not more logical to say that Eve is superior to Adam rather than inferior to him. If the animals are beneath Adam, then "logic" would dictate that Adam is beneath Eve. The woman would be the climax of the whole creation process, not the anticlimax. She would be "the crowning achievement of God, the most perfect work of God."[19] If man is the head, then woman would be the crown *over* that head.[20] After all, Adam merely provided the raw materials for Eve, making him inferior to her.

The truth of the matter is that neither of these "logical" claims to superiority represents a biblical view of Adam and Eve. Both viewpoints are wrong because Scripture presents the first man and woman as being equal. But the point is well made that any logic-based argument for Adam's order in creation securing for him preeminence over Eve is matched and exceeded by the argument saying the very opposite.

The second pool of evidence for the claim that order determines primacy is drawn from Old Testament scriptures that have to do with firstborn sons. Primogeniture is the technical term used to refer to culturally and/or legally acknowledged special rights of the firstborn child, usually the son. There is considerable debate over whether the firstborn position simply involved twice the inheritance or if it actually involved leadership over the family. Though a son is labeled "firstborn" as early in Scripture as Genesis 10, the first reference to primogeniture is found in the story of Esau and Jacob in Genesis 25 & 27. The practice is given mention in the law in Deuteronomy 21:15–17.

Upon closer scrutiny, however, the Bible does not support any claim to special leadership status for Adam due to primogeniture. His sons are chronicled without any undue significance to birth order as are Noah's sons; consequently, the practice may not have existed during these early years. The Esau and Jacob incident and several other Old Testament accounts spotlight not the automatic, binding rights of primogeniture but the exceptions to it. The New Testament portrays Esau, the older of the two brothers, as rejected by God because of his sinfulness (Hebrews 12:16–17). Later, Jacob's firstborn son Reuben lost his rights to Jacob's eleventh-born son Joseph (1 Chronicles 5:1–2) who ruled over all of his brothers (Genesis 48:22 NIV; 50:18). The Messiah was brought through the line of Judah,

Jacob's fourth-born son (Genesis 49:10), rather than through Reuben or Joseph. When the elderly, dying Jacob blessed his grandsons, he deliberately pronounced a greater future for Joseph's younger son Ephraim than for the older son Manasseh (Genesis 48:8–19) though such a prophecy was contrary to primogeniture. Moses, not his elder brother Aaron (Exodus 7:7), was God's choice to lead Israel from Egypt to Canaan. David, the youngest of eight sons, was chosen by God to become Israel's greatest king, making him ruler over each of his older brothers (1 Samuel 16:3,10–11). And Solomon, the son who followed David to the throne, was not David's firstborn. In each of these significant examples, whatever primogeniture meant, the right of leadership was not automatic.[21] Even the reference to primogeniture in the law does not so much condone it but uses it as a check against the ills of polygamy.

With the biblical evidence as it is, it is difficult if not impossible to argue that the cultural practice of primogeniture is responsible for elevating Adam to a position of leadership over Eve simply because he was made before her. First, the custom does not appear to have been existent for the first family. Second, its presence many generations later or in an accommodating provision of the law does not justify projecting the practice backwards into a creation account that makes no mention of it but, instead, speaks plainly about Adam and Eve being equal recipients of God's blessings. Third, most of what the Bible does with primogeniture beyond recording its existence is to override it.[22]

Even if there were any application of primogeniture to Adam and Eve, how would that affect anything today, specifically the issue of women ministers? Not all women are born after men or are even the sisters of men (Numbers 27:8). Are women to be allowed ministry depending upon such factors? Are men to be permitted ministerial leadership only if they are firstborn sons? Is everyone in the church to be under the rulership of the eldest sons of the congregation and to receive less inheritance from their parents than these oldest brothers? Such suggestions are absurd. However, if those who use primogeniture as an argument are not willing to apply its regulations in the very areas over which it originally functioned, then they cannot justify extending its application to an area over which it has no original claim, namely, the question of women ministers.[23]

In summary, then, though Adam was made before Eve, there is absolutely no reason to conclude from that fact any natural or automatic positioning of Adam over Eve. Any such idea cannot be supported by logic or by Scripture.

Eve as Adam's Helpmeet

The word "helpmeet" comes from the KJV translation of Genesis 2:18: "And the Lord God said, 'It is not good that the man should be alone; I will make him an helpmeet for him.'" Modern versions may read, "helper suitable" (NIV). The old English word "meet" means "fit, proper, or suitable;"[24] so, the translations are accurate enough, both in 2:18 and again in 2:20.

The problem arises when any expression using the word "help" is misconstrued as automatically implying that the one doing the helping is subservient to the one receiving the help. Those who allege that all women are to be subordinate to all men (or, at least, wives are to be subordinate to husbands), use this passage to support their argument. They say that because Eve was Adam's helpmeet, she was positioned by God in a servant-like role, basically to assist him with his family and home. Involvement outside these spheres, especially activities that position women/wives "over" men/husbands, they claim, are thereby scripturally forbidden. Actually, nothing could be further from the truth of what the wording of the creation passage really says and means.

The Hebrew words "ezer kenegdo" stand behind the term "helpmeet" or "helper suitable." "Ezer" ("one who helps") is responsible for the "help" portion of the expression. In addition to its use in Genesis 2:18,20, it appears 19 other times in the Old Testament (not counting the times individuals bear the proper name Ezer): 15 times of God helping His people (Exodus 18:4; Deuteronomy 33:7,26,29; Psalms 20:2; 33:20; 70:5; 115:9,10,11; 121:1,2; 124:8; 146:5; Hosea 13:9), one time of God providing help to His people through David (Psalms 89:19), and three times of military powers giving help to Israel (Isaiah 30:5; Ezekiel 12:14; Daniel 11:34). In all three categories of use, the one doing the helping is equal to or superior to the one receiving the help. Certainly in the majority of occurrences, 15 of the 19, God is far superior to the people He is helping. There are no instances in all of the Old Testament of the word being used of a subordinate or an inferior doing the helping. There are other Hebrew words that could carry the connotation of a "lesser" offering help, but none of these words is used of Eve.[25]

The idea of "ezer" is of strength, not weakness, usually of a stronger party coming to the aid of a weaker party.[26] The one who helps has something to offer the one needing help.[27] In fact, the one receiving help is frequently depicted as not only needy but as absolutely vulnerable, desperate, and powerless. It is indefensible to interpret the word "helpmeet," at least according to its biblical usage, as meaning that Eve was subordinate or inferior to Adam. She was not given to serve Adam but to *serve with* Adam, to share the same tasks.[28] This proper interpretation of the word corresponds well with the fact that in Genesis 1:28 they were given identical assignments.

The other Hebrew word standing behind "helpmeet" or "suitable helper" is "kenegdo," accounting for the "meet" or "suitable" portion of the expression. Though the first word "ezer" may have a meaning of equal *or* superior, the second word "kenegdo" modifies it and determines that the meaning of the two words together must be equal and not superior. It would be wrong for one camp of extremists to use Genesis 2:18,20 to say Adam was superior to Eve, but it would be equally wrong for the opposite camp of extremists to say the verses indicate Eve was superior to Adam.

"Kenegdo" means "corresponding to, counterpart to, equal to, matching." The connotation is not one of being identical but of being an equal complement as with the notion of a perfectly fitted partner. Thus, the biblical portrayal of Eve in Genesis 2 continues the portrayal begun in Genesis 1, presenting her as Adam's equal. If women/wives in early civilization or in modern society are made the servants of men/husbands, if they are relegated to domestic activities, it is not because a creation ordinance supports such an arrangement.

Eve Taken From Adam

Evidently to help Adam realize that he had no equal counterpart, all of the animals were brought before him (Genesis 2:19–20). Obviously, he had many subordinates, so that is not what was missing. But each animal seemingly had its complement in the opposite sex, and Adam had no such corresponding equal. After letting him name the animals, God put Adam to sleep to remove bone material from his side with which He made Eve (2:21–22). A corresponding equal for Adam was missing, and a corresponding equal is precisely what the text indicates God created in Eve.

It has already been made clear that God's creating of Adam *before* Eve does not imply man's priority over woman. A similar explanation is appropriate for God's creating of Eve *from* Adam. The fact that Eve's body is "derived" from Adam's body does not mean that women are to be subordinate to men. If that were the case, then men would have to be subordinate to the dust of the earth since Adam's body was derived from it in the same way that Eve's body was derived from him. The truth is that Adam was no more responsible for Eve's creation than dirt was responsible for Adam's creation; Eve no more owes her existence to Adam than Adam owes his existence to dirt. Consequently, there is no sexual hierarchy established by the "Eve from Adam" arrangement.

Perhaps there was more to Adam's "deep sleep" (2:21) than just anesthetic. If men have claimed some responsibility for Eve even though Adam was sound asleep during the whole procedure, it is hard to imagine what claims might be made if Adam had been available for consultation or participation! God the Creator is *solely* responsible for the creation of *both* Adam and Eve. He is Adam's superior, and He is Eve's superior; but it cannot be argued that Adam is Eve's superior.

Even though derivedness does not imply subordination, it does have significant meaning in the creation account. Had Eve been created exactly as Adam was created, from the dust of the earth, there would have been a separateness to the two creations. The relationship of Adam and Eve to each other would have been less clear, and their "sameness of substance" would have been less certain. After all, God made many different things from the ground (2:9,19), including the human being Adam; maybe Eve was something other than a second, equal human being. But all such doubts and speculations are put to rest with God's "Eve from Adam" creation of woman.

Though somewhat aside from the issue at hand, it should be noted that no animal was a suitable partner for Adam (2:20). It is equally valid to argue that the problem of Adam's aloneness was not solved by creating a second man, though God certainly could have made two men with procreative capacities between them. Just as much as woman is portrayed by the biblical account as God's intended partner for man and, conversely, man for woman; it must be acknowledged, according to the same scriptural authority, that homosexuality, lesbianism, and bestiality are outside God's plan. True to its consistent nature, the Bible continues throughout the Old Testament and New Testament to depict these sexual deviations as totally displeasing to God and as extremely harmful to the participants. There is no room for debate or alternative conclusions on this matter.

By creating Eve *from* Adam, the implication is that man and woman are of identical human substance, that they share the same human essence. Eve is essentially like the one from whom she is taken;[29] she partakes fully of Adam's humanity and of everything humanity entails. The emphasis is upon their unity, their mutuality, their likeness. This understanding, not surprisingly, is perfectly consistent with the proper interpretation of "helpmeet." The impression is that of sameness and of equality, not of superiority and inferiority. She stands side-by-side with the one out of whose side she was formed.

It was this essential likeness, this sameness of being that Adam recognized in Eve when God first presented her, and Adam described her as "bone of my bones and flesh of my flesh" (2:23). With a slight play on words, the man [Hebrew 'ish'] calls his new partner "woman" [Hebrew 'ishshah']. The Hebrew words are identical except one adds a feminine ending. So, even Adam's response implies an understanding of their relationship as being one of unity, of sameness, of equality.

The very next verse (2:24) uses the words "for this reason" to introduce marriage, clearly connecting the taking of woman from man in creation with the joining of man with woman in marriage. Again it must be said that only man and woman are designed and ordained by their Creator to engage in such a relationship. In creation, two came from one; in marriage, two become one.[30] Both instances involve the male and female, not any other combinations.

Caution should be taken, however, against a theology of sexuality or a theology of marriage that results in unintentional errors. It is questionable to say that a man is incomplete without a wife or that a woman is incomplete without a husband. Similarly, there is no intention of a husband or a wife forfeiting individual identity to a mate or to the marriage. The emphasis of the creation account is upon the man and woman being so alike that they are compatible and complementary to the fullest extent. But their sameness does not negate their individuality and their distinctions. Eve was a complete individual, as *separate* from Adam and *different* from Adam as she was *from* Adam and *like* Adam.

As is frequently the case with theological truths, it is not a matter of "either-or" but a matter of "both-and." Just as there is the possibility of reflecting the image of God both as an individual and as a couple, an individual man or woman can live a very full life outside of marriage and yet marriage can offer a fullness-of-life all its own. Adam and Eve were similar and equal enough to enter a mysterious oneness within the bonds of marriage; however, they were in various ways separate from and different from each other. God is the great master of "both-and." After all, He is one yet He is three. Only He could create a person who would be the same as Adam and equal to Adam but simultaneously distinct from him and perfectly complementary to him.

Theological error results if either side of the balance is given more weight than the other side. It is a great blessing to be a wife and mother, indeed, one of the greatest blessings of life. But such a woman is more than a wife and mother; she is also an individual person, just as she was before marriage, with talents and responsibilities that impact the home but also extend beyond the home. One side of the truth about women does not have to threaten the other side. Today's feminists must realize that Eve was not a duplicate of Adam; she was as unlike him as she was like him. Today's chauvinists must realize that Eve was not an extension of Adam; she was as separate from him as she was taken from him. May none of us force God's magnificent "both-and" creation into an inferior "either-or" distortion.

The Naming of Eve

It is sometimes said that Adam's naming of his new partner implies his position of authority over her just as his naming of the animals was an exercise of his rulership over them. This argument contains several serious flaws, any one of which renders it erroneous. First, the text (Genesis 2:18–20) does not indicate that Adam's naming of the animals was a demonstration of his authority over them. Instead, the text offers a very different purpose for God's presenting of the animals for naming—to reveal the absence of a corresponding partner for Adam.

It was a demonstration of who was lacking, not a demonstration of who was lord. To disregard the biblical explanation and impose an almost opposite, personal explanation is, indeed, faulty handling of the passage.

Second, the naming in 2:23 is not a naming at all. The word "woman" is not a proper noun but a common noun simply designating the feminine gender. It was used by God (2:22) before it was used by Adam, so Adam is not even its originator. Adam is simply recognizing and acknowledging the "same but different" counterpart personhood of Eve with the play on words. Verse 23 reads: "The man [Hebrew 'ish'] said...she shall be called 'woman' [Hebrew 'ishshah']." The word that God and then Adam used for woman in Hebrew is simply "man" with the addition of an ending that renders it "woman." There is no indication in the text that God is presenting the new creation for naming, and Adam is not naming her; he is simultaneously recognizing her humanity and her sexuality, receiving her as the creature God made her to be.

Third, the naming formula that is typical of Old Testament "official" naming is not present in 2:23.[31] The formula contains the verb "to call" and the noun "name." Though the two components are blended and thereby obscured by the smoothness of the NIV's wording, both are present in the Hebrew text of Genesis 4:25 and are evident in the KJV rendering: "And Adam knew his wife again; and she bore a son, and *called* his *name* Seth." As would be expected, both words are used for Adam's naming of the animals in 2:19, but that is not the case in 2:23.

Fourth, it must be admitted that Adam did name his partner in 3:20, complete with proper noun (Eve) and naming formula ("*called* his wife's *name*," KJV), but it must be noted that this occurs within the fall narrative rather than within the creation narrative. In other words, if naming someone is indicative of rulership over that someone, and that assumption is less than proven, there is no evidence of such a hierarchy existing as a result of God's perfect creation and original plan. Instead, it is a direct and immediate result of sin entering the world with all of its damaging effects. The creation account depicts sexual equality and harmony, but the post-fall account opens (3:20) with immediate indications of sexual hierarchy.

Leaving and Cleaving

In instituting marriage for Adam and Eve in Genesis 2:23–24, not only did God reveal the unity and intimacy of its bonds by indicating that through marriage the two shall become one, He also provided a significant stipulation as to how that oneness is to be accomplished. "For this reason" or "therefore" connects verses 23 and 24 in a very tight "cause-effect" or "reason-result" fashion. The taking of Eve from Adam in verse 23 is to result in two behaviors on the part of a husband toward his wife, and then they together as a couple are to experience the third and final result, namely, becoming one flesh. In emphasizing the third component of becoming one flesh, the other two components of verse 24 are frequently ignored. According to God's instructions, the man is to "leave his father and mother" and is to "cleave unto his wife" (KJV) or "be united to his wife" (NIV). These two stipulations deserve further attention.

Though both a husband and a wife would normally have parents, the husband alone is told to leave his parents. And though it seems that both the husband and the wife should cleave to their mate, again, the husband alone is given the instruction. The Hebrew word for "man" in verse 24 is "ish" rather than the possibly generic "adam," so the command is definitely given to the male rather than to humanity in general. A complete and certain explanation of this passage may not be possible, but some conclusions seem obvious enough to trust.

Marriage somehow reverses or re-balances certain aspects of creation, not like a positive and negative balance each other but like two equally valuable weights balance each other. In creation one became two, which was good; in marriage two become one, which is also good. Similarly, the woman came from the man in creation, but the man is to move toward the woman in marriage. And again, both arrangements are to be seen in a positive light, with neither indicating superiority or inferiority.

This imagery is absolutely opposite from the notion of marriage causing a wife to be lost in her husband's shadow or to be left to her husband's service. She is not to be an attachment to his life; *he* is to attach *to her*, to add his life to her life. There is absolutely no hint of the husband possessing or ruling the wife. In fact, he is to sacrifice his most precious earthly relationship, that which he shares with his parents, in order to have a relationship with someone he treasures dearly. It would be difficult to portray a woman as being any more valuable than this arrangement pictures her. The imagery aligns well with the New Testament's portrayal of Christ renouncing His heavenly home and leaving His Father in order to give His all to His bride, the church.[32]

It would also be difficult to establish a clearer or firmer barrier against the ills of a fully patriarchal society than this arrangement establishes.[33] Though many modern cultures manage a considerable mix of patriarchal and matriarchal tendencies, a definitive mark of a truly, extremely patriarchal society is the settling of a newlywed couple with the husband's parents. Such an arrangement all too often results in considerable and permanent degradation of the wife. She moves from the authority of her father to the authority of her husband *and* his entire family. The biblical mandate given at the very inception of marriage virtually prohibits any such practice. If Eve coming from Adam in creation can in any way be seen as favoring Adam, then the direction of marriage is to reverse or balance this and favor Eve with Adam moving toward her.

Of course, none of this means that it would violate Scripture for a young married couple to live in the home of the husband's parents, especially as a means of assisting the couple. Genesis 2:24 presents a principle that has more to do with the attitude of the husband than with the address of the couple. Upon marrying his life-mate, he is to move his identity and his existence in her direction. It is this willingness to give of himself for her sake that the New Testament describes as continuing throughout the marriage, mirroring the relationship between Christ and the church (Ephesians 5:25–31).

3

The Fall Account

It is not known how long Adam and Eve lived in the Garden of Eden under the perfect conditions intended and provided by God. What does seem evident is that God desired voluntary, free-will devotion from them. This necessitated choice because without choice their service was no different from that of rocks or trees. So God gave instructions of things to do and of one thing not to do. The couple was not to eat of the tree of the knowledge of good and evil. If God were to remain supreme in their lives, they would obey Him and continue enjoying His presence and the perfect world He was providing. If they wished to dethrone Him, they would disobey His wishes and, instead, follow their own desires, resulting in separating themselves from Him, their life source.

The fall did not involve a bite into an apple; it involved a bite into sin. And with one bite mankind's whole being and, indeed, the whole universe was contaminated by it. At Satan's prompting, humanity chose to dethrone God and enthrone themselves, the very sin that was so familiar to Satan. The temptation began with the suggestion that sin, disobeying God, would not have negative results but positive results. How amazing that a lie so old has been so effective throughout human history. The intimation was that God was withholding from Adam and Eve something good which they could and should secure for themselves. It would, of course, require them to follow their wisdom instead of God's words. And in deciding to do so, in deciding that they knew better than God, they attempted to replace Him with themselves.

The consequences of their sin should not be seen as the punishments that a sore-loser, big bully God arbitrarily and angrily imposed upon them and upon everyone to follow. If that were the case, then any resistance to those punishments would be further rebelliousness on their part or on our part. Actually, nothing could be further from the truth. The consequences were just that—consequences. With God on the throne, certain conditions naturally result, namely, perfection and eternality. But with self or sin on the throne, certain conditions naturally result, namely, chaos and death.

What all of this means is that Genesis 3:16–19 should not be put before the church as God's desire for men and women. Every detail in the passage is as far from God's desire as it can be. The passage is a listing of sin's results, not God's desires. God is *describing* what "life after sin" will be like; He is not *prescribing* what He wants life to be like. He sent His own Son to make the difference, to change life from what it will be as a result of sin to what He wants it to be as a result of returning Him to the throne. He could not have made His desires any more clear.

God's ideal for humankind is found in Genesis 1 and 2, not in Genesis 3. And, as has been shown, Genesis 1 and 2 depict a man and woman made to be equal and made to live harmoniously. The same Son of God who came to earth to reverse the death of Genesis 3 also came to reverse the sexual chaos of Genesis 3. Male dominance is just as antithetical to God's original, ideal plan as is human death; both are the result of sin, not the desire of God.[1] Jesus came to reverse sin's consequences, not to reinforce them![2] Of all people, Christians should know this and should wholeheartedly demonstrate it in their daily lives. The complete and final reversal of sin's consequences will not be possible until the "prince of this world" is driven out by the King of Kings and Lord of Lords; but until that great victory, surely Christians should be able to discern the male-female relationships that God desires from those sin causes.

Satan and Eve

Some contend that Satan spoke to Eve in Genesis 3:1 because her inherent intellectual or spiritual inferiority made her a more vulnerable target than Adam. The assumption is that if Satan had spoken to Adam, the temptation would have been recognized and refused and the whole story would have had a considerably different ending. Knowing this, the argument goes, Satan chose to approach Eve, the weak creature, rather than Adam, the strong creature. Thus, the fall account is taken as proof that women are less competent than men.

Not only does this scenario manipulate the text according to personal bias, but it does so with the help of bad theology and bad logic. It is bad theology to interpret the fall of Adam or Eve as indicative of inherent inferiority. God did not create any inferior creatures, not even one. His assessment of the entire creation was that it was "very good" (Genesis 1:31). That's quite an appraisal from the greatest perfectionist to ever create a masterpiece! If Eve was inferior, then Adam was equally inferior because there is nothing in the Genesis 1 and 2 creation account to indicate that they differed other than in their sexuality. Their essential sameness and equality are made quite clear by the text. The truth is that neither Adam nor Eve was inferior. The fall was a result of both individuals exercising their freedom of choice which was very much under God's pronouncement of "very good."

It would be most difficult to build a solid case for the inherent intellectual or spiritual inferiority of women in light of the evidence to the contrary found in the Old Testament, in the New Testament, and throughout history. When God's people Israel sent twelve select leaders to spy out the Promised Land (Numbers 13:3), ten of those men were not able to believe that God could give Israel the land. Their lack of faith was so repulsive to God that they were struck dead by a plague. When Israel approached Canaan the second time with an almost identical number of people, a heathen harlot was able to proclaim that God had already given the land to them (Joshua 2:9). Because of such faith her life was spared, and she was given the great honor of becoming one of Jesus' ancestors (Matthew 1:5). In preparation for the eventual coming of the Messiah, an angel appeared before the priest Zechariah and told him to expect a birth though the mother-to-be had been barren. His response was disbelief which was met by nine months of punishment (Luke 1:20). Shortly thereafter an angel appeared before a lowly maiden and told her to expect a birth though the mother-to-be would be a virgin. Her response was belief which was heralded as follows: "Blessed is she who has believed that what the Lord has said to her will be accomplished!" (Luke 1:45).

Are all women intellectually and spiritually inferior to all men? Surely the ten tribal leaders had an advantage over the heathen harlot, but she was perceptive and they were not. Surely the temple priest had an advantage over the lowly maiden, but she was responsive and he was not. Throughout history, if given enough opportunity, women have stood side-by-side with men in insight and in accomplishment, both in the intellectual and in the spiritual arenas. Any claim to the inherent incompetencies of women simply does not stand up against the reality of the biblical and historical record.

It is possible to locate women, many women, unfortunately, who have never been given adequate opportunities to develop their innate abilities. Even today in cultures and in sub-cultures around the world there are little girls who are never encouraged to wonder, who are never challenged to think. In fact, any such endeavors are labeled as inappropriate and are sharply rebuked. As a result, by adulthood the women of these societies seem dull and dense in comparison to the curious, clever men who function so impressively all around them. But their incompetence is not inherent within their gender; it is the end result of years of conditioning that stifles to extinction their inborn abilities. The same treatment would produce the same results in the male gender.

It has been said that the vast majority of spiritual leaders throughout history have been men, that the thinkers and doers in every field of study or enterprise have been, for the most part, men. Is this proof of anything? It is proof that religious and cultural prejudice has crippled half of society's valuable resources throughout most of history. How tragic to realize that this need not have been. What would the world have been like had the other half of the human population been given adequate encouragement and opportunity to develop their God-given talents?

A further problem with the argument that claims Satan's speaking to Eve implies her inferiority is that it is just as logical, if not more logical, to argue the very opposite. It is just as logical to claim that Satan was aware of Eve's superiority, perhaps due to her creation being the culmination of God's creative work, and that he was equally aware of Adam's tendency to follow her lead. Knowing if he approached Adam first, he would still have to persuade Eve, he, instead, chose to approach the stronger individual, Eve, knowing that the weaker individual, Adam, would follow. After all, if Eve was able to convince Adam to disobey God, then isn't that proof that her mind was capable of outwitting his mind? So who was superior to whom?

Actually, any and all arguments based upon who was approached first may be mute because there is strong evidence that Satan approached Adam and Eve together.

Of course, only the serpent and Eve speak. However, when the serpent speaks to the woman it uses the plural "you," not the feminine singular "you." Contemporary English employs only the one word "you" to signify one or more than one person. The King James Version, though, retains the now archaic plural "ye": "Ye may not eat," "Ye will surely not die," and "ye will be like God." As well, the [Hebrew] text reads: "your (pl) eyes will be opened." God had used the singular "you" ("thou") in Genesis 2:16 when speaking only to Adam. Thus, the serpent is not merely repeating God's command. Probably the serpent employs the plural "you" because it wants to ensure Adam falls along with Eve. It may also be possible that the serpent employs the plural "you" because it addresses Adam as well as Eve. Adam may have been present although not speaking.

The possibility that Adam is present during the dialogue is confirmed in verse 6. After Eve eats the fruit, she gives it to her husband "with her," as in the King James Version. Many English translations tend to omit the words "with her" ('mmah) because they are difficult to translate. In English they appear unnecessary. But, in Hebrew they are also unnecessary, unless the writer wants to specify that Adam was present with Eve.[3]

Verse 7 of Genesis 3 sounds as if the eating of the fruit by both Adam and Eve occurred at essentially the same time, of course meaning that they were together for the eating, and the text seems to intimate that the temptation and the eating were one continuous event. So the evidence is more supportive of the serpent approaching Adam and Eve together than of an initial encounter between only the serpent and Eve.

Consequently, any contention that Satan's approaching of Eve implies inferiority or superiority is not worth entertaining. Even if Satan did converse with Eve without Adam being present, it is no more indicative of inferiority than it is indicative of superiority. It is indicative of neither.

Innate competencies aside, there still may be a difference between Satan's tempting of the two individuals, and the difference may explain why Satan addressed his remarks to Eve. If, as the text seems to indicate, God forbid eating from the one tree (2:16–17, using the Hebrew singular "you" which KJV reflects with "thou") before the creation of Eve (2:18–22), then her knowledge of God's stipulations may have been secondhand, via Adam. This may explain why her rendition of the command (3:2–3) seems to add stipulations that do not appear in the original version (2:16–17). Interestingly, the serpent asked, "Did God really say, 'You must not eat from any tree in the garden'?" Perhaps Satan was hoping that a second-hand account would be less reliable or less convincing; maybe that's why he spoke directly to Eve instead of Adam.

Caution must be taken against saying that God left Eve more vulnerable than Adam. Eve was no more vulnerable than any modern-day Christian who must receive all accounts second-hand through the prophets and apostles. Just as today's Christian is fully capable of believing and obeying, it must be assumed that Eve was left fully capable of the same even though she may have heard God's commands second-hand through Adam. Satan *perceiving* her as being more vulnerable does not mean she was more vulnerable. Proof of this is found in the very fact that Adam, having heard God's prohibition with his own ears, did the very same thing Eve did, and did so without a single word of debate or protest.

Eve's Influence Upon Adam

It has been relatively easy over the centuries to argue that the weight of the fall rests upon Eve's shoulders. Not only did Satan address his comments to her, but after she partook of the fruit she gave some to her husband. Thus, Eve is said to be depicted by Scripture as Adam's temptress, Adam's downfall. This "biblical indictment" is all many have needed to dump enormous amounts of guilt and punishment upon all women thereafter and forevermore. Inexcusable treatment of women has been justified, and inaccurate interpretations of other biblical passages have been defended by this understanding of the fall.

Unfortunately, this "understanding" is more of a misunderstanding than it is an understanding. The erroneous impressions and behaviors it produces are all too similar to others that have wrecked havoc upon society, frequently in the name of Christ. Christians should be able to recognize the error of labeling Jews as "Jesus-killers!" Christians should be equally capable of recognizing the fallacy of viewing women as "Adam-tempters."

The Eve-blaming camp claims that Genesis 3 records the first instance of male-female role reversal, that Eve violated God's prescribed scheme of authority by stepping into Adam's leadership role. Not only did she act independently by deciding to partake of the fruit, which alone would have been a serious violation, but also she grabbed her husband's reign over himself by tempting him to partake, which is the worse possible violation. From this interpretation of the account, it is easy to argue that men should never again relinquish to women their God-given prerogatives of leadership over the human race and that women should never again try to seize that authority.

In order for this interpretation to be accurate, however, it would have to have the support of the biblical text, which it does not have. It has already been shown that no aspect of creation positioned Adam in authority over Eve, not as male over female, not even as husband over wife. Both are positioned over the rest of creation and both are positioned under their Creator, but there is no indication of any hierarchy between the two creatures. Not only does the creation account fail to support the faulty interpretation, the rest of the Bible also fails to support it and, in fact, suggests a very different view.

It is best to let Scripture speak for itself as what was and what was not done wrong in the Garden. After the two had sinned, God approached Adam first. Advocates of male dominance claim that this is indication of Adam's leadership role, a contention that will be refuted below. What is pertinent to the issue at hand is God's description of what Adam did wrong: "Have you eaten from the tree that I commanded you not to eat from?" (3:11) God had given only one restriction, not to eat of a certain tree, and Adam had violated that command. Adam had disobeyed God; that was his sin. God had not said anything about Adam leading his wife or listening to his wife. God's inquiry was not, "Have you sinned by failing to lead your wife though I told you to lead her?" or "Have you sinned by listening to your wife though I told you not to listen to her?" The question was not, "Have you let Eve take authority?"[4] Adam's sin had nothing to do with influence or authority; it had to do with disobedience, *his* disobedience of God's direct command about the tree.

Only after Adam offers the excuse of Eve's role (3:12), does God comply and corner him with the double indictment, "Because you listened to your wife and ate from the tree about which I commanded you, 'You must not eat of it...'" (3:17). Such an accusation may be taken in either of two ways: either the act of listening was in itself wrong, thus, Adam was guilty of two sins, listening and eating; or the listening was wrong only because the content of the advice was faulty, leaving Adam guilty of the one sin of eating the fruit. Because there had been no command against listening and because the rest of Scripture faults Adam not for obeying Eve but for disobeying God, it can only be assumed that God was still accusing Adam of the same one thing—eating of the forbidden fruit. "Listening to his wife only provided the occasion for the sin."[5] The sin was disobeying God's direct command about the fruit.

Parents are known to preface a corrective remark to one of their children with a somewhat similar statement, "Because you listened to your brother...," and then some punishment follows. The parent is not saying it was wrong and it will always be wrong to listen to the sibling. The parent is saying it was wrong to listen on that occasion *because* the advice was wrong. The listening is not inherently wrong; it only becomes wrong if the content of the counsel is wrong. Even if a spiritual leader had been present in the Garden, it would have been wrong to listen to that spiritual leader had the advice been wrong; and yet it is certainly not wrong to listen to spiritual leaders.

It is interesting to notice that many men are still trying to do the very same thing that Adam did, namely, shift the bulk of the blame for sin onto Eve. Adam's response to God's inquiry was: "The woman you put here with me—she gave me some fruit from the tree, and I ate it" (3:12). Actually, he was also trying to blame God by saying, "the woman *you* put here with me." If sin does indeed destroy, it makes sense that immediately upon sin entering the world, Adam's relationship with God and with Eve showed signs of serious deterioration. So it was not some mandate of God in 3:16 that first placed Adam over Eve; it was Adam himself in 3:12, as a direct result of sin, who ended the unity and equality that the couple had originally enjoyed by trying to portray himself as better than Eve.

After confronting Adam, God confronted Eve with the simple question, "What is this you have done?" (3:13). Obviously, there is no rebuke for acting independently of her husband, for suggesting that her husband follow her lead, or for anything else having to do with role reversal or violating sexual hierarchy or seizing male prerogatives or assuming leadership. If it is Eve's great sin, it is amazingly absent from the text.

Even though it is true that witnessing someone else's behavior can press an individual to act in a similar way, the Bible never represents Eve as Adam's tempter. As a matter of fact, the

Bible seems to say that Adam and Eve were guilty of two somewhat different things, making it difficult if not impossible for Eve's behavior to be fully responsible for Adam's behavior. Yes, both ate of the forbidden fruit, first Eve and then Adam. But Eve's sin was due to deception while Adam's sin was due to defiance. And because of the differences, the scriptural account does not rest the weight of sin on Eve's shoulders but on Adam's shoulders. How different this is from the interpretation that men have plagued women with for centuries.

Deception Versus Defiance

According to Scripture, both Adam and Eve were guilty of sin (Romans 5:14; 1 Timothy 2:14), and both experienced terrible consequences because sin entered the world (Genesis 3:16–19). Because they share that world with Adam and Eve, men and women today continue to experience sin's presence and sin's effects. And yet, Scripture differentiates considerably between the two's actions. Though no attempt is being made to in any way exonerate Eve, the Bible does not agree with the tendency of tradition to overly blame her. Further, perhaps surprisingly, the Bible does not even seem to equally blame her.

Debate continues as to whether Eve, like Adam, was trying to shift blame or was simply giving an accurate account when she responded to God's inquiry of, "What is this you have done?" (3:13) with, "The serpent deceived me, and I ate" (3:13). That is exactly what occurred. Satan, whose native language is deceit (John 8:44) and who is a most skillful masquerader (2 Corinthians 11:14), deceived, tricked, fooled Eve into sinning. This master of trickery faced his greatest opponent when he attacked Jesus in the wilderness. Presumably on that occasion he must have used his most powerful weapon. And interestingly, that weapon, misrepresenting God's Word, is the very weapon he wielded against Eve. The result? The New Testament says, "Eve was deceived by the serpent's cunning" (2 Corinthians 11:3), and, "it was the woman who was deceived and became a sinner" (1 Timothy 2:14).

It is true that Eve must have been capable of resisting Satan's temptation. God would not have left her without the ability to do so, and the capacity to decide in either direction would have been a necessary part of her free-will nature. So Eve could have and should have resisted the temptation, but this does not change the fact that Adam's sin is treated by Scripture as more serious and significant. The major difference is that Adam is not said to have been deceived, not by Eve or by Satan. In fact, the Bible states very emphatically, "Adam was not the one deceived" (1 Timothy 2:14). This means that Adam sinned knowingly and defiantly. Eve didn't seize control of his faculties; with his eyes fully open, Adam chose to disregard and defy a direct command of God. This is, indeed, an odd way to earn the exaltation of the male gender.

Evidently there is enough difference between the couple's sins that the Bible specifically identifies Adam—not Eve, not Adam and Eve together, but Adam alone—as being responsible for the sin and the death that is present in the world today. Romans 5:12 states: "…sin entered the world through one man, and death through sin, and in this way death came to all men, because all sinned." It is true that the "all men" of this passage is a clear reference to all humanity, male and female. It is, therefore, possible for the "one man" of the passage to be speaking in equally general, generic terms of both Adam and Eve (though hardly likely that such a masculine term would be used to refer to Eve alone). The Greek word "anthropos," a form of which is used for "man" in this verse, is used in Paul's writings in both ways, as a reference to one individual male and as a reference to humanity, the vast majority of times referring to humanity. But verse 14 seems to specify that the discussion is focusing upon Adam, thus, clarifying which use of "anthropos" verse 12 intends. And unlike in the Hebrew Old Testament, in the Greek language "adam" does not have the dual rendering of a proper noun and a common noun. In Greek it can only mean the proper name of an individual male.

1 Corinthians 15:22 states: "For as in Adam all die, so in Christ all will be made alive." There is absolutely no room in this passage for any reference to Eve, neither individually nor collectively. Paul is saying that the individual man Adam is as responsible for death as the individual man Christ is responsible for life. It is a weak argument to claim that Paul is simply using poetic language in this verse, that he is desiring a parallel to the man Christ so he refers to the man Adam even though everyone knows that Eve is the real culprit. Paul does use various literary techniques in his writings, but he never sacrifices clarity and accuracy, especially in dealing with weighty theological matters, for the sake of poetry. Adam is undeniably

implicated by Scripture as introducing sin and its awful consequence, death, into the world.

Consistent with the New Testament, death is not mentioned
in God's words to Eve in Genesis 3:16 but in His words to Adam
in 3:17–19. God had said that death would result from sin (2:17).
If Eve was solely or evenly equally responsible for introducing
sin into the world, it is odd that no mention of death is found in
God's response to her. Of course, Eve and every woman after her
must experience death once it is present. But it is in God's words
to Adam that this direct consequence of sin is announced. So,
both the Old Testament and the New Testament differentiate
between what Adam did and what Eve did. And, though it would
not in itself justify any binding conclusions, it is interesting that
God's words to the serpent in 3:14–15 open with a "because"
reference to what it did, and God's words to Adam in 3:17–19
open with a "because" reference to what he did, but no such
preface is given to God's words to Eve in 3:16.[6]

Regardless of our complete understanding or our personal
approval, the Bible differentiates between Eve's sin which was
a result of Satan's deceit and Adam's sin which was a result of
his own deliberate defiance. It is also worth remembering that
Adam definitely received the prohibition about the tree directly from God; whereas, Eve probably received it indirectly
through Adam. Though both could have and should have
refused to sin, "from the one who has been entrusted with
much, much more will be asked" (Luke 12:48). How can
Scripture indicate greater culpability on Adam's part, but
Christian tradition insist upon greater culpability on Eve's
part? And if someone dares to suggest that the centuries of
blame upon womankind should be removed and the resulting
stereotyping and stigmatizing should be stopped, that someone will very likely be accused of bending to societal pressures.
Why not, instead, applaud that person for advocating scriptural teachings?

Adam, Priest of Eden?

As mentioned earlier, God's approaching of Adam first after
the fall has been misconstrued by some as meaning that Adam
was in some way Eve's spiritual guardian, somewhat of a priest
of Eden. This is an erroneous interpretation on three counts.
First, God did not approach Adam on behalf of Eve; He ap-

proached Adam solely on behalf of Adam. In 3:9 God "called to
the man, 'Where are you [singular]?'" In 3:11 God said, "Who
told you [singular] that you [singular] were naked? Have you
[singular] eaten from the tree that I commanded you [singular]
not to eat from?" God is clearly inquiring of Adam as an
individual rather than as Eve's representative.[7] Though Eve
had eaten of the fruit, had felt naked, had participated in sewing
clothing, had heard God's voice, all side-by-side with Adam, and
though Eve was hiding with Adam, God says nothing and asks
nothing about her. Not only is God not looking to Adam to
represent Eve, He is rather conspicuously omitting Eve from
His encounter with Adam.

Second, Adam did not function in any way as Eve's spiritual
overseer, in fact, far from it. When his hiding was questioned,
he explained only his own behavior, not his wife's: "I [singular]
heard you in the garden, and I [singular] was afraid because I
[singular] was naked; so I [singular] hid" (3:10). When his sin
was investigated, he did even worse. Rather than acting as
Eve's priest, he acted as her accuser: "The woman you put here
with me—she gave me some fruit from the tree" (3:12). "He tried
to absolve himself by incriminating her."[8]

Third, God summoned Eve to give account for herself. She
answered to Him just as directly and just as much for herself as
Adam answered directly for himself. And when the consequences of the fall were enumerated, Eve's list was separate
from Adam's list. There was no hierarchical headship operating
in the Garden of Eden.

Why, then, did God approach Adam first when Eve was first
to eat of the forbidden fruit? It was perhaps because Adam had
been created first and had been instructed first against partaking from the tree. The one who had been given the precious gift
of living in fellowship with God first and the one who had been
directly and personally warned against losing that fellowship
(2:16–17 being in the singular) was naturally the first one God
would approach when found hiding in the trees.

Paradise Lost

Satan was obviously present in the world before the fall
because he was available to approach the couple, but he evidently was not positioned in the way that the fall left him
positioned. The wound that he was able to inflict upon God's

perfect creation was temporary but, nonetheless, enormous. Jesus called him the "prince of this world" (John 12:31; 14:30; 16:11). Paul called him the "god of this age" and spoke of him blinding people's eyes to the light of Jesus (2 Corinthians 4:4). And it is not just humanity that suffers under the effects of the fall. The New Testament describes the whole creation as groaning (Romans 8:22) and says, "the whole world is a prisoner of sin" (Galatians 3:22). When the very foundation of order, right relationship with God, was displaced, all of nature was thrown into disorder.

What resulted from sin was not God's desire for His creation but the outworking of Satan's "wish list" for disrupting and destroying God's plan. One must simply read the Genesis 3:16–19 passage to see that sin's consequences reversed the original, ideal conditions of the Garden. It is difficult to imagine how any biblical scholar could interpret this list of struggles, contrary as it is to the harmony of the creation account in Genesis 1 and 2, as anything other than the handiwork of Satan.[9] To loyally embrace any aspect of the list, including husband/male dominance, as God's desire for humanity reflects an extremely poor understanding of the first three chapters of Genesis. Indeed, to mistake Satan's wishes for God's wishes is the height of faulty scholarship.

Because of God's grace, life would continue after the fall; but because of Satan's impact, life would be plagued with hardships and with death. The major arenas of human activity and identity were each affected: male-female relationships, childbearing, work, and life-death. Again it must be underscored that God's desire for each of these areas is found in Genesis 1 and 2, not in Genesis 3. The creation account of chapters 1 and 2 contains God's model for humanity; the fall account of chapter 3 contains the list of things that "will be but ought not be."

Rather than endorsing the tragic consequences of sin found in Genesis 3:16–19 as God's will or as some irreversible scriptural mandate, Christians should present Genesis 3 as the wrongs Jesus gave His life to make right. None of them will be made completely or permanently right until Christ establishes His eternal kingdom, but until then Christians should not position themselves as advocates of sin's effects but as its adversaries. If Jesus' sacrifice was all about reversing sin's effects, then surely the Christian should favor reversal and not reinforcement. The conditions described in Genesis 3:16–19, including husband/male dominance, are the wounds of war inflicted upon the human race by its enemy, Satan. Though total healing of these wounds will only occur in eternity, none of them should be welcomed; instead, all of them should be resisted.

The Curse

"The curse" is glibly blamed for all of the ills of a woman's fertility cycle and for her endless struggle to receive proper treatment from the men in her life. Technically, that's not accurate, and the correcting of this misconception may be more significant than a mere adjustment of a small technicality. The biblical text speaks of God cursing Satan and the ground but says nothing about God cursing Adam or Eve. Is it possible that neither Adam nor Eve, neither men nor women, bear God's curse in all the ways that have been presumed?

In Genesis 2:16–17, God said that sin would result in death, not male sweat or female subordination, but death.[10] The remainder of Scripture is consistent with those first words of warning. None of the ills of Genesis 3:16–19 are identified in the Old Testament or in the New Testament as the curse or the punishment of sin except death. But regarding the connection between sin and death, the Bible is emphatic: "the wages of sin is death" (Romans 6:23) and "sin entered the world through one man, and death through sin, and in this way death came to all men, because all sinned" (Romans 5:12). Only when the river of the water of *life* and the tree of *life* become available to the saints does the Bible say, "No longer will there be any *curse*" (Revelation 22:3), clearly equating the curse with death.

Human experience lends further support. Women have given birth to babies without suffering pain, women have escaped the dominance of a husband by not marrying or by marrying into a relationship of equality, and computer technicians sit in air conditioned offices awaiting scrumptious evening meals without ever feeling a dot of sweat on their brows. But death is different. All of humanity is bound by the warning God gave in Genesis 2, making death the one and only unavoidable, universal result of sin, just as God said it would be. Death, then, is the curse, the punishment of sin. The other situations described in 3:16–19 must be of a different nature.

Why is death so firmly tied to sin? Because holiness is so firmly tied to God. God is absolutely holy. God is so holy, sin cannot dwell in His presence. Consequently, sin separates men and women from God. The prophet Isaiah decried this same condition in the lives of God's people Israel: "your iniquities have separated you from your God" (Isaiah 59:2). And left without God, the source of all life, death results, both spiritual death and physical death. Even the final, eternal death of sinners is described not only in terms of torture but also in terms of total separation from God (2 Thessalonians 1:9). This cycle is inescapable, fixed, because it is based upon the very nature of God. It is an inevitable result of who He is.

The sin-separation-death cycle is exactly what happened with Adam and Eve. After their sin, they hid from God's presence (3:8), indicating the spiritual separation that had already transpired. God's response to their sin was to banish them from the Garden in which He had been manifesting His presence (3:22–24), also denying them access to the tree of life and leaving them to the eventual death that would result. Quite different from the other consequences of sin described in 3:16–19, this punishment, separation leading to death, was clearly unchangeable and permanent, evidenced by the posting of a fierce angelic guard. No enforcement whatsoever was set over the other consequences of sin because, again, they are of a different nature.

Death, then, is the curse of sin, the punishment for sin, in a way that nothing else is. It is firmly fixed to sin because of the very nature of God. The other consequences of sin found in Genesis 3:16–19 are considerably different. They are not based on the divine nature of God; they are based on the fallen nature of humanity and on a creation left to disorder and to death. Sexual inequality exists because humanity is out of proper relationship with God. Suffering in childbirth and in tending the land exists because death is constantly pushing upon life, pushing upon the giving of life and pushing upon the sustaining of life. These conditions are simply the natural results of an imperfect world, not in any way situations that should be epitomized or encouraged.

If it is all right for humanity to resist the physical and spiritual death that separation from God causes, and that is exactly what is done through science and through salvation, then surely it is right to renounce the other consequences listed in the fall account, since they are even less "necessary." If world evangelization is all about reversing the sin-separation-death cycle by encouraging people to receive the substitutionary death of Christ and thus enter into a relationship with God that is characterized, again, like in Genesis 1 and 2, by fellowship and righteousness and life, then surely it is right to encourage an end to all of the other consequences of sin. The more sin is dealt with in a society, in a church, in a home, the more the effects of sin should be dealt with, including husband/male dominance.

Descriptive, not Prescriptive

It was so necessary, because of God's nature, for separation and death to follow sin that it took the giving of Himself to fulfill the sin-separation-death cycle and at the same time rescue humanity from it. It is accurate, then, to say that death was prescribed (ordered, dictated) by who God is. But the other consequences of sin found in Genesis 3:16–19 were not *prescribed* by God's *nature*; they were *described* by God's *foreknowledge*. Knowing their fallen nature and the condition of a universe taken prisoner by sin, God was able to warn Adam and Eve about the life they were stepping into and sending the rest of humanity into as the consequences of their sin began to unfold.

The distinction between death being prescribed and the other consequences being described is extremely important. Death *must* result from sin, but the other consequences simply *will* result from sin. Again, human experience bears this out in that death is universally experienced by *every* person; whereas, the other consequences are generally experienced by *many* people. Death is not avoidable once sin enters a person's life, and sin has entered every person's life. Death is only transferable—from a sinful person to an amazingly loving Son of God. The other consequences of sin *are* avoidable because they were simply described by God, not prescribed by Him. As previous comments have shown, they are different from death in every way.

God's knowing something and warning about it does not mean God is causing that event to happen and, of course, does not mean God is wanting that event to happen. This misconception results in people misunderstanding other passages of Scripture as well as the fall account and results in people misunderstanding God. God exists outside our sphere of time and space, so He is able to see what *we* do before *we* do it. But this does not mean He *causes* it or *wants* us to do it. It may be difficult for the finite human mind to fully understand, but

God's omniscience does not eliminate humanity's free will. His knowing does not determine our doing.

God's predicting of sexual hierarchy in Genesis 3:16, then, is not what theologians call causative—God is not *causing* (or desiring) male dominance and female subordination to occur. God did the predicting, but people do the causing. And the causing of sexual inequality by people is as much a result of sin today as it was a result of sin originally. God's words in this passage are not a command; they are a warning.[11] If verse 16 were a command, then the more dictatorial a husband was over a wife, the better he would be fulfilling God's wishes.[12] But God is not prescribing the pattern He wants men and women to "follow or institutionalize in the family, church, or society."[13] He is not presenting the consequences of sin as universal norms that have His approval. He is simply acknowledging that certain conditions will result from fallen humanity living in a fallen world. To use this passage as a defense for male dominance and female subordination is to totally misrepresent it and its author, God.

Physical Versus Relational

Perhaps part of what is confusing is that some conditions in the Genesis 3:16–19 list are physical while others are relational. Pain in childbirth is clearly a physical phenomenon as is toiling to grow food. However, the sexual hierarchy between husband and wife which features male dominance and female subordination is very much a relational situation. However, even though these consequences function in different spheres, do they not share in common a hope for relief?

Evangelical Christians view scientific advances as "graces" or gifts of God. Even Pentecostals are known to say, "God may heal medically or instantaneously, but either act of God to reverse an otherwise permanent condition or terminal illness is a miracle." If any of this is true, then God provides the means via science whereby various physical consequences of sin can be lessened. Through the insights God has given scientists, both childbirth and agriculture have been considerably improved. And it would be an extremely unusual, radical person who would resist these advances and claim that it is more spiritual to suffer and sweat.

It is not through God-given insights about nature but through equally God-given insights about relationships that the other consequences of sin, male dominance and female subordination, can be lessened. It is easy to understand that once Adam and Eve damaged their relationship with God, their relationship with each other suffered severe damage as well. Still today a person who is out of proper relationship with God cannot expect to engage in proper relationships with others. Complementariness gave way to conflict and competition. Unity gave way to disunity. Sexual harmony gave way to sexual hostility and sexual hierarchy. Equality gave way to inequality.

But if science can impact the physical consequences of the fall, even permitting the prolonging of life and the delaying of death, then surely salvation can impact its relational consequences. As men and women make right their relationship with God, if they will but listen to His voice, He will share with them insights about making right their relationships with each other. Restoration to righteousness, then, will be evidenced not by reinforcing sin's relational damages, but by repairing them.

Offsetting the Consequences

It is not sensible to condone lessening some of the Genesis 3 consequences and to criticize lessening others. It would be hard to locate an evangelical Christian who thinks it's more spiritual to be a subsistence farmer, sweating daily to produce food from the ground, than it is to be a computer technician, enjoying a cool, clean office. It would be difficult to locate a suburban churchman who refuses, for biblical reasons, to use weed killer or to even pull weeds. If it is not wrong for men to offset the results of sin that affect them, why is it wrong for women to offset the results that affect them?

It is true that women are permitted to benefit from the help that science and medicine can provide during childbirth, but even this has not always been the case.

> In the sixteenth century in Scotland, Eufame MacLayne was pregnant...carrying twins. When labor began, things got rough. Sometimes twins do not come the easy way. They can be in odd positions, causing long and difficult labors. Eufame, for whatever reason, requested a certain painkilling herb to be given to her. I do not know how much it helped, but she survived and so did her babies.

However, someone found out what she had done. Painkillers were forbidden to women in childbirth. It was against God's law. He wanted women to suffer in labor. The Bible said so, their punishment for Eve's sin.

So Eufame was brought before those who decided punishment. And they could not of course let her go free (there was also the possibility of witchcraft, you see, because she had not relied solely on the grace of God for relief from her pain). So her babies were taken from her arms and given to someone else's care. Eufame was tied to a stake. Bundles of wood were laid at her feet. Then new mother Eufame was burned alive.[14]

As extreme as this incident may seem, it is based on the very same reasoning that insists upon wives being subservient to husbands. If Genesis 3:16–19 lists conditions that *must* be, then not only must a wife be under a husband's rule, but also women must be denied pain relief during childbirth; and all men must return to earning their food by the sweat of their brows without any technological assistance to minimize their toil. These stipulations are presented no differently in the passage, so they must be applied no differently.

If any such suggestion is ludicrous, and, indeed, it is, then it is ludicrous in its entirety, including the part about wives and husbands. If the church does not preach suffering in childbirth as God's unchangeable will for all women and sweat in farming as God's unchangeable will for all men, then it should not preach sexual inequality as God's unchangeable will for all humanity. These are humanity's enemies, not God's designs. It is not more spiritual or more scriptural to insist upon living in the grip of sin's physical and relational consequences. If anything, it is indicative of a life, either due to remoteness or stubbornness, that is yet untouched by God's gracious intervention. It is not rejecting God's purposes to live differently than Genesis 3:16–19 describes, because, as has been noted earlier, this passage contains Satan's "wish list," not God's.

The "Sense" of the Consequences

If for no other reason than to see how devastating the fall was, its sweeping effects upon God's perfect creation are worth noting. Even though life would continue, its inception would be characterized by pain, its sustenance would be plagued by toil, and its end would be wracked with death. In other words, "suffering as a preliminary form of death" would mar the entire process of life, its beginning, its sustenance, and its ending.[15] Could anything be any further from God's original intention?

Even though *both* Adam and Eve had been told to subdue and to fill the earth, the consequences of sin that Adam would feel had to do with subduing and those that Eve would feel had to do with filling. This seems to suggest that the pre-fall sexual equality would not only be replaced with sexual inequality but also with sexual stereotyping. It is no coincidence that advocates of unbendable gender roles point to the Genesis 3:16–19 passage as supportive of their contention that a woman's place is at home and a man's place is at work. (Of course, in their refusal to let women step outside the house, they fail to realize that most men have left the farm fields.) Regardless of whether Genesis 3 hints at impending sexual stereotyping (and predicting it is not the same thing as condoning it), it is nonetheless true that God's pre-fall assigning of male-female responsibilities was *equal* and was *ideal*; but after the effects of sin were felt, both the equality and the ideal were lost. The sexual stereotyping that was left and that is still plaguing society today is as far from God's original intention as death is from life.

Of course, bearing children and working the land in themselves should never be seen as the negative consequences of sin; both were pre-fall provisions and were part of God's "very good" pronouncement. Neither activity was intended by God to be laborious or in any way negative. But sin's effects touched the entire universe, including its creative processes, so the body and the earth would produce their fruits only with great suffering.[16] The same Hebrew word is used for Eve's pain in childbearing as is used for Adam's toil in farming. Both would be significantly marred by sin, again, completely contrary to God's original plan.

Just as hard labor was added to childbirth and to raising food, inequality was added to marriage. These three activities, bearing children, tending the land, and marriage, were all created to be perfectly positive activities for the male and female to enjoy equally. But because of sin hard labor was imposed, and because of sin inequality was imposed.

Perhaps as a constant reminder of the perfect creation that had been lost, a new antagonism would exist between the creatures and the raw material from which each had been created.[17] Both the man and the woman would be subject to that from which each had been originally made: Adam, created from the ground, would be subject to the ground; Eve created from Adam, would be subject to Adam. The ground would grieve Adam with its powers over him, and Adam would grieve Eve with his powers over her. Neither arrangement was present under pre-fall conditions; both are the inevitable results of sin wrecking havoc on creation.

Another way to see the same turn of events is to remember that in the Garden both Adam and Eve were subject directly and only to God, their actual source of being. But after rejecting His sovereignty in their lives, they were left to be ruled by the secondary, earthly "sources" of their being: Adam by the ground and Eve by Adam.[18] Again, however, neither arrangement was God's desire. God's original, perfect desire was that both men and women be ruled directly and only by Him.

Blessing of God or Consequence of Sin?

It is difficult to understand how some scholars can claim that Adam's dominance over Eve was both pre-fall and post-fall. The same scholars manage to see that suffering was not part of God's original plan for bearing children or for tending the land, and death was not part of His plan in any way. But they fail to see that sexual inequality was not part of God's original plan for marriage, that it was a post-fall, negative addition. Perhaps it helps to be a woman to realize that male dominance and female subordination are not the good and perfect gifts of God! But common sense is all that is necessary on the part of a man or a woman to realize that sexual inequality cannot be both positive and negative, cannot be both a blessing of God and a consequence of sin, cannot be both pre-fall and post-fall. Either it is the desire of God, consequently, it was set and functional in the original creation before the fall; or it is the effect of sin, *but it cannot be both.*

The biblical record bears out the conclusions of common sense. As has been shown earlier, the relationship between Adam and Eve in the creation account was characterized by unity, mutuality, and equality. There was *no* sexual hierarchy in the original creation. The relationship showed its first sign of deterioration immediately after the fall when Adam suggested that he stood in better stead than Eve (Genesis 3:12), the first hint of inequality and hierarchy. Then God predicted that inequality and hierarchy would continue to be the effects of sin (Genesis 3:16)—not the desire of God, *the effects of sin*. This "ruler/subject" arrangement took only six generations (from Adam to Lamech) "to disintegrate into polygamy, the showcase of male dominance in the fullness of its sinful expression."[19]

Many biblical scholars try to explain themselves by saying that the consequence of sin was the *increasing* of Eve's subordination, that she was subordinate before the fall but *more* subordinate after the fall. This is a lame argument, indeed. They use as their defense the increasing of childbearing pain. If this consequence can consist of the increasing of a present condition, then, they say that the same can be true of the subordination consequence. The Hebrew word that is used for "increase, multiply" ("rabah"), however, is not limited to the idea of "make more." It can also mean "make many" or "make great" with none of the total amount existing yet. It is oftentimes used in this way across the Old Testament. Furthermore, to claim that some pain existed in creation before the fall is a faulty view of creation. How can some subordination be a blessing of God but more subordination be a consequence of sin? Such a notion is just as contradictory as the contradiction it is trying to remedy, namely, the contradiction that sexual hierarchy can be both pre-fall and post-fall.

Other scholars explain that the consequence of sin was that woman would desire the man though he subjugates her. This claim usually fails to address the question at hand, whether male dominance was put into practice before the fall or only after the fall. If the contention is that it was present before the fall, then the contradiction of it being both a blessing of God and a consequence of sin has not been rectified. If the contention is that it did not begin until after the fall, then both the male dominating the woman and the woman desiring such a man are consequences of sin, and both should be renounced.

The point is clear and strong and cannot be set aside—Adam's rulership over Eve was not a part of God's original creation but was a consequence of the fall. Therefore, the positioning of a husband over a wife must either be abolished entirely, or if it seems to appear elsewhere in Scripture, such as in the expression "headship," it must be defined according to an accurate interpretation of those and other passages of Scripture, not according to a misinterpretation of Genesis and not according to centuries of societal wrongdoing. Death, suffering in bearing children and in tending the land, and hierarchy in marriage clearly belong to one and the same classification. They are post-fall consequences of sin, not pre-fall designs of God.

The Cursing of the Tempter

Genesis 3:14–15 records the curse that God put upon the serpent and upon Satan for tempting the couple. Though little has been said about it thus far, this curse is of a very different nature than the consequences of sin that Adam and Eve would experience. True, just as there is a "sense" to the results Adam and Eve would feel, there is a similar sense to the curse put upon the serpent:

> The serpent had been "more" sly than all the animals of the field which God had created (3:1). After the fall, the serpent is "more" cursed than all the animals (3:14). The serpent had encouraged Eve and Adam "to eat" from the fruit of the tree of the knowledge of good and evil. Now the serpent will himself "eat," but it is dust he will eat all the days of his life.[20]

Despite this similarity in "fairness," the list of ills affecting the serpent and Satan results from God cursing them. God did not curse Adam and Eve; the list affecting them is simply a description of the natural, inevitable results of sin entering their world. A further difference is found in the fact that Satan is not still deciding his eternal destiny as are men and women, so the punishments affecting him can be of a "must happen" nature; whereas, the consequences affecting humanity are of a "will happen" nature. So, in verse 14 the serpent receives punishments from God, and in verse 15 these punishments blend into the punishments of Satan who was behind the serpent, all of this being the result of God's curse upon them.

It is not directly relevant to the topic at hand to engage in a lengthy discussion of all of the possible interpretations of the enmity that is detailed in verse 15. What is significant is the likelihood that this is the Bible's first reference to the promise of redemption. Though Satan had dealt and would continue to deal a temporary blow ("strike his heel") against the Creator through His creation, Jesus would level a permanent blow ("crush your head") against Satan that would return God's creation to the perfection and the eternal life it was meant to enjoy.

Immediately upon falling into sin, humanity heard God promising redemption from it! It has also been said that God's temporary provision for sin in verse 21, the providing of animal skins as covering, gave Adam and Eve an early picture of how the promise of redemption would be kept. Throughout the Old Testament, God would continue to paint the same picture, requiring the sacrifice of animals to "cover" the sins of humanity. Then one day the perfect sacrifice would offer His body and His blood to atone for all sins once and for all. He would offer more than a covering; He would offer removal.

Contrary to popular theology which overly blames and punishes Eve and her offspring for the sins of the world, the only glimmer of hope that lights the tragic scene of Genesis 3 is that through *Eve's* offspring redemption would come (3:15). In a book that traces genealogies through male descendants, why not through Adam's offspring? The first entry in the genealogy would be Seth who was equally the son of Adam and Eve, so, again, why not through Adam's offspring?

Various speculations are intriguing but are only speculations. What can be said with confidence is that God does not treat Eve the way many have treated her across the centuries. God elevates her, rather than Adam, to being the serpent's enemy and to being the one through whom redemption would come, the progenitor of the Messiah.[21] How ironic that God's Son is welcomed to abolish any consequences of sin that affect men, but He is not equally welcomed to free women from the consequences of sin that affect them. It seems that in the community of redemption, both men and women should be freed from sin's consequences and restored to the mutuality and equality that Jesus gave His life to restore.

Even though it is sometimes interpreted as an exercise in male dominance for the husband to name his wife in 3:20, perhaps Adam was primarily reaching toward the promise that was made in 3:15. By naming his wife "living" or "mother of all living," he was seemingly acknowledging God's promise of hope and was simultaneously acknowledging Eve's role in the fulfillment of that promise. Through her, God would bring forth life, and through her, God would bring forth redemption. If Adam could reach toward redemption in his naming of Eve, surely Adam's sons should reflect the impact of that redemption upon their lives in their treatment of Eve's daughters.

Eve's Consequences

None of the efforts to balance Eve's role in the fall of human-ity should be perceived as efforts to depict her as innocent. Eve did participate in the fall, and she would suffer consequences as would all women after her. The consequences are detailed in Genesis 3:16.

As has been noted earlier, the curse of sin, death, would constantly press upon life, upon the giving of life through pain in childbearing and upon the sustaining of life through pain in tending the land. As sexual inequality would increasingly entrench itself in early society and thereby fix firm gender roles, a woman would repeatedly feel the one consequence while a man would repeatedly feel the other. The use of the same Hebrew word for "pain" in verses 16 and 17 further underscores the evenness with which these two consequences were felt by Adam and Eve. Sin entered the perfect world of creation. It is still so present in the world, even though it is essentially a spiritual entity, that its very physical presence is felt in two of the most basic activities of life—the birthing of a baby and the farming of a field.

There is little discussion made over the first portion of verse 16. But, of course, considerable debate encircles the latter portion: "Your desire will be for your husband, and he will rule over you." Before anything else is given consideration, it should be understood that the passage concerns husband-wife rela-tionships, not male-female relationships. Because Hebrew and Greek can use the same word for man and husband and the same word for woman and wife, the distinction must be dis-cerned from the context. In this instance, the Hebrew wording *"your* man" signals a clear reference to the husband. Unless men are ready to transfer all husbandly behaviors to the male population at large, they should be careful not to condone the transfer of any one behavior such as dominance. And, of course, if God is not even advocating the dominance of husbands over wives but simply predicting it, He is certainly not to be repre-sented as instituting the dominance of men over women in general.

It should be noted that Eve was not told to be subordinate to Adam. Eve's subordination would not be the result of any voluntary act on her part; it would be forced upon her by the dominance of Adam. The words "he will rule over you" read quite differently from "submit to your husband's rule." Sin left Adam willing to exchange a "horizontal relationship of equality and mutuality" for a "vertical relationship of master and slave."[22]

As straightforward as it may seem in English, it is difficult to understand with certainty the Hebrew phrase that stands behind the line "your desire will be for your husband." The word for desire, "teshukah," appears only here and two other times in the Old Testament (Genesis 4:7 and Song of Solomon 7:10), with considerably different meanings each time. Applying the Genesis 4:7 sense, some argue that Eve and wives after her would wish to possess or rule their husbands. Even this interpretation has two different twists available to it. Those who claim (wrongly) that God gave Adam headship over Eve before the fall, say that Eve's descendants would continue to do exactly what Eve did, namely, try to seize the husband's authority. Those who, instead, see sexual hierarchy as post-fall, say that the wife will be trying to counter her husband's self-appointed rise to rulership over her with her own rulership over him. (It should be noted that wanting to rule him is totally different from wanting equality with him.) Whichever of the two twists is taken, according to this rendering, the phrases "your desire will be for your husband" and "he will rule over you" end up depicting the battle of the sexes that is about to be waged, with the wife wanting it one way and the husband pushing it the other way. How contradictory that a wife's effort to dominate her husband can be seen as sinful, while the exact counterpart effort on a husband's part is called divine design.

Applying the Song of Solomon sense of the word "desire" produces a different understanding, the idea of "turning toward" or "wanting" or "longing after" the other person. This interpretation has in its favor the tying together of everything God says to Eve. Though childbirth will threaten the wife with enormous pain, she will nonetheless gravitate toward a husband, the very originator of the pregnancy; and her desires will be further abused by his response of rulership over her. This view predicts a cycle of frustration and disappointment that has been the lot of many wives. The gravitating toward the husband may not be as much physical or sexual as it is emotional. Instead of the mutually nurturing companionship that she expects, featuring closeness and oneness, the wife repeatedly encounters self-serving dominance.

Of course, those who are comfortable with male dominance are also comfortable with the "marry or die" drive of a woman. It is true that most women will marry, and it may even be true that it is God's will for most women to marry. But the *undue* desire for a husband or the *undue* dependency upon marriage that throws all too many women into wrong relationships may be just as unhealthy and just as much a consequence of sin on the part of a woman as dominance is on the part of a man. After all, "your desire will be for your husband" is an item in the Genesis 3:16–19 list of sin's effects. It is unlikely that it should be read as the only positive or neutral item in the list.

Adam and Eve were first made by God to be individuals and were then joined by God in marriage. A healthy individual has a wholeness and a richness of identity to offer a marriage partner. But if a woman is driven into marriage by an unhealthy dependency upon a husband due to her own personal incompleteness or if a man is distinguished in marriage by an unhealthy dominance over his wife due to his own personal insecurity, both are far from God's creation intention.

Adam's Consequences

Genesis 3:17–19 is straightforward enough that it needs no further commentary. What is worth noting, however, is one item that is *not* in God's words to Adam. The sovereignty of the husband is in Eve's list; it is not in Adam's list. In other words, contrary to how many men behave and contrary to what many men claim, husbands are not told to rule over wives. God warns Eve that it will happen, but He does not command or even suggest that Adam carry it out. If this is God's design for marriage and, indeed, for society and eventually for the church, one would expect Him to instruct Adam accordingly or to at least mention it to him. But it is nowhere to be found in the entire Genesis 1–3 text except in a list of negative things that are about to happen to Eve and to women after her. Men who operate according to this principle, then, are not operating according to God's directives but according to a "bad news" list of woes that is so far from God's design it will require the sacrifice of His Son to reverse it.

4

Old Testament Stipulations About Women

If the role of the Old Testament in the overall plan of God is not understood, then many of its passages will be read in isolation and will be terribly misunderstood. Excerpts that deal with women are no exception and, in fact, may be particularly vulnerable. Against the backdrop of a modern consciousness of women's rights, certain Old Testament passages could be seen as archaic at best or chauvinistic at worst. But the Bible is neither out-of-touch nor faulty; it is relevant and reliable when understood properly.

As has been stated in an earlier chapter, the Old Testament stands between the fall of humanity in the Garden and the redemption of humanity in the Gospels. Its laws were given for a post-fall, pre-redemption period as a means of temporarily curbing sin's effects and thereby preserving and preparing a people for the day when sin's power could be broken (Galatians 3:19). Because its recipients were ungodly, its provisions were incomplete and imperfect (Romans 8:3; Hebrews 7:19), impaired by humanity's depth of sinfulness (Romans 8:3; 1 Timothy 1:9–10).

So, to read the Old Testament as a depiction of God's ideal is to misread it. Its "giants" were guilty of serious sins—Abraham, Moses, David. God's best were touched by Satan's worst. All too often God's people moved back and forth between the pull of sin and the pull of righteousness, and the Old Testament gives a candid account of the details. Likewise, to represent Old Testament law as a manifesto of God's ideal is to misrepresent it. It was meant to check people's behavior. It was meant to prevent sin from causing further damage by meeting humanity in the midst of its sinfulness, individually and societally, and building a blockade at that point. There are multiple instances of the law actually "accommodating" sin, holding it at bay rather than totally forbidding its existence, such as with the regulating of divorce, while awaiting redemption from it. The law left images of God's ideal, but it stopped far short of embodying that ideal or of elevating people to that ideal because it did not have the power to change souls (Hebrews 10:1).

Because the Old Testament was on the right track but was not capable of reaching the final destination, the New Testament explains that Jesus both fulfilled and superseded the law. In one sense He didn't abolish it (Matthew 5:17), but in a different sense He did abolish it (Ephesians 2:15). By exceeding its demands and fulfilling its ideal intent, He honored it while rendering it obsolete (Colossians 2:14; Hebrews 7:18–19; 8:13). By giving people new hearts, He lifted them out of external regulations to internal motivations (Jeremiah 31:33; Ezekiel 36:26).

All of this means that it is incorrect to use the Old Testament's seemingly uneven portrayal of women as grounds for denigrating them. The negative effects of sin damaged the relationship between Adam and Eve even before God announced that it would happen (Genesis 3:12). Not surprisingly, early civilization became extremely patriarchal. From the world of male dominance, God chose an individual, Abraham, through whom He would bring forth His people. Abraham, a product of his culture, was patriarchal and polygamous, and he remained so. The biblical account records his shortcomings, and in future years the law would regulate those very shortcomings. But this should not be misconstrued as the Bible condoning or endorsing patriarchy or polygamy.

Of course, God did not tolerate everything from Abraham's sinful background. Not only did the fall damage the relationship between men and women, it primarily damaged the relationship between humanity and God, resulting in early civilization becoming idolatrous. Abraham's own father was a worshiper of other gods (Joshua 24:2). But for Abraham's descendants, idolatry would be a sin punishable by death (Deuteronomy 17:2–5). Similarly with Moses, God chose him to lead Israel even though he had wrongfully taken someone's life and had made God angry with his resistance to the call. But God would not tolerate him failing to circumcise his son (Genesis 17:9–14; Exodus 4:24–26).

The Old Testament should not be misunderstood. God's mercy and grace regarding certain shortcomings did not mean that He would allow any and all sins to exist in His people's lives. But it also did not mean that the wrongdoing He was willing to "work with" was in any way an acceptable or commendable way of living. Rather than faulting the Old Testament for favoring men, it should be understood as simply recording the favoring of men that was characteristic of the culture. And, if anything, the stipulations about women given in the law were efforts to protect them from the far more serious violations that would occur if no barriers were set.

Polygamy, Divorce, and Adultery

As has been mentioned, some of God's chosen spiritual leaders participated in polygamy. Two of the patriarchs were guilty—Abraham and Jacob. The great judge and warrior, Gideon, had many wives. King David had numerous wives and concubines, and King Solomon had hundreds of each. Although adultery may seem to be the worst way in which a husband can disrespect his wife, polygamy is even worse. It is probably the rankest possible violation of God's original "one flesh" intention for marriage.

Is the Old Testament's depiction of polygamy and lack of direct denouncement of it grounds to engage in this despicable practice or at least grounds for a low view of women? Of course not. First, this is one of many examples of having to read the Old Testament in light of its position in the overall picture. God's revelation of truth is progressing toward perfection in Jesus, but it is far from final arrival. Second, if the Bible's representation of discrimination against women is read as a commendation of the practice and its underlying prejudices, then all of the other sinful behaviors and attitudes recorded and regulated in the Old Testament would have to be embraced as godly living as well. Third, what is said about marriage before the law, within the law, and following the law stands in direct opposition to this desecration of women. God's institution of marriage in Genesis 2:24 is very much in the singular: one man and one woman are to become one flesh. The many references within the law are to one wife rather than to multiple wives. (The only possible exception is the Deuteronomy 21:15–17 passage which is clearly trying to restrict the inevitable ills of polygamy, *if* it happens to exist, rather than in any way presenting it as a desirable option.) The psalmist promises several blessings to the righteous man, including the fruitfulness of his wife, not his wives (Psalms 128:3). The final book of the Old Testament warns, "Do not break faith with the wife of your youth," again, not the wives of your youth (Malachi 2:15).[1]

Whereas polygamy permits a man to have multiple wives concurrently, divorce permits him to have multiple wives successively. This, too, culturally acceptable as it may be, is diametrically opposed to God's design and desire. The Bible is clear on the matter: "'I hate divorce,' says the Lord God of Israel" (Malachi 2:16). The Old Testament does make provision for divorce in Deuteronomy 24:1–4, but the New Testament clarifies that it was done only as a concession to the people's sinfulness (Matthew 19:8). And upon reading the Deuteronomy passage, it is clear that men were being restrained from the harm they would otherwise do to women and to society. As has been said, the law acted to preserve a people *and to protect its women* while Abraham's descendants were being taken, slowly but surely, from a world ridden with sin to an eventual kingdom of righteousness.

There was no provision made in the law for a wife to divorce her husband because the practice did not exist in Israel. Providing for it could have resulted in producing it. However, with it already very existent among men, detailing it in the law would have just the opposite effect, specifically, a curbing effect. Society let husbands treat wives like property, to be put aside at will for no legitimate reason. By legislating the divorce activity of men, the law was not causing or condoning the sin; it was checking and containing it from the wanton excesses society would otherwise permit. To interpret this different treatment of husbands and wives by the law as indicative of husbands having a different standing in God's eyes than wives is to totally misunderstand the intent of the law. Different situations were simply given different but appropriate treatments. What curbed sin for men would have caused sin for women. The difference in the law's treatment of husbands and wives is due to God meeting people where sin left them, not to any gender bias on God's part.

This understanding of the law's "seemingly uneven" treatment of husbands and wives is confirmed by its extremely even handling of a sin that *was* present among both men and women—adultery. If a man and woman were involved in adultery, both of them were to be put to death (Leviticus 20:10;

Deuteronomy 22:22). This "same situation, same provision" for adultery is the logical counterpart of the "different situation-different provision" for divorce. The world is guilty of treating men and women unevenly, but God's treatment of them is dependent solely upon their individual circumstances rather than upon their gender.

Because sinful society gave a husband the upper hand over his wife, he was able to make untrue accusations about her chastity and faithfulness. To keep such accusations from resulting in any type of undeserved punishment for the woman, the law made special provision for her protection. If a husband wrongfully accused his wife of sexual promiscuity prior to their marriage, there was a means by which her innocence could be proven, and he was punished (Deuteronomy 22:13–19). Of course, if she was guilty, then the punishment for adultery was enforced—death. Similarly, if a husband suspected his wife of unfaithfulness during their marriage, a test of her faithfulness was available (Numbers 5:11–31). Its results and her fate were put into the hands of an all-knowing God rather than left to the whims and dictates of any man.

The fact that women were not given any mechanism for testing a man's chastity or faithfulness is probably because the culture would not permit any such allegation. It is also possible that a woman's purity had to be especially guarded in order to ensure the legitimacy of children for inheritance purposes.[2] With God's presence and blessing being associated with possession of the land and with the assigning and bequeathing of land being according to tribal-clan affiliation, it was imperative for the legitimacy of children to be as certain as possible.

Perhaps, like today, women in antiquity were automatically accused of playing the role of temptress in certain instances of improper sexual activity. The law gave the woman extra protection in these situations as well. A man is referred to as the one doing the seducing of a virgin in Exodus 22:16–17 and is held responsible for marrying her or for paying her bride-price. The raping of a woman by a man is given a means of detection so as to distinguish it from consenting sex, and appropriate punishment is dictated (Deuteronomy 22:23–29).

Cleansing and Redeeming

Leviticus 12 designates periods of "ceremonial uncleanness" after a woman gives birth to a baby. In the case of a son, there were to be 7 days of one level of uncleanness and 33 more days of a different level of uncleanness, totaling 40 days. In the case of a daughter, the two periods were exactly double, 14 and 66 or a total of 80 days. This "unevenness" is frequently interpreted as indicative of God's positioning of the male child as somehow better than the female child. This conclusion is nothing but speculation because the reason behind the differentiation is unknown. Other guesses, then, would be just as valid as this guess.

Before proceeding further, it should be noted that the unclean status put upon the woman is not a demeaning of women. The giving of children is, according to Scripture, an act of God and a great blessing. The uncleanness had more to do with the bodily fluids involved in the birthing process than with anything else. Men were similarly restricted from religious activities in conjunction with the discharging of bodily fluids (Leviticus 15:1–18). Further evidence that the stipulation does not imply inferiority is found in the fact that both Mary and Jesus are said to have been affected by it. Luke 2:22 refers to completing *their* time of purification (KJV being faulty in its use of "her" to translate the Greek text's plural pronoun).[3]

As to interpreting the differentiation between male and female babies, two feasible explanations have been proposed.[4] First, perhaps the 14 days is cut in half for the male baby by the even more important ceremonial duty of circumcision which was to occur on the eighth day after birth. It only followed that the correlating period of 66 days would be cut in half as well, leaving the male child with half the term of uncleanness as the female child. Second, in light of the fact that extreme patriarchy has typically resulted in very hard lives for little girls, perhaps God was legislating an especially lengthy period of bonding between the mother and daughter. The long period of isolation together would also practically guarantee the direct care of the baby girl by the mother, thereby even strengthening the child physically. Either of these explanations is more likely than jumping to the conclusion that God values boys over girls, a position that is not supported by the rest of Scripture. If God did have this bias, it would be difficult to explain the fact that the purification sacrifice was identical for a boy and a girl, a clear indication of their equality in God's sight.

Leviticus 27:1–8 details the procedure for redeeming various categories of people from religious service. The dedication of an individual to a period of tabernacle/temple work could be exchanged for the "equivalent" value in currency. With every example, the value of a male exceeds that of a same-age female. Again, this can be and has been misconstrued as indicating that God regards men more highly than women.

The correct understanding seems, instead, to lie in the text itself. First, it is interesting that females could be dedicated to tabernacle/temple service at all. Many women throughout church history have wanted to make similar commitments of themselves to ministry but have been denied the privilege of doing what the Old Testament obviously permitted.

Second, the gender differentiation must be interpreted in the same way that the age differentiation is interpreted. The passage gives four different age divisions, with the redemption price changing for each category. Surely no one would suggest that God has a low opinion of young children or of the elderly, yet their redemption price is set considerably lower than that of young people and adults. In fact, there is far more difference between a man and either a young male or an elderly male than there is between a man and a same-age woman. The scale must reflect the fact that tabernacle/temple work involved duties that the very young and the very old were *physically* less able to do— probably actual physical activities.[5] At every age the female would have less physical ability than the male. The more *physically* fitted for the work the person was, the more valuable his or her service would be and the higher the redemption price should be. The stipulations, then, are dealing with nothing but body build and body strength, not exactly the deciding factor in selecting a pastor today. Ironically, some denominations that will not allow a woman to minister in a plush suburban pastorate will let her enter inner-city ministries and foreign mission fields that will not only tax her physical strength but will even put her life in danger. In claiming to follow Scripture, today's practices misunderstand, misrepresent, misapply, and even disobey the very passages they claim to honor.

It is also possible that lesser amounts of redemption money were designated for females because the culture did not value them enough to pay full amounts. In such a patriarchal system, females would have had very little in personal resources and would have been very dependent upon family finances. If the full amounts were seen by the male leadership of the family as excessive, then the father or husband would have exercised his right to veto the vow that had been made by the daughter or wife (Numbers 30). Setting lesser amounts for females seems to be very much in line with God's regard throughout mosaic law for classes of people who have less to give. The lesser amounts would have encouraged women to make these spiritual commitments and would have encouraged the men in their lives to honor their vows.[6]

Genealogies, Firstborn, and Inheritance

The Old Testament lists only the sons in most genealogies, speaks only of a son being the firstborn, and refers to the sons receiving the family inheritance. Do these tendencies reflect a bias favoring men? Yes, they do, but the important question is, "Whose bias?"

These are clearly examples of the Old Testament reflecting the culture of the people God was trying to redeem without always correcting and changing every detail of that culture's wrongdoing. In the same way that polygamy existed alongside God's prescription for monogamy, other ills of a patriarchal society were very much evident within Israel. It was the culture, not God, that had a bias against women. God was willing to work within and through that culture in order to provide redemption for its people.

The ancient middle-eastern world, of which Israel was a part, positioned husbands over wives just as God had warned in Genesis 3:16. But the biblical prediction of sexual hierarchy was not given in isolation; it was given with an explanation of its cause. All of the Genesis 3 warnings were presented as consequences of sin. If a society positions husbands over wives, it's an easy step to the positioning of all men over all women and just one more step to the disregarding and devaluing of all women. The world surrounding Israel was indeed sinful enough to be entrenched in this cycle of sin, and Israel was, to varying degrees, a product of that culture and guilty of its wrongdoing.

So, it is not surprising that the generations were traced through the male offspring. The women who actually bore the generations were consigned to being represented by their husbands, their individual identity virtually lost. Scripture simply reports the genealogies as the culture recognized and recorded them. It has been said, however, that only one genealogy really matters, the one found not in the Old Testament but in the New Testament, the ancestry of Jesus. In it (Matthew 1:1–16) God seemingly intentionally violates societal norms by injecting not only five women but five unlikely women: Tamar the trickster; Rahab the prostitute; Ruth the foreigner; Bathsheba the wife gained by sin; and the quiet, humble Mary. Unlike the Old Testament genealogies, the only designation Joseph carries is "the husband of Mary." Mary, on the other hand, is said to be the one "of whom was born Jesus." This same New Testament proclaims the "good news" that Jesus "bore our sins…so that we might die to sins and live for righteousness" (1 Peter 2:24). May we allow Him to bear not only our sins but also the consequences of our sins, including any inclination to diminish the worth of women.

A culture with a secondary or inferior view of girls would not bestow upon a daughter the special honor thought to be due the firstborn of a family. Consequently, "firstborn" automatically meant firstborn *son* in the world of the Old Testament. Though scholars disagree on various details, special favor was given to a family's firstborn son. Of course, if God does not view a firstborn son more highly or even any differently than He views a second-born son, then it cannot be concluded that He views sons any differently than He views daughters. Both the favoring of sons and the favoring of firstborn sons were cultural practices, not godly preferences. God was willing to work within and through the customs of the ancient world without condoning those customs for that day or prescribing them for this day.

God was simply talking Pharaoh's language when He said, "Israel is my firstborn son" (Exodus 4:22). He was saying that Israel was His favorite child. And because Egypt would not release God's favorite child, God would strike dead each Egyptian family's favorite child, the firstborn son (Exodus 4:23). God didn't view that child as more valuable than the others. God's favor or disfavor always stems from what He finds within an individual's heart, and He is frequently seen in Old Testament Scripture "preferring" an unlikely person over a likely person for this very reason. But the Egyptians saw the firstborn son as the most valuable child; consequently, the death of this child, in particular, would be one of the most painful blows God could deal.

As a perpetual reminder of God's miraculous deliverance of Israel out of Egypt, He claimed for Himself the favorite child of every family of Israel. Not surprisingly, the favorite child for them was the same as it was for the ancient cultures surrounding them, the firstborn son. A daughter, even firstborn, would not have represented, in *their* estimation, the same costly demand. God's right to the firstborn son and His provision for redeeming him back into the family are explained in Exodus 13:1–2, 14–16 and in Numbers 3:11–13, 40–48; 8:14–19; 18:15–16. God used ancient, flawed customs to paint a picture of what He would require of Himself. His *only* child would one day stand in the place of all of the first fruits, best animals, and favorite sons. God's first, best, and favorite would provide the final, perfect sacrifice for humanity's sins.

Ancient patriarchal societies, including Israel, typically extended their regard for sons into their inheritance practices. This, of course, left out the daughters. A daughter was viewed as an indirect recipient of her husband's inheritance just as she was seen as an invisible extension of her husband's identity in the genealogy. After all, the couple was perpetuating *his* family line, not hers. Only if she was fortunate enough to have brothers who were fortunate enough to have sons would her family line continue, and yet after marriage it wasn't even her family line any more. So, with the family line went the family fortune.

The "fortune" that God had interest in passing from generation to generation was the land itself. Possessing Canaan was symbolic of living in God's presence and enjoying God's blessings. Because of its spiritual significance God was insistent upon the land being divided fairly—first between the tribes and then clan by clan within each tribe. He was equally insistent that tribes and clans not lose possession, at least not permanently, of whatever portion had been given to them. Various laws guarded the loss of land such as those pertaining to the Year of Jubilee and to the Kinsman Redeemer.

Obviously, land could not be divided between a husband's family and a wife's family without resulting in strife between the two families and without dividing it into nonexistence. It had to stay either within the husband's family or within the wife's family. Though God's original plan for marriage (Genesis 2:24) may or may not suggest matriarchal succession, by the time the law was given Israel was quite patriarchal. It is understandable, then, that the law's provisions specified that sons would inherit the land, thereby accommodating cultural custom.

The fact that "male versus female" was not the point is made clear by the provision for daughters to inherit land whenever a family had no sons (Numbers 27:1–11; 36:1–12). Five daughters whose parents had not had sons petitioned Moses for their father's inheritance saying, "Why should our father's name disappear from his clan because he had no son?" Obviously the point, the *only* point, was to perpetuate the heritage, not to favor sons. It could be done through sons *or* daughters, but not both; and, of course, it would be done through sons in a patriarchal society. If neither sons nor daughters were available, other relatives were sought because the point was to keep the land within the family. Even the five daughters were required to marry within the tribe and clan of their father because that was the point, maintaining possession of the land clan-by-clan and tribe-by-tribe as God had originally allotted. Caleb, one of only two first generation Israelites permitted to enter Canaan, gave land to his daughter (Joshua 15:19), and Job, whose connection to mosaic law is unclear, seems to have divided his wealth equally between his sons and daughters (Job 42:15).

Vows

The mosaic law was quite firm in holding men to vows and pledges that they made to God. Extensive exceptions were granted, however, for identical vows and pledges made by women. According to Numbers 30, a single woman's vow could be nullified by her father or later by her husband, and a married woman's vow could be nullified by her husband. This provision has been used to support a host of negative stances toward women, ranging from the claim that God has positioned them under the authority of the men in their lives to the claim that they are incapable of sound spiritual judgment without male supervision.

Faulty conclusions drawn from Numbers 30 are a result of failing to let the passage interpret itself. The provisions for canceling vows are not due to any distinction between men and women on God's part. This is made clear by the fact that widowed and divorced women are just as responsible to keep their vows as are men (30:9). If women were in some way incompetent or requiring male guardianship, then these two categories of women would not have been left to themselves.

Then what is the reason behind the special provisions allowing fathers and husbands cancellation rights? The closing verse of the passage states that the stipulations were being made "concerning relationships" or "as between" father and daughter and "as between" husband and wife (30:16). If, as has been shown, God did not dictate that men should dominate women, then the only possibility is, once again, that God was establishing His rule within the confines of the culture, which had, indeed, determined that family relationships would be patriarchal. In the ancient middle-east, daughters and wives did not operate as independent individuals, at least not in a way that would violate the authority that fathers and husbands exercised over them. Religious vows could have involved abstaining from certain routine responsibilities or giving up valuable possessions. No such decision could be made by a girl or a woman without the approval of her father or husband. Culture had set these relationships, not God.

Perhaps the provisions of Numbers 30 were meant to emphasize and legislate what women *could* do rather than what women *could not* do. If this is the case, then the passage should be read not as limiting women's participation but as securing for women the opportunity to make vows. Many ancient cultures, including Israel perhaps, would not have allowed their women to make serious religious pledges. By binding daughters and wives to their vows except in the case of father/husband nullification, God was acknowledging and protecting their place in the worshipping community, not lessening it. With the cancellation clauses, God arranged for women to exercise their devotion in a way that was culturally tolerable, thereby further encouraging the possibility of them making spiritual vows.

Circumcision

A major claim to God positioning men over women in the Old Testament is based upon the rite of circumcision. This was to be the outward sign of God's covenant with Israel and of Israel's consecration to that covenant and to God. But, of course, only males could participate, so it is said that men were thereby chosen by God to be the spiritual leaders of the nation of Israel.

Circumcision was established between God and Abraham in Genesis 17, but several significant incidents preceded the occasion. In Genesis 12 God promised to make Abraham the father of a great nation of people. But the fulfillment did not occur immediately, so in Genesis 15 God covenanted with Abraham assuring him again of His promises. But the fulfillment still didn't come, so in Genesis 16 Abraham tried to produce the first descendant himself. It was after this incident that God introduced circumcision. Abraham and all male descendants that followed him were to observe it.

Why circumcision? Is there any "sense" to this symbol? Why was it introduced in chapter 17 rather than in 12 or in 15? All of what God was promising Abraham revolved around the miracle of *God* bringing forth a great nation of people from this man. God was evidently waiting for Abraham to be too old to produce offspring himself in order for there to be no doubt as to God's role in the miracle. The point was for Abraham to trust God, not himself. But even with the assurance of God's promises in chapter 12 and of God's covenant in chapter 15, Abraham was struggling with such trust. So God reconfirmed His commitment to Abraham with a very significant symbol. He reconfirmed that He would do exactly what He had promised and had covenanted to do, that *He* would provide the descendants. And He told Abraham to literally etch a reminder of his total reliance upon God on the very instrument Abraham viewed as the producer of descendants. Further, God insisted that this same mark be worn by every man who would follow Abraham, providing a perpetual reminder that God, not man, was producing this great nation of Israel.

As far as can be determined, ancient peoples viewed men as being more responsible for producing children than women. Probably because the man's sperm was "visible" via the semen and the woman's contribution, the egg, was not visible, the male was seen as the cause of babies, and the female was seen as simply the carrier of babies. This explains the pressure women felt to conceive children and the stigma assigned specifically to them if the marriage did not produce offspring. If the husband could emit semen, he had to be all right. If there were no children, the wife had to be the problem. It was also generally true in the male dominated societies of antiquity that the husband determined the frequency of sexual intercourse within the marriage. The wife complied and bore the children that resulted. So the very one who thought he was responsible for producing offspring would be asked to wear a mark on *his* body proclaiming that *God* was producing the offspring of His special people Israel.

It is more sensible to conclude that circumcision was a reflection of a society characterized by male dominance and particularly a purposeful "check" put upon the confident men of that society than it is to conclude that circumcision means God wants men and only men to be spiritual leaders. The first conclusion does not require the big jump that the second conclusion requires. Further, the Old Testament, as will be seen in a subsequent chapter, does not support the second conclusion. It does not contain "men only" in its roster of great spiritual/national leaders. Circumcision, then, had to do with the position of men in a sinful society rather than with the position of men in the eyes of God.

It has been said that because they were circumcised, husbands functioned as spiritual representatives or "priests" of their families in somewhat the same way as priests functioned as spiritual representatives for the whole of Israel because they were consecrated. This is extended into today and interpreted as meaning that husbands/men are positioned by God more highly than wives/women and are actually *over* them. It does seem that God was trying to instill in His people a sense of collective, corporate identity. Because of this a priest was able to offer a sacrifice for an entire nation and a man was able to visit the tabernacle or temple on behalf of his entire family. Of course, in a patriarchal culture it would be the husband/father, certainly not the wife/mother and not even the couple together, who would be expected to fill such a post of leadership. Again, God was working within societal practices for His purposes, but He was not prescribing their customs for the future.

What did God desire for the future? Two New Testament stipulations shed considerable light on the answer to this question. First, with the coming of the perfect priest Jesus Christ, the New Testament abolishes *all* spiritual representation by earthly priests (Hebrews 7 & 8), be they over a congregation or over a family. Instead, every individual Christian is made a member of the priesthood of believers (1 Peter 2:5; Revelation 1:6) with direct access to God and with equal standing before God. Interestingly, Protestants are quick to cite this truth as sufficient grounds for dispensing with the position and authority of a congregational priest, but many refuse to make the same application to their Old Testament view of family priests.

Second, the outward sign of participating in the *new* covenant is not circumcision, which includes only men, but water baptism, which is equally available to both men and women. The New Testament does not instruct Christians to be circumcised; in fact, it says, "Circumcision is nothing and uncircumcision is nothing" (1 Corinthians 7:19). So much for any claim to male superiority or female inferiority based upon this Old Testament rite! The very command of Jesus that commissions believers to evangelize the world instructs them to baptize each convert (Matthew 28:19). This is the outward sign of membership in the covenant community of the New Testament, and it is totally without male-female preference.

Unless the church is willing to require the rite of circumcision of all adult male converts as God told Israel to do (Exodus 12:48–49), it should not impose any implications of uncircumcision upon its women, especially implications that are erroneous to begin with. However, if God's reasons for requiring circumcision are over, then any superiority men claim over qualifying and participating must be over as well, especially any that never truthfully existed in the first place.

Male Priests

Probably the loudest argument drawn from the Old Testament against women ministers is that there were no female priests. When God first appointed Aaron to serve as Israel's priest, He appointed Aaron's sons to serve with him (Exodus 29:4–9). Similarly, when the tribe of Levi was appointed to replace the firstborn of each family in assisting with tabernacle/temple duties (Numbers 1:47–53; 3:5–8,11–12; 8:26), only the males were counted (Numbers 3:14–16). Though there is some dispute among scholars between the exact duties of the priests versus the Levites, the intention of God's original appointment seems to be that Aaron's male descendants would serve as priests; and the male descendants from the tribe of Levi would serve in assistant capacities. There is no record in the Old Testament of a woman serving in either position. The argument, then, is rather obvious: if women were not priests or assistants in the Old Testament, they should not be ministers today.

This argument fails to acknowledge two important possibilities. First, there may have been reasons for excluding women from the priesthood which had nothing to do with their spiritual/ministerial fitness per se, especially as it pertains to filling a post of church leadership today. Second, the close connection that is being drawn between the Old Testament priest and the New Testament minister may not be valid and may result in more excluding than the church realizes.

The first possibility that deserves careful investigation is the likelihood of there being other reasons for the all-male priesthood that actually explain it better than claiming that God prefers the spiritual/ministerial leadership of men over that of women. There are, indeed, five such reasons worth consideration.

(1) Certain duties of the Old Testament priesthood may have been physically prohibitive for the build and strength of a woman. Without getting lost in a maze of intricate details, it can be said that there were multiple daily sacrifices, plus the many occasional sacrifices and the annual festival sacrifices. Most offerings involved the slaughter of animals, sometimes by the male worshipper but other times by the priest. Though there was provision for doves and pigeons to be offered by the very poor, the sacrificial animals were typically quite sizable. It is feasible that a female priest could not have fulfilled the physical demands of the position.

(2) It is possible that the constraints of motherhood presented an additional obstacle. God was raising up a great nation in Israel, a people growing from 70 upon entering Egypt to several million upon leaving Egypt, a people that would eventually number "as the stars in the sky and as the sand on the seashore." A fruitful womb was a sign of God's blessing upon a couple. Put quite bluntly, the women of Israel were probably carrying a child, birthing a child, or nursing a child much of their fertile years. Though both parents were equally responsible under God for child-rearing, the mother's childbearing responsibilities were, of course, unique to her and extremely restrictive by nature. A woman could not possibly be available on any regular, long-term basis for morning-till-evening assignment outside the home unless she was celibate, and God chose not to design celibacy into the priesthood. Eventually, the priests were orga-

nized into 24 divisions, with each division given one week of service twice a year. Again, the feasibility of aligning such a schedule with the women's various cycles of carrying, birthing, and nursing their babies made female priests physically impractical if not impossible.

(3) A major "legal" restriction was imposed upon the viability of female priests by the law itself. Though ceremonial cleanness and uncleanness may seem like remote concepts to Christians today, God used these provisions to teach Israel important lessons that would help ready them for redemption. One of the causes of uncleanness was the emission of bodily fluids produced by the reproductive organs. This, of course, affected both men (Leviticus 15:1–3, 13, 16) and women, but it affected women for seven days every menstrual cycle (Leviticus 15:19), 33 or 66 days every time a baby was born (Leviticus 12:1–5), and additional days under various other circumstances (Leviticus 15:25,28). This should not be interpreted as discriminatory against women. It was simply a spiritual lesson about God's presence and holiness that was so crucial it could not be compromised in any way (Leviticus 15:31), not even for the sake of "sexual fairness." Because men and women have different sexual discharges, the restrictions affecting each had to be different, reflective of the gender. It would be difficult, then, for a woman to serve as a priest in light of the fact that she would undergo such regular, lengthy intervals of ceremonial uncleanness during which she could not engage in religious service. Her menstrual cycle alone would render her unavailable one fourth of the days each month, plus the possibility of additional disqualification numerous times during every nine-month pregnancy. Such frequent periods of uncleanness made it difficult if not impossible to expect of a woman the dependable service that was necessary to administer a system of daily sacrifices.

(4) It is very likely that Israel's patriarchal culture played a role in God's excluding of women from the priesthood. The office of the priest held a high degree of stature and authority which would have been incompatible on an everyday basis with the social standing of Hebrew women. Though there were exceptions, women were generally not seen as independent of a father, a husband, or some other male relative; nor were they viewed as representatives of a family. Perhaps it would have been difficult to accept them as representatives of an entire nation, especially spiritual representatives, though exceptions

did arise. The priesthood was also a profession in that the priest and the priest's family were supported by its "proceeds." It was not the role of a Hebrew woman to provide the family's primary livelihood; that was the role of the man.[7] As in the many other instances of God dealing with Israel within the confines of its culture, the all-male priesthood was probably, at least in part, a result of patriarchal preferences and practices that were extremely entrenched in the customs of the ancient world.

(5) A strong argument can be made for the possibility of God establishing an all-male priesthood in order to distinguish Israel's true religion from the false religions of Canaan and the surrounding areas. What plagued Israel's neighbors is known today as the Earth-Mother religions, the fertility cults, or the mother goddess cults. Their prevalence and influence are attested to by modern archeology and anthropology. And the Bible is clear that Israel was to avoid any association with their practices.

These ancient agricultural peoples thought that the fertility of the earth (plants, animals, and people) was tied to the sexual activity of male gods and female goddesses.[8] In order to stimulate the deities to fruitfulness, male priests and female priestesses would typically imitate the deities' sexual activities by engaging in "sacred prostitution" with each other and with worshippers. So, even though Israel's contemporaries were quite familiar with "female ministers," they were very much associated with ritual prostitution and with the goddesses who were the lewd partners of a multitude of false gods.

According to Scripture, these religions were *the* enemy of God's people, constantly threatening to undermine their loyalty to Jehovah. Unfortunately, Israel fell victim again and again to their powerful attraction. The god Baal and the goddess Asherah (Ashtoreth, Ashtaroth) were male-female counterparts and were probably the supreme deities of the fertility cults. Each took various local forms and was denounced many times by God. Nonetheless, Israel began worshipping these two deities not long after settling into Canaan (Judges 2:13) and returned to them many times.

It is possible that Asherah eventually became more prominent than Baal because far more idols and poles (KJV "grove" or "high places") bearing her image have been found throughout Palestine than those bearing his image. Perhaps this corresponds with ancient women feeling such pressure to conceive children and such blame if the marriage was childless. God's people were warned in particular against the worship of this goddess (Deuteronomy 16:21, NIV). The worship of her is identified in particular as being associated with the fall of Israel (2 Kings 17:7–13, NIV). It was Asherah who was set up in Jerusalem in the temple, not by an invading people but by one of Judah's kings (2 Kings 21:7, NIV; 23:4–7, NIV). It was the "Queen of Heaven" to whom a large throng of Judah's citizens still claimed defiant allegiance even after being sent into exile for their idolatry (Jeremiah 44:15–18).

Because both the priests and the priestesses of these false religions performed sexual rites, and because there were as many male prostitutes in their temples as there were female prostitutes, women should not be accused of bearing more blame in the fertility cults than men. Why, then, would it help maintain Israel's dissociation from the cults to exclude women from tabernacle/temple service? God's people had to be kept from *any* notion of multiple deities, but the pitfalls that were *most* threatening because they surrounded them were the fertility cults that featured male and female deities. By using priests and priestesses to depict the activities of these gods and goddesses, there was clearly a link between the false religions of Israel's neighbors and the makeup of their clergy. Consequently, Israel's priesthood could only be distinctly different if it was either *all* male or *all* female, completely avoiding the sexual connotations that a dual-sex priesthood would convey in the ancient world. If it were male *and* female, then a replica of heathen leadership and an opportunity to imitate false worship would be ever present. In light of the other likely reasons for instituting a male priesthood, there is little doubt as to which way the choice would lean.[9]

Without wanting to extend the discussion unnecessarily, it should, nonetheless, be made clear for the sake of thoroughness that the five explanations for excluding women from tabernacle/temple service are not only applicable to the position of priest but to the position of Levite as well. (1) With the Levites being responsible for disassembling, transporting, reassembling, and maintaining the worship facility, the physical demands of their service equaled or exceeded those of the priests. Even after the temple was in use, the Levites' tasks were still quite physical (2 Chronicles 35:11). It is likely that a woman's strength would not have been adequate. (2) The constraints of motherhood would have posed as many problems for the schedule demands of a Levite as for those of a priest. (3) As the priest's appointment began with a ceremonial consecration (Exodus 29), the Levite's appointment began with a ceremonial purification (Numbers 8). This cleanness would have to be maintained because of handling the very elements of worship. But a woman would experience frequent and lengthy periods of disqualification because of her bodily functions. (4) Because of their involvement in Israel's worship of Jehovah, the Levites were definitely seen as holding positions of spiritual leadership. Repeatedly placing women in such a position of prestige and power would have run contrary to Israel's entire societal structure. (5) As assistants to the priests, it would have been just as problematic in terms of identifying with the fertility cults to have female Levites as it would have been to have female priests.

Each of the explanations for an all-male priesthood (including the Levites as assistants) is compelling. All five put together are more than compelling and are far more believable than any notion of God viewing men as inherently more spiritually/ ministerially fit than women. But what is most significant is that none of the five reasons for excluding women from the Old Testament priesthood is applicable to ministry within the church today. Pastoring doesn't require slaughtering oxen. Childbearing is not as primitive or as restrictive as it was thousands of years ago. Bodily fluids do not disqualify someone from preaching the gospel. Women serve as presidents of corporations and as prime ministers of countries; surely one could serve as a youth pastor. And as long as the desire to open the ministry to women is driven by the call of God and by the truth of Scripture rather than by a secular feminist agenda, then their presence would not risk confusing the church with false cults.

No one is saying that the Old Testament is irrelevant, simply that the reasons and purposes behind *certain ceremonial stipulations* are not present today. If the meaning behind a provision is gone, if the situations that a provision was meant to fit do not exist anymore, then continuing to apply its demands is nothing but empty legalism. And, of course, if someone insists upon being legalistic, then he must be consistent in applying *everything* the Old Testament says about priests. If the demands on a priest's beard (Leviticus 21:5) or testicles (Leviticus 21:20) were applicable in the past but are not applicable today, isn't it right to understand the gender requirements in the same way?

If men with physical defects of any type (Leviticus 21:21) were barred from the Old Testament priesthood but are welcome in church ministry today, isn't it right to understand the gender restrictions in the same way? According to the Old Testament, over 99% of today's ministers do not qualify to be priests because they are not descendants of Aaron, the absolutely first and foremost qualification of the priesthood (Exodus 29:9; Numbers 18:7). If non-descendants can be New Testament ministers, why not non-men?

The preceding lengthy treatment of five likely reasons for there being no female priests addresses only one of the two problems associated with barring women from the ministry on the basis of the Old Testament priesthood, namely, the problem of overlooking very compelling explanations that render Old Testament practice unique to the Old Testament. The second problem is even more serious. The New Testament abolishes the Old Testament priesthood! This leaves absolutely no room for defining a New Testament minister according to an Old Testament priest, either in role or in requirements.

If the New Testament minister derives from any Old Testament position, it derives from the Old Testament prophet, and there *were* female prophets in the Old Testament. Whereas the priest was an ecclesiastical, institutional office, the prophet had a charismatic calling.[10] Which of the two rings true to the New Testament? Whereas the priest had to be ceremonially clean, the prophet only had to be spiritually clean. Which reflects the criteria of the New Testament? John the Baptist, the minister who bridged the Old Testament and the New Testament, had both a priestly ancestry (Luke 1:5–13) and a prophetic anointing (Matthew 11:9,14).[11] Which ministerial opportunity did he choose? The priest spoke for the people to God (Hebrews 5:1, NIV), but the prophet spoke for God to the people (Hebrews 1:1).[12] Which would be the higher office? The answer to all of these questions is the prophet—the Old Testament office that provides the model for the New Testament minister, the office that was very much open to women in both the Old Testament and the New Testament, the office that still exists after Jesus fulfilled and concluded the priesthood.

As important as a "collective identity" was while God was establishing and preserving Israel as a nation, the New Testament opens covenant citizenship to everyone and emphasizes, indeed *requires,* an individual relationship with God through

Jesus Christ. In the Old Testament a man was able to represent a family before a priest, and the priest was able to represent the entire nation before God. But in the New Testament Jesus is said to have served in a representative, priestly capacity for the final time. Everyone, men and women, *everyone* who trusts in Jesus' representation is made an "individual priest" before God, not to offer further ceremonial offerings but to offer continuous spiritual offerings (1 Peter 2:5,9).

The Old Testament sacrifices that men offered for their families and that priests offered for their nation were simply "markers" anticipating the one and only sacrifice that was able to actually atone for sin. Once the perfect, final priest sat down at the right hand of God, His sacrifice complete, the ceremonial sacrifices *and the clerical priesthood* were over. The imperfect was replaced with the perfect; the temporary was replaced with the final (Hebrews 7:11–12,18–19,23–28; 8:1–2; 10:1–12).

The role of the priest, then, was to offer sacrifices for the sins of the people, and that role is over. The New Testament minister does not serve in a priestly capacity because there are to be no further collective representations and no further offerings for sin. If the New Testament minister does not fulfill the role of the priest, then there is no reason to expect him *or her* to meet the requirements of the priest, not the ceremonial requirements or the gender requirements. The various versions of the word "priest" (priest, priesthood, priests, priest's, priests') are found over 150 times in the New Testament, but, not surprisingly, not one ever refers to a Christian minister.[13] It is used of the priests of the old covenant, of first-century Jewish priests, of Jesus, and of all believers. None of the New Testament ministers is portrayed as a priest.

Even if there is some non-ceremonial way in which the New Testament minister represents the body of believers to God, this fact does not close the door to women ministers but opens it. If Christians are likened throughout the New Testament to Christ's bride, then it seems like women could serve well in representing them. And if there are seemingly always more women than men in local assemblies, surely a predominantly female group could be represented effectively by a woman.

So this "weightiest of all" arguments from the Old Testament for barring women from the ministry has absolutely no basis. First, there are at least five likely reasons for the all-male priesthood that are not applicable to the ministry today. Second, the model for the Christian minister is not found in the priest but in the prophet, which was open to both men and women in both testaments. And even if some thread of the representative function still lingers, women qualify as much as men to serve the New Testament church in this capacity.

The number of times in this discussion and in previous and subsequent discussions that God's sensitivity to culture is noted deserves careful attention. Of course, those who would explain God's dealings with a chauvinistic interpretation need to realize that there are other, better explanations that have everything to do with culture and nothing to do with preferring or positioning men over women. But God's awareness of cultural constraints must be acknowledged as well by overly zealous women who may be tempted to ramrod their way into the ministry waving biblical proof of equal access. Christian women must be sensitive to the culture of their society *and* to the culture of their church. Slowly but surely God readied His people for redemption and for the life-changing levels of righteousness that redemption would make possible. He continues to deal with His people in the very same way, patiently moving them along in a process of spiritual maturation. May the Spirit of God who has orchestrated these masterful step-by-step accomplishments give women the love and patience and wisdom that are necessary to deal with people as He deals with them.

Other Stipulations

Space does not permit a lengthy discussion of every Old Testament stipulation that "seemingly" favors men over women. Some of the most frequently cited have been examined to provide a model for understanding others. The Old Testament is the Word of God, so it must be read as providing truth for today. But in order for its message to be understood accurately and universally, it must be read within its cultural and historical context, realizing that its pages do not always present God's desires but oftentimes present Israel's customs. Sometimes the far-from-ideal practices of the ancient world are simply being reflected and recorded. Sometimes God is allowing these practices to temporarily coexist alongside His long-term efforts to move a people toward redemption. Sometimes, He even uses the "concessions" to teach truths that are foundational to being ready to receive redemption. And sometimes, though accused of condoning wrongdoing, God is actually restraining it and protecting women from its full potential.

This is not an effort to *"explain away"* Scripture. It is an effort to simply *explain* it and to do so in a hermeneutically sound fashion. It is an effort to explain Scripture so that many passages about men and women fit together consistently and holistically. It is an effort to explain Scripture so that the Old Testament and the New Testament each have their own unique identity but together have a progression and a unity. It is an effort to read Scripture in light of God's known character as revealed in Jesus Christ, so that it resounds with testimony to His integrity rather than shouting with confusion and contradiction.

After all, the same Old Testament that reports discrimination against women reports the practice of slavery and other societal evils. One example is probably sufficient: "Your male and female slaves are to come from the nations around you; from them you may buy slaves. You may also buy some of the temporary residents living among you and members of their clans born in your country, and they will become your property. You can will them to your children as inherited property and can make them slaves for life" (Leviticus 25:44–46). To put such a reference to slavery found in the law within its proper cultural and historical context is not said to be "explaining away" Scripture, at least not by advocates of the Bible. It is simply interpreting Scripture according to sound hermeneutical principles. The same treatment must be afforded the passages about women. If the bigotry that frequently stands behind slavery can no longer be defended by misrepresenting Scripture, then the male chauvinism that frequently stands behind the excluding of women from the ministry must be denied this dangerous practice as well.

Perhaps the most interesting "other Old Testament stipulation" regarding women is actually the absence of a stipulation. It is true that an argument from silence is not the most compelling argument. However, in light of the fact that Israel's very relationship with God was regulated by the mosaic law, and in light of the fact that the smallest detail of everyday living was addressed by these portions of Scripture, it is most interesting that the Old Testament nowhere commands a wife to obey her husband. Neither is the hierarchy of husbandly dominance and wifely subordination ordered by the Old Testament. Disrespectful and disobedient children are addressed in more than one location as is the authority of parents over children, but the authority of the husband over the wife is noticeably absent from God's dictates. In a document that details how God's people are to live their daily lives, the absence of any such stipulation is striking.

Spiritual Privileges and Responsibilities

Sense can be made of every Old Testament stipulation that may seem, on the surface, to discriminate against women. It is not hermeneutically necessary, nor is it even hermeneutically accurate to extend any of these provisions into a disqualification of women for ministry today. But there are still other Old Testament stipulations—those which *favor* the involvement of women in Israel's religious activities.

Even without circumcision, women were as much a part of the covenant as were men (Deuteronomy 29:9–15; 31:12). In fact, oftentimes "sons" refers to children in general, even to grandchildren, great grandchildren, and descendants in general. Women were just as responsible for knowing and obeying the law of the covenant as men were (Deuteronomy 17:2–5). Daughters were to participate in the ceremonial worship activities on an equal par with sons (Leviticus 10:14; Numbers 18:11,19; Deuteronomy 12:17–18). Women were to enter into the rejoicing of worship (Deuteronomy 12:12), and they are recorded as doing so through singing and dancing (Exodus 15:20–21; Judges 5:1,12). At least at one point, they comprised part of the temple choir (Ezra 2:65). In fact, nowhere in the Old Testament is the worship participation of women silenced or in any way restricted. If quietness in the sanctuary service is indeed a timeless, universal dictate of God, then any commandment to that effect is surprisingly missing from this large portion of Scripture that regulates worship to the smallest detail.

If the Psalms address everyone, not men only, then *everyone* is told to be very vocal in worship and in witness, in praise and in preaching. "Sing to the Lord, all the earth" (96:1). "May the peoples praise you, O God; may all the peoples praise you" (67:5). "Sing to the Lord, you saints of his; praise his holy name" (30:4). "Sing joyfully to the Lord, you righteous; it is fitting for the upright to praise him" (33:1). "Sacrifice thank offerings and tell of his works with songs of joy" (107:22). "Shout for joy to the Lord, all the earth" (100:1). "Let us shout aloud to the Rock of our salvation" (95:1). "Let everything that has breath praise the Lord" (150:6). Is all of this to be done only in private? No! "Enter his gates with thanksgiving and his courts with praise" (100:4). "Sing to the Lord a new song, his praise in the assembly of the saints" (149:1). "Praise God in his sanctuary" (150:1). And the commands not only include ministry *to* God but also ministry *for* God. "Proclaim among the nations what the Lord has done" (9:11). "Declare his glory among the nations, his marvelous deeds among all peoples" (96:3).

The women are specifically mentioned as being present for pivotal occasions in Israel's worship history:[14] the renewal of the covenant at the threshold of Canaan (Deuteronomy 29:9–15), the reading of the law when Joshua succeeded Moses (Deuteronomy 31:12), the renewal of the covenant after entering Canaan (Joshua 8:30–35), the return of the ark (2 Samuel 6:17–19), the spiritual preparation of the nation for a great military battle (2 Chronicles 20:13), the prophetic call for repentance before the people were sent into exile (Joel 2:12–17), and the reading and reestablishing of the law when the people returned from exile (Nehemiah 8:2).

Mothers shared with fathers one of the most important duties given to Israel, perhaps second only to serving God themselves—transferring the knowledge of God to the next generation (Proverbs 1:8). As KJV indicates, the word used of the mother, different from the word used of the father, is the Hebrew word "torah" or "law." This being Israel's designation for the mosaic law, the authoritative role being ascribed to mothers is made exceptionally clear. What the father and mother do for the child is combined into one entity in the next verse (Proverbs 1:9). Perhaps partially because of this great assignment, mothers were due the same honor as fathers (Exodus 20:12; 21:15,17; Leviticus 19:3; 21:1–3,10–11; Deuteronomy 21:18–19; 27:16), definitely a correction of what would otherwise be the case in a patriarchal culture. "These laws made no distinction between mother and father. Both parents shared the position of authority and responsibility in the care of their children."[15]

One of the greatest individuals in Israel's history, Samuel, was more a product of his mother's spiritual influence and family leadership than his father's. It was his mother Hannah, not his father Elkanah, who sought God for his birth and made a vow to return him to God's service (1 Samuel 1:9–11). It was Hannah's decision that Samuel would be given to God: "She said to her husband, 'After the boy is weaned, I will take him and present him before the Lord, and he will live there always.' 'Do what seems best to you,' Elkanah her husband told her" (1:22–23). The account continues, "After he was weaned, she took the boy with her, young as he was, along with a three-year-old bull, an ephah of flour and a skin of wine, and brought him to the house of the Lord" (1:24). The Bible says "they" took the child to the priest (1:25), evidently meaning Hannah and Elkanah, but the spokesperson before the priest was Hannah (1:26–28). Her dedicatory *prophetic* prayer is written into Scripture (2:1–10), and the Bible quotes her as saying, "I give him to the Lord" (1:28) and credits her as being the one responsible for doing so (2:20, NIV).

In various situations that specifically affected women, they were told to offer their own sacrifices for cleansing (Leviticus 12:6–8; 15:28–30). This involved approaching the door of the place of worship and presenting an offering to the priest, just as the men did with their sacrifices. No man was to act as the woman's spiritual guardian and offer the sacrifice for her; instead, she was to function as an independent individual. It can only be assumed that the same direct participation was expected of her any time a sacrifice was required of individuals under the law. The holy altar was just as approachable for her as it was for men.

The Leviticus 12 provision for cleansing after childbirth recognized two stages of uncleanness: first, 7 or 14 days during which the new mother's uncleanness was contagious, and, second, 33 or 66 additional days during which she was not contagious but could not "touch anything sacred or go to the sanctuary" (12:4). It seems reasonable to interpret this special provision as meaning that outside of these occasions, women approached the sanctuary and touched holy things as a part of their worship in the same ways anyone else did.

Provision was made for women to attend each of the three major feasts that men were required to attend—Passover, Pentecost, and Tabernacles (Deuteronomy 16:16). With the physical constraints and the ceremonial contamination associated with being female and bearing children, women could not, realistically, have been commanded to attend these events, but they were invited to attend. They were, of course, very much present and participatory in the first Passover (Exodus 12:47) and seem to have partaken in subsequent celebrations (Numbers 9:1–5; Joshua 5:10–12; 2 Kings 23:21; 2 Chronicles 35:1,7,17–18; Ezra 6:19–22). Explicit invitations were given for their participation in the feasts of Pentecost (Deuteronomy 16:11) and Tabernacles (Deuteronomy 16:13–15; 31:9–13). Women, then, were welcomed by God into Israel's highest expressions of corporate worship.

The discrimination against women in the temple did not occur until the intertestamental period, totally contrary to the provisions God had made within the law. In Solomon's Temple and in the Second Temple, both of which were built by the command of God, there were no separate, exclusive courts such as the Court of Women or the Court of Gentiles. These did not appear until Herod's Temple was built several years before Jesus' birth. It was in Herod's Temple that women were kept outside the Court of Israel, further away and at a lower elevation level than Jewish men were permitted. These, however, were man's restrictions, not God's. According to God's design, only the priests were to move into areas off-limits to fellow Israelites. And this restriction was abolished during the Crucifixion when the temple curtain was torn in two, signifying that God's special dwelling place would henceforth be within human hearts. So, God's "temple" in both the Old Testament and the New Testament was to be totally nondiscriminatory.

There is even a reference in the Old Testament to women ministering at the entrance of the tabernacle (Exodus 38:8). Their specific duties are unknown, but the Hebrew word used for their service is used elsewhere in the Old Testament only of military activities and of the work of the Levites in tabernacle/temple service.[16] It was at the entrance of the tabernacle that God met with Moses and with Israel and that sacrifices were made (Exodus 29:42–43), that priests were consecrated (Exodus 29:4) and Nazarites were dedicated (Numbers 6:18), that the people gathered (Leviticus 10:3) and were called to worship by the pillar of cloud (Exodus 33:9–10). It was from this location that the Promised Land was divided. It seems to have functioned very much like the altar area or platform of today's sanctuary, and it was here that women ministered.

One other spiritual honor bestowed upon Old Testament women is well worth noting. Both men and women were invited to voluntarily devote themselves to God in a special way through the Nazarite Vow (Numbers 6:1–21). Many scholars view the Nazarite as approaching the consecration level of the priest, perhaps even the high priest. There are certainly similarities in the ceremonial requirements, such as abstinence from wine (Leviticus 10:9; Numbers 6:3) and refraining from touching a dead body, even of a parent (Leviticus 21:1–3; 10–11; Numbers 6:6–7). Whatever the ministerial status of the Nazarite, it is significant that God would command a patriarchal people to allow women to join men in making a distinct dedication to spiritual matters. Whatever the New Testament counterpart would be, all too many will not permit women the same opportunities in the church today.

5

Old Testament Examples of Women

The Old Testament presents several women who served in high-level positions of spiritual leadership within Israel, indeed, sometimes *over* all of Israel. Of course, far more men than women ministered in such capacities because Israel was predominantly patriarchal, and God did tolerate certain cultural inclinations. But the women who led God's people did so with God's approval and anointing, and they did so with unusual distinction and effectiveness.

There is no way to rectify this with a narrow, superficial interpretation of the two brief "silent and submissive" passages in the New Testament. In fact, the weight of Old Testament history to the contrary is one of the most insurmountable obstacles to any claim that the Bible forbids women from serving as authoritative, spiritual leaders. Scripture does not deny female leadership; Scripture depicts female leadership. The traditions of a culture or of a church may paint women as incapable of leadership or as ineligible for leadership, but the Bible paints a very different picture.

There is no indication that any of the female leaders of the Old Testament functioned under the supervision of a man. Anyone who claims this has no evidence to support it and is basically just inventing details that are not found in the biblical account. Further, there is no indication that a position, when filled by a woman, was in any way different from the same position filled by a man. A female prophet was fully a prophet, and a female judge was fully a judge. The Old Testament makes absolutely no distinction in its presentation of women in positions of authority versus its presentation of men in the identical positions. Any claim to the contrary is, again, nothing but imagination and invention. The women are never presented as temporary, emergency replacements for unavailable men. They are most certainly not presented as something contrary to the nature of humanity or to the will of God. There is no hint of their appointments being God's "permissive will" rather than God's "perfect will." Again, such notions are imposed upon the text. Even though they were rare exceptions rather than common occurrences, due to the people's cultural prejudices, they are in no way depicted by Scripture as novelties or oddities. They are simply matter-of-fact-likely portrayed as God-called, God-used individuals who happen to be women. Their record of righteousness and boldness stands for itself, and they become models for both men and women to emulate.

The biblical account does not even mention their facing any confusion or resistance on the part of the people who were to follow them. Every indication is that Israel acknowledged their authority and leadership exactly as male leaders were acknowledged. Evidently even within ancient, patriarchal Israel there was an ableness, a willingness to recognize true handmaidens of God. Oh to God, for such a capacity today! If God's Old Testament people saw women do great things for Him, surely God's New Testament people should encourage even greater opportunities and accomplishments.

Lofty Honors

The spiritual privileges afforded New Testament believers far exceed those available to their Old Testament counterparts, both in quantity and in quality. Surely two of the highest spiritual distinctions bestowed upon any Old Testament saint were, first, a visitation of the Lord and, second, the opportunity to compose Scripture. Both of these honors were given to women.

Numerous times the Old Testament records a visit by "the angel of the Lord." Though it is possible for this reference to identify one of the heavenly hosts, more often it seems to refer to a manifestation of God Himself. Theologians label this occurrence a "theophany." Because the word "angel" means "messenger," it is appropriate for it to refer to anyone bearing a message. The theophanies are believed to involve the person of God because on various occasions the messenger receives worship, accepts an identification of deity, offers an identification of deity, and is said to be able to forgive sins. Because this messenger is frequently distinguished from God the Father, He is thought to be God the Son in preincarnate form.

What a privilege to receive such a visitation. Very few individuals in the Old Testament were so blessed, but women were among the select few. Hagar was ministered to on two separate occasions by the angel of the Lord and was told what would become of her child (Genesis 16:7–14; 21:14–19). In between these two incidents, the angel visited Abraham, and that visit included an inquiry about his wife Sarah and a response to Sarah's lack of faith regarding a child being born (Genesis 18:1–15). Also on two occasions, the angel of the Lord visited Samson's mother (Judges 13). Interestingly, it was to her rather than to Samson's father that the message was first given that the child was to be a Nazarite from birth. When Samson's father sought God for additional instructions, it was not to him but, again, to Samson's mother that the angel appeared a second time. He was only included in the visitation when she brought him to the angel. And in a reversal of the scenario of Abraham having faith and Sarah doubting, Samson's father was lacking in his understanding of the visit while Samson's mother was far more spiritually perceptive.

It's only conjecture as to why these particular women were chosen. What is certain is that women were chosen. They were chosen to receive very special revelations of God's work in the affairs of humankind. If God thought them valuable enough and capable enough to be given a peek into what He alone knew and understood, it's difficult to argue that Eve's deception left all women inferior and incompetent. Obviously, God thinks otherwise, yes, even when significant spiritual insights are involved. It is especially significant that God did not use her husband or any other man to serve as a trustee for Samson's mother. Instead, God rather deliberately bypassed her husband and spoke truth directly to her and assigned responsibility singularly to her.

In addition to the honor of receiving theophanies, women were also given the opportunity to contribute some of the material that was ordained by God to be included in Holy Scripture. Though only a brief chorus in comparison to the "Song of Moses," the words of praise that Miriam wrote are found in Exodus 15:21. Deborah and Barak sang a lengthy song (Judges 5), and she was evidently responsible for composing its words (v. 7). One of Huldah's prophecies is permanently recorded in 2 Kings 22:15–20 and in 2 Chronicles 34:22–28. The magnificent, often-preached passage describing the ideal wife, preserved at length in Proverbs 31:10–31, is credited to the teaching of a woman (Proverbs 31:1). The list continues into the New Testament with the blessing of Elizabeth (Luke 1:42–45) and the song of Mary (Luke 1:46–55). These are not just words spoken by women in conversation but according to the Bible's designations are verses of song, instruction, and prophecy authored by women. Of course, men wrote significantly more scriptural material than did women, but the fact that God chose to include the compositions of several women underscores how effectively they, like men, can be moved upon by God's Spirit to produce and to perpetuate truth. If they can write Scripture, surely they are trustworthy to teach it.

Wise Women

The Old Testament tells the stories of two different wise women whose counsel superseded the decisions of Israel's highest ranking officials. The first is detailed in 2 Samuel 14:1–21. After David's son Absalom ordered the murder of another of David's sons, Absalom went into exile from his father. Though David longed for Absalom, he was evidently unwilling to reconcile with him. So David's military commander Joab sent for a wise woman from the town of Tekoa to do the clever, sensitive persuading of the king that was necessary. She did so quite impressively and successfully. King David did exactly what she encouraged him to do.

The second account is found in 2 Samuel 20:14–22. After David's son Absalom led a revolt against his father and was killed, David had to mend the rift that was left between the tribes. A man by the name of Sheba took advantage of the disunity and instigated his own rebellion against the king, resulting in a very large following. David's military commander Joab chased Sheba to the city of Abel Beth Maacah and laid siege to the city. Just as Joab was about to ram through the city's wall, a wise woman called from inside to talk with him. She proceeded to reason with Joab and to negotiate terms for lifting the siege. She then met with the people and convinced them to comply with the arrangement. They did so, which meant delivering Sheba's head to Joab, and with that the siege was over.

The Bible presents both of these wise women in a positive light. One reasoned with a king; the other reasoned with a general and with an entire city. Both acted in noticeably influential, extremely authoritative capacities. Both set out to change the mind and the conduct of a man, a man in a high position of leadership. In one instance the man was the king of Israel. In the other instance the man was the ranking military officer of Israel. One of the women put herself in leadership over a whole community of God's people. However, there is not the slightest hint of wrongdoing on the part of either woman. They are presented as perceptive in their thinking and as competent in their accomplishment. They were able to converse with a king, a general, and a city and to direct their audience wisely and rightly. One functioned privately, and the other functioned publicly; but both seemingly functioned with God's blessing.

At an earlier time in David's life, another woman, Abigail, was similarly used in the wisdom of God. She was able to reverse his plans, which were terribly wrong, with her counsel, and she is said to have been sent by God to do so. "David said to Abigail, 'Praise be to the Lord, the God of Israel, who has sent you today to meet me. May you be blessed for your good judgment and for keeping me from bloodshed this day'" (1 Samuel 25:32–33). She is depicted by Scripture as intelligent and capable, while her wealthy husband is depicted as too insolent to do right and her soon-to-be king is depicted as too impetuous to do right. She reversed the bad decisions of both men with her own better judgment.

Long before David's time another man, Abraham, was overruled by his wife. Sarah literally told her husband what to do in regards to problems that were arising with Hagar and Ishmael. God told him to do as she said, and he did so (Genesis 21:8–14). One can only imagine the import the words "listen to *whatever* Sarah tells you" would have today if they had been spoken in the opposite direction. But because a husband was told to "obey" a wife, the incident is virtually ignored. It is true that Sarah had been wrong regarding Ishmael's birth, but she was right about his future. Abraham's will in the matter threatened to thwart God's plan, but Sarah's will promised to advance God's plan.

Long after David's time, yet another woman took the lead in her family. The Shunamite woman was clearly more sensitive and responsive in spiritual matters than was her husband (2 Kings 4:8–37). She, not her husband, realized Elisha was a man of God for whom provision should be made in their home. It was of her, not of her husband, that Elisha inquired regarding returning the favor. It was to her, not to her husband, that the promise was made of a child being born. When the child became ill and died, it was she, not her husband, who traveled to Elisha for help. And when the child was raised from the dead, Elisha delivered him back to her, not to her husband. None of the woman's spiritual initiative and forwardness was met with correction but with blessing.

These Old Testament examples do not align with a "wife obey husband" view of marriage and family. Instead, they demonstrate the viability of a woman exercising authority and leadership in the home. They depict this role as being ordered, used, and blessed by God. Some of the examples show that her competencies should be empowered outside the home as well. Obviously, Eve's deception has not left women so prone to deception that they must be kept from positions which would allow them to have influence over men. Each of these Old Testament women did quite well with her influence over men, whether a husband, a general, a king, or an entire city of men. In each case she was extremely right, and one or more men were extremely wrong.

Prophets

The word of the Lord came to Moses, Samuel, Elijah, Elisha, Isaiah, Jeremiah, Ezekiel, Daniel, and several other select Old Testament prophets, including women. The Old Testament priest represented the people to God, which Jesus did once and for all, thereby ending the office. The Old Testament prophet, however, represented God to the people, a much loftier position, in fact, the loftiest position in all of the Old Testament. Scripture itself was known to first-century Jews as "the law and the prophets" (Matthew 7:12), not "the law and the priests" or "the law and the kings." The responsibility of speaking for God entails the highest level of spiritual intimacy and authority possible.[1] The fact that this function is still needful and active in the New Testament church, and the fact that women were used in this capacity in both testaments speaks volumes about their qualification to serve at all levels of spiritual leadership today.

Whereas a priest could function by simply knowing the ceremonies of Judaism, a prophet had to know the mind and will of God. And the prophet not only received a message from the Lord, he or she then spoke that word. Prophesying involved preaching as much as or more than it involved predicting. It is extremely significant that women served just as effectively as men in such intimate, authoritative, and instructional capacities. And they did so not over a small local gathering but over the entire nation of Israel, over all of God's people. Indeed, their messages frequently had not only spiritual ramifications but also social and political effects which were felt nationally and internationally. How, then, can a woman not qualify to serve as a deacon or a pastor in a local church today?

These women did not position themselves; God selected and appointed them. They were the recipients of God's call and of the accompanying gifts. If God, rather than individuals or organizations, is still calling ministers, then how can there be resistance or refusal when He calls a woman just as He did in the Old Testament? If under the old dispensation, in the midst of Israel's extreme patriarchalism, God-called and God-anointed women were allowed to speak for God, shouldn't equal or greater opportunities be granted to women under the new covenant?[2]

Because the presence of female prophets in the Old Testament impacts the legitimacy of female ministers in the New Testament, special precaution must be taken against attempts to explain the prophets out of existence. The typical arguments are identified at the outset of this chapter. With the exception of Miriam probably functioning under the leadership of Moses, the female prophets of the Old Testament did not serve under the supervision of men. In whatever way the prophet Miriam was under Moses, the priest Aaron was also under Moses. If there are no carryover effects upon male ministers due to Aaron's position, there should be no carryover effects upon female ministers due to Miriam's position. The Bible gives no indication of any difference in what a prophet was or in what a prophet did depending upon whether the position was filled by a man or a woman. And it was a position, an office, not just a momentary, charismatic activity. The women are not simply said to have prophesied; they are called prophets. There is no hint that they were positioned by God because men were not available, nor is there any suggestion that they were seen by Israel as peculiar because of their gender. No such suggestions are made about the male prophets, and there is no reason to do so regarding their female counterparts.

The Hebrew word for prophet is "nabi." The same word with a female ending is "nabiah" in Hebrew and "prophetess" in

English. It is used of four women of God in the Old Testament: Miriam (Exodus 15:20), Deborah (Judges 4:4), Huldah (2 Kings 22:14; 2 Chronicles 34:22), and Isaiah's wife (Isaiah 8:3). The same word is also used of Noadiah (Nehemiah 6:14) who was evidently a problematic prophetess. She was grouped with "the rest of the prophets" who were in error, no distinction being made between males and females.

It is possible in reference to Isaiah's wife that the word is used as an honorary title for the wife of a prophet, but it is just as likely that the two were a "ministerial couple." The fact that the verse refers to her within the context of conceiving his child may invite the conclusion that she was simply the wife of a prophet. However, the Old Testament makes a clear designation to this effect when it is the case elsewhere (2 Kings 4:1). Further, it was not common in Israel for a woman to receive the feminine title of her husband's profession.[3] Since all of the other Old Testament uses of the word "prophetess" are clearly referring to female prophets, there is considerable weight on the side of her being exactly that.

Whatever the case with Isaiah's wife, Miriam, Deborah, and Huldah were women of God who ministered as Old Testament prophets. There is no way to minimize or invalidate their positions of authority and leadership in Israel. If they gave forth true prophecy, and they did, it had to have come from God. He, then, was the originator and the source of their ministries. Even women who prophesied falsely were not denounced for anything having to do with their gender but were condemned solely on the basis of their false message and false practices (Ezekiel 13:17) as were men who did the same thing (Jeremiah 23:31). The female false prophets are, of course, far outnumbered across the pages of the Old Testament by the male false prophets.

Prophetess Miriam

Though little is known about the individual or her ministry, Miriam, the sister of Moses and of Aaron, is called a prophetess (Exodus 15:20–21). She cannot be dismissed simply because she was guilty on one occasion of challenging Moses' leadership (Numbers 12). Aaron was an equal participant in the wrongdoing and was also guilty of a seemingly more despicable sin in regards to erecting and worshipping the gold calf idol (Exodus 32). Moses himself was found with sin and was forbidden from entering Canaan because of it (Numbers 20:1–12). Nonetheless, Moses was the deliverer, Aaron was the high priest, and Miriam was the prophet of Israel.

Many years after Israel's Egypt-Canaan trek, God spoke the following words to them: "I brought you up out of Egypt and redeemed you from the land of slavery. I sent Moses to lead you, also Aaron and Miriam" (Micah 6:4). According to Scripture, then, Miriam, was appointed by God Himself to a position of national leadership over all of Israel. She was one of three individuals commissioned with the responsibility of leading God's people out of Egypt into Canaan. She was viewed by God as in a category with the great deliverer Moses and as being side-by-side with the high priest Aaron. The three of them were more highly positioned than anyone else in Israel—the leaders of the twelve tribes, the judges chosen to assist Moses (Exodus 18:24–26), the Levites chosen to assist the priests, and the priests chosen to assist Aaron. All of these individuals were, of course, men; and Moses, Aaron, *and Miriam* were spiritual leaders *over* all of them.

Acts 7:37–38 uses the very same word for the people of Israel (Greek "ekklesia") as is used throughout the New Testament for the church.[4] Israel was indeed an assembly or body of believers, a congregation, a church. And Miriam was one of three spiritual leaders over that church. Because of the size and spread of Israel, a local pastorate would not even be the equivalent of her position; high-level denominational leadership would be the counterpart today. This prophet and spiritual leader of Israel stands in sharp contrast to any insistence today that women be kept from congregational ministry and be kept from authority over men.

Prophetess Huldah

After God's people divided into two kingdoms, Israel basically plummeted into sin while Judah went through cycles of sin, repentance, and renewal. One of the most sweeping renewals was during King Josiah's reign. He ordered the restoration of the temple; and in the process of obeying his order, the high priest found the "Book of the Law." When it was read to the king, he was extremely upset over Judah's obvious disobedience of its decrees. He gave the following order to the high priest and to four of his high-ranking national officials: "Go and inquire of the

Lord for me and for the people and for all Judah about what is written in this book that has been found" (2 Kings 22:13). The five-man delegation went to the prophetess Huldah (2 Kings 22:14–20; 2 Chronicles 34:22–28).

King Josiah was asking for a commentary from God regarding the Scripture that had been read to him; he was asking for a direct word from God regarding Judah's spiritual situation. And he was asking for this insight on behalf of a king and an entire kingdom. It is interesting that the high priest was not able to interpret God's Word. It is also interesting that the men did not seek the counsel of Jeremiah or Zephaniah who were ministering in Judah at this time. Instead, Huldah was the one who knew the word and will of God in the matter. She served as God's mouthpiece to the priest, the officials, the king, and all of God's people. Over and over again in her response she proclaimed, "Thus saith the Lord." Is there any higher claim to authoritative words?

After Huldah's words were reported to him, King Josiah gathered all of Judah's elders, priests, prophets, men, and people together and read to them the book that had been found (2 Kings 23:1–3). Evidently Huldah had authenticated it, had confirmed that it was indeed God's Word. He also renewed Judah's covenant with God and enforced drastic changes in their religious practices (2 Kings 23:4–25). Huldah had impacted the spiritual behavior of the entire nation.

Very little is known about this woman other than that she was married to a rather low-ranking temple official. So, she was not the wife of a prophet as was the case with Isaiah's wife; she was the prophet. Though she is not known to have penned any other portions of Scripture herself, the words of her prophecy about the eventual fall of Judah are recorded and fulfilled in Scripture.

What may be most significant about the prophetess Huldah is the way her ministry presses itself upon any view of women in ministry that is truly biblical. Obviously, she was not positioned and used by God because competent men were not available. A righteous king, a high priest, two notable prophets, and a contingency of national leaders and temple officials were all available. Obviously, she did not operate under the auspices of male supervision. Her husband is no more than named. The male officials were not giving her counsel; they were seeking and following her counsel.

Huldah's authority and leadership were not small. She spoke for God. Her words affected the course of a king, the assignments of the clergy, and the fate of a nation. How can anyone claim that, according to the Bible, women cannot pastor local congregations? She interpreted Scripture, and some scholars contend that in authenticating it as God's Word she literally canonized Scripture. How can anyone claim that women cannot teach Scripture? Her insight and influence were given to her by God, obviously for the furtherance of His divine purposes. When she had audience with the high-ranking religious and political men of her day, she was neither silent nor subordinate. She spoke boldly and she ministered powerfully because her gifts and her position were of God.

Prophetess and Judge Deborah

In between Miriam and Huldah was a woman who was both a prophetess and a judge, Deborah. She, too, led men and was instrumental in determining the destiny of God's people. After the initial conquest of Canaan, the individual tribes were to drive out the small pockets of ungodly inhabitants left within various tribal boundaries. They failed to do so and instead were pulled into ungodliness themselves. To correct their wrongdoing, God allowed Israel to be oppressed by people groups both inside and outside of Canaan. Each time they cried out to God in repentance, God raised up a deliverer (KJV "savior" in Nehemiah 9:27). These individuals were called "judges" because they administered justice against the oppressors and then oversaw justice within Israel for the years of peace that followed. Unfortunately, Israel went through this sin-servitude-sorrow-salvation cycle over and over for more than four hundred years until they finally demanded of God an earthly king to lead them, again, trying be like the peoples around them.

The judges were not put into position by inheritance or by election. They were directly appointed by God (Judges 2:16; Acts 13:20). They were definitely leaders, first in a military capacity and then in a civil capacity. Several had rather surprising spiritual shortcomings, evidently explained by the fact that their primary role was not spiritual. It must be understood, however, that even though some of their activities were not sanctioned by God, their position of leadership over Israel was by divine commission.

There was one distinct exception to the "non-spiritual" leadership of these deliverers. Out of the twelve judges detailed in the book of Judges, one and only one, was also a prophet. One out of twelve judges, then, was called by God to be a military leader over Israel, a civil leader over Israel, *and* a spiritual leader over Israel. That judge was the woman Deborah. Without question she held the highest position of authority and leadership in Israel in her day. Only Samuel, detailed outside the book of Judges, also served as both judge and prophet, and yet his military contribution did not match that of Deborah. There is probably no ministerial position available today as high as that which was held by this woman.

Deborah's story is told in Judges 4 and 5. After a Canaanite group located in the northern part of Israel had oppressed God's people for twenty years, God raised up this woman as the solution. She summoned Barak, evidently a military man, and ordered him by the command of God to lead an army of 10,000 men against their foe. She spoke to this high-ranking man authoritatively, even claiming to speak for God (4:6). She offered to lure the opposing commander, Sisera, into their hands, but that was not enough for Barak. He said, "If you go with me, I will go; but if you don't go with me, I won't go" (4:8). She went with Barak and the troops, and she gave the decisive order to "charge" (4:14). Sisera's entire army was killed by Israel's swords. Sisera himself managed to flee but was later killed by a neighboring woman and handed over to Barak (4:17–22). Forty years of peace followed this significant victory (5:31).

Deborah, like Huldah, was married, but her husband received no more than an identification (4:4). She is said to have "held court...and the Israelites came to her to have their disputes decided" (4:5). In a culture in which the men made most of the decisions for the family and for the tribe, it can be assumed that these clients were men far more often than they were women. And yet a woman was put in position *by God* to be the final authority in their disputes. Her judgments would have affected entire families and entire tribes. Just as the people took their difficulties to Moses and later to Samuel, they sought Deborah's decisions in the same way. All indications are that her judgments were met with full acceptance and obedience.

As a judge, then, this woman exercised military, political, and judicial power. She was appointed by God to lead a nation out of servitude and into freedom, which she did. She was the leader in battle and the ruler in peace.[5] She was the only legal system the people had, the only government they had. As a prophet, she spoke God's truth and will to the people. She instructed them in the things of God. It can be assumed that if correction was necessary, she did that as well. Neither judges nor prophets functioned under man's authority; they functioned directly under God's authority, and the people, including the men, submitted to their leadership.

Any determination that is made today regarding what women can and cannot do in the work of God must reflect the biblical account of this woman Deborah; otherwise, the conclusions are not fully reflective of Scripture. This includes any conclusions that are drawn regarding the rightful positioning of married women. As a judge-prophet she stood in authority over the entire nation of Israel. Her leadership was clearly ordained by God and was mightily used by God, and all of this was accomplished without violating God's design for marriage. If Old Testament Israel was spiritually astute enough to discern and welcome God's hand upon a woman, it is difficult to understand why many Christians fail to do so today. Regrettably, if models such as Deborah are not put before the girls and women of the church, they too may fail to hear the voice of God calling them into ministerial service.

Queen Esther

The example of Queen Esther is frequently disregarded in studies of Old Testament women in leadership. It is true that certain questionable details are part of her story. As an exile from Jerusalem, Esther was able to become the queen of the foreign nation Persia only because the king's first wife was dismissed for disobedience to him. It was Esther's physical beauty and then her personal charm that won the position for her, and throughout the application process her Jewish identity was deliberately kept secret. This is quite different from the callings of judges and prophets.

Nonetheless, once Esther was made queen, she used her access and authority to oversee God's people. She demonstrated an amazing level of courage that women are sometimes not thought capable of exerting, risking her own life to save her people. She ordered a whole city of Jews to a fast. She was spiritual (Esther 4:15–16), assertive (4:17), diplomatic (7:3–4;

8:5–6), and brilliant (5:1–8; 7:1–6). These very qualities enabled her to save the Jews from utter annihilation and to position them within the favor of a powerful empire. She then continued to exercise leadership over them (9:29–32).

The Ideal Wife and Mother

Many who argue against women in ministry insist that the Old Testament examples of female leadership should be seen as exceptions rather than as models. They say that most Old Testament women saw their primary role as being a wife and a mother; consequently, women should aspire to the same domestic pursuits today. There are a few problems with this line of thinking. First, even if female leaders were exceptions, why are the opponents of women ministers not open to exceptions today? The attitudes, policies, and practices of many denominations regarding women in ministry are so absolute and all-encompassing that there is no room to recognize and receive the ministry of any woman, even an exception. How can New Testament believers defend being more rigid than Old Testament believers in this one area?

Second, as has been established earlier, the rare positioning of women in the Old Testament was more likely a result of *society's* biases than a reflection of *God's* biases. If God did not favor women in ministry, *no* women would have been called, anointed, and used. The fact that several were positioned by God indicates that He favors such roles for women. The problem, then, which limited their number must have had to do with the cultural chauvinism of the ancient world. Indeed, Old Testament Israel was so patriarchal that it is striking that any women were able to rise to leadership.

Similarly, societal resistance has restricted the role of women throughout history. What is tragic, however, is that it is the church more than the culture erecting the barriers today. Modern culture allows women opportunities that ancient culture forbid, but the church remains resistant. Not only in western societies but even in third world countries, women are moving into positions of leadership in practically every sphere of life—*except the church*. If God did not bar women from leadership in the Old Testament, Christians should not do so in the New Testament. If God allowed women as much leadership as the culture would accept, Christians should do the same.

The third problem with the idea of restricting women to domestic pursuits is that the Old Testament does not actually support this picture. The passage that is preached most often as the model for the ideal wife and mother is Proverbs 31:10–31. A closer look at this passage, however, reveals a women who is involved in far more than homemaking. The text identifies several outside-the-home activities that are thought by some to be the exclusive domain of men. She engages in real estate transactions (16) and in profitable trading (18). She has independent earnings which she invests into agricultural ventures (16). She operates a business of manufacturing and marketing goods (24) which requires the securing of raw materials (13). In short, she is a skillful, successful business woman with numerous commercial undertakings. In addition, this ideal woman, not her husband, manages the affairs of the household (27) and is known for her wisdom and for her teaching abilities (26). What a different picture from the restrictive conclusions that are drawn from certain New Testament passages.

This woman's accomplishments are independent from the involvement or supervision of her husband. He is not even mentioned other than to say that he has complete confidence in her (11) and praises her (28), which must include her business competence since it is the primary focus of the passage. Her career work is in no way shameful but brings honor to him (23) and equal honor to her (31).

Two mistakes must be avoided in forming a proper, biblical view of the role of wife-mother. One mistake is to *so devalue* the role that women think it necessary and acceptable to neglect their family members for the supposedly more meaningful pursuit of outside-the-home work. The ideal wife and mother of Proverbs 31 does not do so. Her attentiveness to her family's needs for food and clothing are mentioned (15,21). Her husband and her children do not feel neglected; they feel blessed (28). The second mistake is found at the opposite extreme, to *so overly value* the role of wife-mother that a woman is confined exclusively to that role, not permitted to invest her talents in outside-the-home activities. The Proverbs 31 passage obviously contradicts this notion. The ideal wife and mother of this passage is able to work outside the home without lessening her value inside the home. If the Bible does not force a woman into an either/or choice, neither should anyone else.

It must be remembered that if a man is a husband-father, then he is just as accountable to God for fulfilling these responsibilities as his mate is accountable for being a good wife and mother. In fact, men are probably admonished in Scripture about fulfilling their roles more often than are women. And yet no one would conclude from this that a man must not pursue a profession. Relationships inside the home and roles outside the home are two different things; one does not necessarily preclude the other for a man, so one does not necessarily preclude the other for a woman. For *either* a husband-father or a wife-mother, a career *can* interfere with family obligations, but it does not have to do so. Both spouses must give utmost attention to the marriage, and both parents must give utmost attention to the children—regardless of outside-the-home involvement.

Of course, a woman's body is different from a man's, and these distinctions are not to be denied or disdained. She will carry, birth, and perhaps nurse any babies that are produced by the couple. She is typically less muscular than her mate, unable to perform some of the physical tasks that he is able to perform. She seems to be somewhat different emotionally, although many of these differences are environmentally produced rather than genetically produced. Any male-female differences that are genetic in nature are God-ordained and must be respected, but many of the ramifications of these differences are not specified by God and are thereby left to be decided by people. Numerous family, household, and wage-earning assignments that are "decided" by one's gender are actually decided culturally and individually; they are not prescribed by Scripture. The woman of Proverbs 31 crosses lines that some individuals and some cultures draw, but she evidently crosses no lines drawn by God.

It is possible that another book written by Solomon reveals the secret to less restrictive gender roles. Song of Songs (Song of Solomon) describes a relationship within which there is "no male dominance, no female subordination, and no stereotyping of either sex. The woman is independent, fully the equal of the man."[6] She approaches him as readily as he approaches her. He belongs to her as much as she belongs to him. Every aspect of the relationship is dictated by mutual respect for the qualities, desires, and potential contribution of the other person. Out of such a relationship can flow the beautiful combination of individuality and unity that marriage was meant by God to foster.

6

God's Gender

It is commonly assumed that ministers should be men because they serve as God's representatives and, of course, God is male or at least more male than female. Is there any truth to this claim? Is God in any way male? Is God in some way more male than female? Do a male minister and God share more in common than a female minister and God? These questions must be addressed because this alleged affinity between maleness and divineness is not only one of the most frequently voiced arguments against women ministers, it is a subconscious impression and a nagging hang-up even in the minds of many people who agree to accept women ministers. After all, God the Father, God the Son, and the vast array of masculine pronouns referring to God make for a compelling case in favor of God's maleness.

The Challenge of Revealing God

Theological truth is frequently found at the intersection of two opposing positions. If the tension wire is loosened on either side, if the scale is tipped in either direction, error results. This type of error is especially deceiving because it consists of an overabundance of one of the two ingredients that would otherwise produce truth. An example is found in viewing God as overly personal or as overly impersonal. Many false religions throughout history have proposed a god who is personal to the point of taking on the very characteristics of humanity. Other false religions have featured a god who is impersonal to the point of being an abstract principle or force. Cults of antiquity seem to have been particularly vulnerable to the first mistake, while modern cults seem more likely to fall prey to the second mistake.

The true God is neither personal to the point of human nor impersonal to the point of abstraction. The true God is spirit, which is difficult for humanity to comprehend. How can such an identity be revealed? The Bible presents God through the use of figurative language. Human-like characteristics and relationships are assigned to God, but these are not meant to be taken literally. God is said to see, but a Spirit God doesn't have actual eyes; God is said to hear, but a Spirit God doesn't have actual ears. In addition, analogies or "controlled comparisons" are made. Comparing is different from equating in that comparing always means "God is like this, but God is also not exactly or fully like this." Language in general as well as imagery and analogy are frail instruments to reveal a proper understanding of God. Even the effort of all efforts, the incarnation of God into human flesh, can be misunderstood. It is imperative that the revelation of God be approached with the utmost of care and without any self-serving preconceptions.

Masculine Pronouns

Throughout Scripture God is referred to as "he." This is not the choice of a modern translation team; it is the language of the original text. Does this mean that God is male? No, not necessarily. Hebrew, Greek, English, and most other ancient and modern languages do not offer a generic personal pronoun. Generic (not specifying gender) is available using "it," personal is available using "he" or "she," but the combination of generic and personal does not exist in the pronoun selection of most languages. "They" can be used if the reference is plural, but what is done if the reference is to an individual who is simply a person, not necessarily male or female? No matter how much it may violate modern sensitivities, "he" is the pronoun that must be used. Either by rule or by common usage, then, "he" has two possible meanings: specifically referring to a male or generally referring to any individual person. Both uses are frequent and are equally legitimate.

Why isn't "it" used of God? "It" cannot be used because it is not a personal pronoun. It would not reflect the personal character of God and would thereby invite the theological error of viewing God as an abstract principle or force. Why is the inserting of "he/she" or the interspersing of "she" throughout the text an unacceptable approach? Because "she" unavoidably connotes gender, and any connotation of gender invites the theological error of viewing God as human-like. What about using "they" for the "three-in-one" God? In a world of multiple false gods, it evidently was and probably still is essential that God's unity be given special emphasis. The only pronoun, then, that can be used of God in Hebrew, Greek, English, and many other languages is "he." The point of using the word is not to acknowledge God's sexual nature but to emphasize God's personal nature. It is being used in its general sense as a personal pronoun, not in its specific sense as a masculine pronoun.

The Error of Gender

To attach gender significance to any of the references to God is to make a far more serious mistake than many people may realize. To say that God has sexuality is to assign to God physical, human qualities. This is exactly what the ancient pagan cults did, especially the fertility cults that were denounced throughout the Old Testament. Not knowing the truth about God, these people simply defined their deities according to what they understood about themselves. They were sexual beings, so their deities became sexual beings. And as sexual beings, their male gods and female goddesses had sex organs and were capable of sexual activity.

Knowing the truth about God, Israel was to do no such thing: "You saw no form of any kind the day the Lord spoke to you at Horeb out of the fire. Therefore watch yourselves very carefully, so that you do not become corrupt and make for yourselves an idol, an image of any shape, whether formed like a man or a woman" (Deuteronomy 4:15–16). It wasn't just the wood or stone statue that was wrong. The prohibition opens by denouncing the wrong thinking underlying the wrong doing. It is wrong to think that God is in any way physical or human. And perhaps there is no characteristic more physical or human than sexuality. According to this passage, it is equally wrong to depict God as female-like as it is to depict God as male-like.

The fact that humanity carries the image of God cannot be turned into the notion that God carries the image of humanity. God says, "I am God and not man" (Hosea 11:9). God transcends creation, which means God transcends things as physical as sexuality. It is the height of heresy and heathenism to propose that God has the sex organs that constitute either gender. This would be equating the Creator with the creation. What follows this type of thinking? Does a male deity require the presence of a female deity? As children of God, are we in some way sexually produced by God? Is Jesus the product of an actual sex act between divinity and humanity? Such suggestions are repulsive. But each of these perversions begins with the claim that God is somehow male. The Bible is clear: "God is spirit" (John 4:24).

The Predominance of Masculine Imagery

Once it is understood that the scriptural revelation of God uses human language and human-like descriptions in an attempt to reveal an infinite being to a finite creation, and once it is understood that these expressions must be interpreted as meaning only what they are intended to mean and no more, the fact remains that the Bible uses more masculine word pictures to describe God than it uses feminine word pictures. Is there any explanation for this other than that God is more male than female? If God does not possess the physical, human characteristic of sexuality, then there must be some other explanation.

In the same way that God is revealed through the vehicle of human language, it is very likely that human culture provides some of the means through which God is revealed. In fact, there is such an overlap between language and culture that it would be difficult if not impossible to remove from language the influence of culture. The Old Testament world was patriarchal. The man was the central figure, and the husband-father was the authority figure. He was to be respected and obeyed because of his role as the family's primary protector and provider.

It is understandable, then, that masculine terms would be the common choice in describing a God who is the great protector and provider. They would be the obvious choice for describing a God who is independent rather than dependent, strong and able rather than vulnerable, deserving of utmost regard rather than frequently suffering disregard. In the same way that Scripture likens God to various animals (Deuteronomy 32:10–12; Hosea 5:14; 11:10; 13:7), certainly not because God is an animal but because an animal has a hint of a characteristic that would help humanity better understand God, Scripture likens God to males, not because God is male but because of certain roles assigned to men by ancient cultures. Male imagery then, any amount of it, does not in any way indicate that God is male.

The Use of Feminine Imagery

Any argument for God's maleness that is built upon the use of masculine imagery should be silenced by the fact that Scripture also contains a significant amount of feminine imagery for God. In light of the patriarchal culture of Israel and surrounding peoples, this is rather remarkable. Evidently, a God who is not male cannot be adequately described using only male terms and comparisons.

The first author of Scripture, Moses, was led by the Spirit to record God's words when the law was first given on Mount Sinai, and those eventful words include the likening of God to a mother eagle (Exodus 19:4). On another momentous occasion, the end of Moses' ministry and his final preparation of Israel to enter Canaan, Moses described God as being both the one who fathered them and the one who birthed them. (Deuteronomy 32:18, KJV wording "formed" instead of "birthed" ignores the wording of the Hebrew text "writhe in pain" and ignores the fact that this wording was usually used in reference to childbirth.) The words of God to His special servant Job also speak of the Almighty's combination of fathering and mothering qualities (Job 38:28–30).

Feminine imagery is common in the poetical writings. God is depicted as a midwife, definitely a female activity (Psalms 22:9–10, NIV). He is likened to both a male master and a female mistress (Psalms 123:2) and to the mother of a young child who has been breast-fed (Psalms 131:2). The Proverbs extol God's wisdom in feminine terminology, actually presenting this wisdom as a woman (Proverbs 1:20–21; 4:5–9; 8:1–11; 9:1–6). This, of course, stands in sharp contrast to any accusation that women are inherently less intelligent or perceptive than men. Proverbs 8:22–36 is a particularly interesting passage—God's wisdom which has been the focus of the preceding verses and which has been likened to a woman is identified as the Eternal One who is said to be Jesus in John 1.

The prophet Isaiah uses a considerable amount of female imagery in his references to God. He describes God as being like a woman in the pains of childbirth (42:14), like a woman who has given birth (49:14–15), and like a woman breast-feeding her baby (49:14–15). He quotes God as saying Jehovah has functioned toward Israel like a woman who conceives and carries a child (46:3) and like a mother comforting a child (66:13).

Female imagery is continued into the New Testament. In a series of three parables, Jesus likened a sinner to a lost sheep, a lost coin, and a lost son (Luke 15:3–32). In the second parable, the character who portrays the role of God is a woman. Jesus described Himself as being like a mother hen longing to gather her children under her wings (Matthew 23:37; Luke 13:34).

Of course, none of these analogies means that God is female, no more than the masculine imagery means that God is male. The Spirit God is neither male nor female and is certainly not bisexual. Again, it must be emphasized, the Spirit God transcends all physical characteristics, including sexuality. Adam and Eve, man and woman, were both made in God's image in an identical, equal way; but their characteristics, especially their physical characteristics, are not to be forced back upon a definition of God. Defining the Creator according to the creation lowers the Creator to the level of the creation and produces serious theological errors.

Feminism's Extremes

If female imagery is used of God in both the Old Testament and the New Testament, especially if the imagery of a mother is used, then are radical, secular feminists right in calling for God's title to be changed from "Father God" to "Mother-Father God"? No! There is evidently a distinction between the use of imagery in talking *about* God and the addresses that are acceptable in talking *to* God. The Bible specifically designates God as being "our Father" (Isaiah 64:8) but nowhere designates God as being "our Mother." Jesus taught the disciples to address prayers to their Father (Matthew 6:9) but did not teach them to pray to their Mother. The evidence of Scripture is against making the change that some feminists urge the church to make.

Is it possible that some extreme feminists have various hidden agendas behind their demands? Are they asking Christians to pray to the God of the Bible or to some other god? Isn't the concept of a "Mother-Father God" reverting back to the ancient fertility cults in which maleness and femaleness were incorporated into the deity rather than transcended by the deity?[1] Doesn't such a title overly establish the sexuality of God rather than neutralize or negate the sexuality of God? Doesn't it leave room for the possibility of bisexuality in God, consequently the acceptance of bisexuality in humans? For whatever reasons, some of which may be known only to God, the God of the Old and New Testaments is to be known by believers as "Father." Everything that is taught about this God by the mix of masculine and feminine imagery should be kept in focus, but the title given to God by Scripture is not Mother or Mother-Father but Father.

Chauvinism's Extremes

One last time it must be emphasized that God's fatherhood does not mean God's maleness. God is father-like relationally, not sexually. As wrong as it is for feminists to impose female gender on God, it is equally wrong for chauvinists to impose male gender on God. Both claims are contrary to Scripture, are theologically dangerous, and are usually self-serving in motive.

Since God is without gender, it is unnecessary to limit the ministry to one of the two genders. But even if God were male, it would still be unnecessary to limit the ministry to that gender. Ministers do serve in certain ways as God's representatives as do all Christians (2 Corinthians 5:20). They do so in ways that are similar to ambassadors serving as representatives of presidents or prime ministers. Being a representative is quite different from being a representation. Ambassadors speak for whoever sends them and act in behalf of whoever commissions them, but they do not have to imitate or impersonate that individual. Indeed, female ambassadors have represented men and male ambassadors have represented women on many occasions.[2] Representation involves reflecting the wishes of a person, not embodying that person's gender.

In representing the person of God, some of the attitudes and actions that the minister reflects are, at least from a human perspective, "feminine." This should be no surprise after seeing the amount of feminine imagery that is used in Scripture to reveal God. Moses likened his leadership over Israel to the activities of a woman (Number 11:12). Paul spoke in the same way on more than one occasion (Galatians 4:19; 1 Thessalonians 2:7). If the characteristics of God and the representative role of a minister, then, are the determining factors, there is as much room in the ministry for women as there is for men. In other words, a woman, who bears the image of God as much as any man, is qualified to represent a God who could only be adequately revealed in Scripture using masculine *and feminine* imagery.

Jesus' Maleness

But wasn't Jesus a male? Yes, of course He was. But the important question is, *"Why* was Jesus male?" Was He male because ministers must be male, or was He male for entirely different reasons? If the answer is "different reasons," then do those reasons have any affect on the gender of ministers today?

What was necessary and, consequently, what was most meaningful in Jesus' birth and life was that God became flesh, not that God became male. The Bible states this very fact: "The Word became flesh" (John 1:14). "Every spirit that acknowledges that Jesus Christ has come in the flesh is from God" (1 John 4:2). Even Jesus' primary title for Himself, "Son of Man," and most other New Testament references to Jesus being a "man" use the Greek word for "human being" ("anthropos") rather than the Greek word for "male" ("aner" or "arsen"). In the same way, the English word "man" oftentimes means human being rather than male as in the translating of "anthropos" to "man" in Galatians 6:7 or to "man" (NIV) or "men" (KJV) in Hebrews 9:27. In the incarnation, God was willing to become what He was wanting to save—humanity. If Jesus' maleness had the theological or spiritual significance that some try to attach to it, then women would not be savable or would not be as savable as men, and, of course, neither is the case.[3]

The fact that Jesus had a sexual identity does have theological significance. In order to be fully human, Jesus had to be male or female. Somehow being neither or being both, as some heresies propose, would mean that Jesus was other than human because humans are one or the other.[4] If the choice could not have been based upon God's gender because God is neither male nor female, and if the choice could not have been based upon God's preference because God does not favor men over women, then what determined Jesus' gender? The likeliest possibility is the culture into which Jesus was born.

The culture of first-century Judaism made it virtually impossible for anyone other than a man to be recognized as a teacher of truth. Women, children, and slaves were not part of the headcount in meeting the quorum that was necessary to form a worship community. Men were not to let women read or study the law. Men were not to speak to women publicly, not even to a wife or daughter, and were to speak even to them only privately and as little as possible. The testimony of a woman was not legally credible. Men said a prayer of thanksgiving every day praising God for not making them Gentiles, slaves, or women. The Messiah simply had to be a man; though it was probably theologically possible to be otherwise, it was culturally impossible to be otherwise.

Interestingly, the human nature that Jesus absolutely had to embrace in order to be the Savior was derived 100% from a woman.[5] The greatest miracle of history, God becoming flesh, was accomplished without the involvement of a man, but it was not without the intimate involvement of a woman. Whatever aspects of humanity that equipped Jesus to be the ideal minister that all other ministers are to emulate were derived 100% from a woman. It seems as if the Savior's gender is very much "balanced" by the unique details of the Savior's birth. Theologically, then, it is indefensible to view the female gender as in any way inherently inferior to the male gender. It is equally incorrect to claim that the female gender is inherently disqualified for the ministry. Whatever the mix of reasons for Jesus being white, male, Jewish, and working-class, it is not biblically/theologically necessary to require all of these characteristics of ministers today. Therefore, there is no biblical/theological reason to require just one of them, namely, maleness.

Again, however, a word of caution is in order. Just as the Bible refers to the first member of the trinity as God the Father and not God the Mother, the second member of the trinity is said to be God the Son and not God the Daughter. No compromising of this truth should be entertained. First, it is a fact that Jesus was born into this world as a male child. Second, even though Jesus' gender was most likely an adaptation to the culture of first-century Palestine, there may be additional reasons for His maleness. Perhaps, for example, the "male dominance, female subordination" consequence of the fall had to be overturned by the dominant gender rather than by the subordinate gender. Perhaps that the first human was male had to be matched by and redeemed by a Savior who was male. Whatever any additional reasons may be, God's determination of Jesus' gender is not negotiable or changeable. It is not necessary to deny historical fact or to disregard biblical authority in order to realize that Jesus' gender does not dictate the gender of all other New Testament ministers.

7

Jesus' Treatment of Women

Jesus made a clear declaration of His primary purpose for coming to earth: "The Son of Man came to seek and to save what was lost" (Luke 19:10). No other issue or activity obscured this singular focus. He did not immerse Himself in other causes, as worthy as several of them must have been, because the work of redeeming humanity was far more compelling. He left a similar mission with His followers: "Go into all the world and preach the good news to all creation" (Mark 16:15). No other effort should displace this most important task. Christians must remember that one thing matters far more than all other good causes—reaching people with the gospel.

The fact that Jesus' attention was not distracted by societal shortcomings, however, does not mean that He did not recognize and address such matters. Regarding the plight of women, He was nothing short of revolutionary in the things He said and in the things He did. His attitudes were particularly striking against the backdrop of the attitudes that surrounded Him. Israel had fallen to an all-time low in its view of women, but Jesus was emphatic in His regard for their person and for their potential.

Women in First-Century Israel

Approximately 400 years stand in between the close of the Old Testament and the opening of the New Testament. It was during this period that many Jews who had been taken captive by surrounding empires journeyed back to their homeland and rebuilt their lives. It was also during this period that Judaism began its development, the name originating from the large number of returning exiles who were of the tribe of Judah. Though it did not reach full development until after the destruction of Herod's Temple in A.D. 70, Judaism was very much present in first-century Israel and was extremely influential in shaping daily life.

Whereas the religion of the Old Testament was based upon the role of the sacrifice, the foundation of Judaism was an extreme emphasis upon the study of Scripture. In an effort to painstakingly apply mosaic law to every detail of life, rabbis generated extensive interpretations of Old Testament material. Before eventually being compiled into written form, these teachings were transmitted orally from generation to generation and were basically seen as being equivalent to Scripture in authority. It was the "tradition" to which Jesus made frequent negative reference.

The volumes of rabbinical literature that are available today are invaluable in investigating the Jewish view of women during the time of Jesus. They contain the "oral law" which governed Judaism immediately before, during, and immediately after the first century. Additional information is available through the writings of Jewish historians of the first century such as Philo and Josephus. Collectively these materials are rather conclusive in depicting Judaism as having an extremely negative view of women. In the role of wife and mother, women did receive a mix of commendation and criticism. In any non-domestic ventures, however, they were absolutely unwelcome. In public, they were only present if necessary and even then only within extreme restrictions. In worship, they were relegated to the Court of Women in the outskirts of the temple. Overall, there was a general disregard for their potential and a general disdain for their person.

The following is a sampling of statements against women that can be found in rabbinical literature. "Adam was the light of the world...and Eve caused his death" (Palestinian Talmud, Shabbath 20a). "Happy is he whose children are males, but woe to him whose children are females" (Babylonian Talmud, Kiddushin 82b). "As soon as a male comes into the world peace comes into the world. A female has nothing with her" (Babylonian Talmud, Niddah 31b). "To listen to a woman's voice is indecent" (Babylonian Talmud, Kiddushin 70a). "Talk not much with womankind. [This includes] a man's own wife. He who talks much with womankind brings evil upon himself...and at the least will inherit hell" (Mishnah, Aboth 1:5). "Women are exempt from the study of the law" (Babylonian Talmud, Kiddushin 34a). "If anyone gives his daughter a knowledge of the law it is as though he taught her obscenity/promiscuity" (Mishnah, Sotah 3:4). "There is no wisdom in woman except about woman's work" (Babylonian Talmud, Yoma 66b). "The more women the more witchcrafts" (Mishnah, Aboth 2:7). "The most worthy of women indulges in witchcraft" (Babylonian Talmud, Soferim 41a).[1] "Though a woman be as a pitcher full of filth...yet all speed to her" (Babylonian Talmud, Shabbath 152a).

Frequently throughout rabbinical literature women are categorized with children and slaves and are sometimes positioned beneath them. For example, the testimony of women, children, and slaves was generally not admissible in legal disputes (Babylonian Talmud, Baba Kamma 88a). The testimony of women was viewed as being in the same league as that of gamblers, usurers, and abusers of the Sabbath (Babylonian Talmud, Rosh Hashanah 22a). Women, children, and slaves were not countable in achieving a quorum for establishing a worship community. If necessary, however, nine men and a male child or nine men and a male slave could qualify, but nine men and any number of women could not qualify.[2] The daily prayer of men, which is found in three different locations in rabbinical literature and which is attributed to a first-century rabbi,[3] praised God for not making him a Gentile, a slave, or a woman (Babylonian Talmud, Menahoth 43b).

First century historians confirm that these attitudes were very much in the hearts of most men. Josephus wrote, "Let not the testimony of women be admitted, on account of the levity of their sex" (Antiquities, Book IV, Chapter VIII, Section 15). He claimed to be quoting Scripture but was actually reflecting oral tradition when he wrote that "a woman is inferior to her husband in all things" (Apion, Book II, Section 25). Philo said that women should not leave the home except to go to the synagogue and to do so only when most other people would not be present (The Special Laws, III, XXXI, 171). He said that a woman is by nature "easily caught by the persuasions of false-hood," whereas a man is "competent to disentangle the notions of seduction" (Questions and Answers on Genesis, I,33); "woman is accustomed rather to be deceived than to devise anything of importance out of her own head but with the man the case is just the contrary" (I,46); woman is "imperfect and depraved by nature," whereas man is "the more excellent and perfect crea-ture" (I,43); and woman was originally created from man "in order that the woman might not be of equal dignity with the man" (I,27).

Of course, many cultures leave room for a range of acceptable behaviors, and this may have been the case within first-century Judaism. Sometimes city versus country or upper-class versus lower-class can result in considerable differences. Furthermore, Israel was surrounded by the ethnic diversity of the Roman Empire which was very much in a state of cultural transition during the first century.[4] It seems that the role of women, in particular, was undergoing change throughout the empire.

But even though there is evidence of some Roman girls attending school and of some Roman women rising to positions of prominence, there is also evidence of widespread opposition to these changes.[5] Cultural conservatives were quick to associate such deviations from the norm with the radical feminism promoted by the goddess religions which they vehemently opposed. Also, the rare opportunities for education or leadership were available only to upper-class girls and women. Most girls were not admitted to schools. Most women did menial work, were under the rule of their husbands, and were seen as inferior persons. And overall, openness to changing the status quo was found less within Israel than it was in many other parts of the Roman Empire. So, even though individual exceptions were possible, generally within Judaism "women were to be seen as little as possible and heard even less."[6]

Jesus' Birth

It was into the everyday world of the first century that Jesus was born. Into a world plagued with sin, the gift of God came to free people from sin. As has already been noted, the humanity of this perfect one was drawn entirely from the flesh of a woman, without the initiation or involvement of any man. And yet simply because she was a woman, this mother of the Highest One was among the lowliest of her world. Indeed, each of the women who are identified in Jesus' genealogy (Matthew 1) felt the pain of being a woman in a world ruled by men. Tamar, left alone by four men, stooped to incest rather than bear the stigma of being a childless widow. Rahab was caught in the abusive throes of prostitution. Ruth, also a childless widow, was dependent upon charity for each morsel of food that she ate until she was able to convince a relative of her late husband to marry her. Bathsheba was victimized by the lust of a man who already had a harem of wives and concubines. And Mary was found to be with child outside of marriage. These women were each very personally and very keenly aware of the effects of sin which brought Jesus to earth. How interesting that they would make this striking appearance as early as in His birth record.

Oh, good news! The promise that had been given to Eve thousands of years earlier was about to be fulfilled through Mary. Eve's offspring would crush the head of the tempter (Genesis 3:15). God would be victorious over Satan, and men and women would no longer have to be held captive to sin or its consequences. Jesus announced this good news at the beginning of His ministry when He declared that He had been sent "to proclaim freedom for the prisoners" and "to release the oppressed" (Luke 4:16–21). Among the most shackled prisoners of sin about to experience this great release were the women of Israel and the women of the world!

It was so unusual for attention or credit to be given to women that one can only wonder if Luke did not intentionally insert into his account of Jesus' birth the highlighting of three men *and* three women: Zachariah, Elizabeth, Joseph, Mary, Simeon, and Anna. Was this a subtle but nonetheless clear way of saying that the Messiah would treat men and women equally, offering them the same spiritual privileges?[7] Luke records that two of these individuals, Zechariah and Mary, were honored with an appearance by the angel Gabriel (1:5–22; 26–38). The man, Zechariah, was a priest who should have been spiritually perceptive, but he was unable to believe the angel's words of truth (1:18–22). The woman, Mary, was a lowly maiden who probably had no formal training in Scripture, but she was commended for her belief (1:38,45).

Yes, it was to Mary that the angel Gabriel appeared, announcing that she was the recipient of God's presence and favor (1:28), announcing that she was being given the opportunity to cooperate with God more intimately and minister for God more significantly than anyone else in human history. The angel did not appear to her father, to her fiancé, or to her priest.[8] The intermediary, the guardian that Judaism prescribed for a woman was not necessary in God's estimation; the announcement of the plan of redemption was entrusted directly and personally to this young woman.

Luke's Gospel, then, marks the opening of the new covenant with the faith of a woman, Mary (Luke 1:38),[9] and with the recognition and confirmation of that faith by a second woman, Elizabeth (Luke 1:39–45). And it is not only with the news of redemption that Mary was entrusted, but also with the early character nurturing and the formative educational training of the Son of God.[10] How can women be said to have a spiritual deficiency that disqualifies them from ministry? How can they be barred from leadership because of what is said to be a divinely-ordered hierarchical scheme? Such claims fail to address the strategic position of spiritual responsibility determined by God for Mary. As she said, "The Mighty One has done great things for me.... He has scattered the proud.... He has lifted up the humble" (Luke 1:49,51,52).

After depicting Elizabeth more favorably than Zechariah and positioning Mary more pivotally than Joseph, Luke relates a third male-female couplet, Simeon and Anna (2:21–38). Again, there is a clear contrast between the two individuals. Simeon is described as a "man" (2:25); whereas, Anna is said to be a "prophetess" (2:36). Simeon "went into the temple courts" (2:27), but Anna "never left the temple" (2:37). Both of these worshippers were discerning enough to recognize that Jesus was God's provision for salvation (2:28–32; 38), something that was not evident to most of the religious leadership of Christ's day. Simeon *and Anna*, then, were shown things by the Spirit that priests, scribes, and rabbis were unable to see.

But Anna is credited with more than spiritual discernment; she is portrayed as having a teaching-preaching ministry. In addition to labeling her as a prophetess which means she spoke forth the truths of God, the account says, "she spoke about the child to all who were looking forward to the redemption of Jerusalem" (2:38). This means that a woman was the first person to make public proclamation of Jesus. Further, it can be assumed that this proclamation was made *in the temple* (2:37). The teaching-preaching ministries that women are being denied in many churches today are no different than what Scripture presents as acceptable and commendable for the woman Anna. New Testament Christians were told that they were built upon the foundation of the apostles *and the prophets* (Ephesians 2:19–20). Surely if a woman could steady Christianity as a foundation stone, then she is capable of spreading Christianity as a building stone.

Bridging the Covenants

The Bible explains that the mosaic law of the Old Testament was given "because of sin" (Galatians 3:19). People who were imprisoned by sin (Galatians 3:22) were held in protective custody by the law (Galatians 3:23). Though it was incapable of freeing them from their sin, it was able to make them aware of their wrongdoing (Romans 3:20) and prepare them for faith in Christ (Galatians 3:24), the one who could rescue them. So the role of the law was narrow and temporary. Once faith in Jesus Christ sets people free from their captivity to sin (John 8:34–36; Romans 8:1–2), then the safeguarding function of the law is no longer necessary (Galatians 3:25). It is replaced with the ministry of the Spirit (Ezekiel 36:27; Romans 8:9).

The Bible could not be any more emphatic than to say that circumcision, the identifying mark of living under the old covenant and of obeying its mosaic law, holds no meaning anymore. "Neither circumcision nor uncircumcision means anything; what counts is a new creation" (Galatians 6:15). This new creation results from receiving the redeeming work of Christ. "If anyone is in Christ, he is a new creation; the old has gone, the new has come!" (2 Corinthians 5:17). The sin that first entered the world through partaking of a tree was finally abolished by God's Son being hung from a tree.[11]

Surrounding the exclamation "the old has gone, the new has come" are other declarations of new covenant truth. One of these is, "From now on we regard no one from a worldly point of view" (2 Corinthians 5:16). Paul confessed that he and others had seen Jesus in this wrong way. Their inability to realize that God was doing a new thing through Christ kept them from receiving that new thing and left them fighting against it. But Paul concluded, "We do so no longer." And regarding Paul's newfound view of others, he wrote, "There is neither Jew nor Greek, slave nor free, male nor female, for you are all one in Christ Jesus" (Galatians 3:28). These distinctions mattered under the old covenant, but they cease to matter under the new covenant. Everyone is to be "one," *equal*.

Still today if people fail to see that God did a new thing through Jesus, they will be found fighting against it rather than receiving it. They will be found viewing Christ *and others* from a worldly point of view. Jesus brought an end to the old covenant by fulfilling all of its demands, and He inaugurated the new covenant, sealing it with His own blood. Whereas the animal sacrifices of the old covenant were able to cover sin, the perfect sacrifice of the new covenant is able to remove sin as well as its consequences and to give new life to a person.

The crux of sin's consequences was and is the breakdown of relationships, starting with the relationship between humanity and God. A broken relationship between an individual and his/her God, then, leads rather naturally to broken relationships between individuals. Every sin, it seems, is traceable back to one of these faulty relationships. The reconciling work of Christ not only restores a right relationship between God and humanity but also makes it possible for people to live daily in right relationship with others, including men with women and women with men.

So, the new life given through redemption supersedes the old creation life that was marred by sin. A new spiritual man replaces the old natural man. The Old Testament with all of its accommodations of the fallen nature is superseded and replaced by the New Testament. A new person in Christ does not have to live any longer in bondage to sin or its consequences, including the chains of unregenerate male-female relationships that have plagued humanity since the fall. As Scripture proclaims, "The old has gone; the new has come!"

Of course, the complete lifting of the curse of sin and all of the consequences of sin will not occur until the tree of life appears once again (Revelation 22:1–3). Then and only then will death and all divisiveness cease to exist. Then and only then will inequality and injustice cease to exist. The delay is unavoidable because the whole world is still imprisoned to sin (Galatians 3:22). It has not yet experienced its re-creation, but that great day is coming (Revelation 21:1).

Until everything is made right, however, Jesus has made it possible for individuals to join the new covenant community and to live according to their new natures rather than according to their old natures. He has made it possible for husbands and wives to enjoy the unity and equality that was present between Adam and Eve before the invasion of sin and for that right relationship to breathe health into all other male-female relationships in the redemption community. If redemption rectifies only the human-divine relationship and fails to change human-human relationships, especially marriage, the most intimate and precious of human relationships, then a great part of the earthly value of redemption has been tragically lost. May the divisions that Jesus gave His life to destroy *be destroyed* among His people: Jew versus Greek, slave versus free, *and* male versus female (Galatians 3:28).

There is another new covenant truth surrounding the exclamation "the old has gone, the new has come" that is well worth noting. According to 2 Corinthians 5:18, there is such a close connection between redemption and ministry that there seems to be the idea that redemption produces ministry. To those who have been reconciled to God is given the privilege of reconciling others to Him. This being the case, ministry becomes a benefit of redemption and like everything else that is available through redemption, it must be equally available to everyone who experiences redemption. This is possible because both redemption and ministry originate with God, not with man. Of course, God may not direct a certain individual to pastor a local church or become a foreign missionary, but this would not be because the individual is a member of the large portion of humanity, womankind, for whom only partial redemption benefits are available.

Presenting Versus Preventing

What a task Jesus had—to turn old thinking into new thinking, to turn old ways of living into new ways of living. It was out of the old covenant that the new covenant was to emerge, so Jesus had to build upon the new without diminishing the worth of the old. He had to cause a change from the old to the new while still bridging the two together. He had to draw people to His message without tempting them to discard that very message. This was, indeed, a challenging course to chart, but He did it masterfully. And He left an example for believers to follow: the *presentation* of redemption must be accomplished without preventing the *acceptance* of redemption.

One illustration in particular is appropriate. Jesus violated all rabbinical teaching regarding the treatment of women. He went out of His way to include them and to elevate them in ways that were absolutely amazing to the people of His day. He also cut across all cultural convention in His treatment of Samaritans and Gentiles. But He did not select a Samaritan, a Gentile, or a woman to serve as one of the twelve disciples. Doing so would have made it impossible to reach those He was sent to reach first, the people of the old covenant (Matthew 10:5–6; 15:24).

Reaching the Jews first was not meant to permanently exclude others; on the contrary, it was meant to provide the means through which all others could be reached (Romans 15:8–12) because the new covenant would be built upon the old covenant. Similarly, excluding women, Gentiles, and Samaritans from the first band of ministers was not meant to permanently bar these three categories of people from Christian ministry. If that were the case, most ministers today would have to resign their credentials. Jesus was simply being sure that His presentation of the gospel through the twelve disciples did not prevent the very people He was trying to reach from accepting the gospel, namely, the Jews.

As will be shown in future chapters, the Apostle Paul led the Early Church in following the example that Jesus set. Sometimes cultural sensitivities could not be violated without hindering the spread of the gospel. In such instances, Paul was insistent that believers exhibit appropriate caution and restraint. The issue of individual freedom had to bow, occasionally and temporarily, to the far more important concern of furthering the gospel.

However, as will be equally evident, the Early Church was just as true to Jesus' example in taking every opportunity available to advance revolutionary change in how men and women viewed and treated each other. Jesus planted the seeds of change. The Early Church watered those seeds with great care and with impressive results. Across church history it is understandable if growth is slow at times because of a hostile environment. What is not excusable is for the church to fail to cherish and cultivate the seeds that Jesus first planted, the seeds of change.

Rewriting the Rules

When Jesus began His ministry, there were rules for women and about women, plenty of rules. Because women were seen as inferior to men by both religion and society, they were to be treated accordingly. As has been shown, the oral teaching of the rabbis as well as the general culture of Palestine was exceedingly restrictive of women. Jesus ignored all of this and treated women as He treated men. He viewed both as being fully capable of spiritual understanding and as being totally responsible for their own spiritual decisions.[12] He did not ignore or patronize women; instead, He treated them as persons fully deserving the same respect and dignity that were given to men,[13] as equal to men in every respect.

That women were present at all in Christ's ministry was a radical departure from the norms of the day. For Him to refer to them, approach them, and include them to the extent that He did can only be interpreted as a deliberate attempt on the part of the Son of God to change how His people would view and treat women from that day forward. Of all of His references to them, not one was derogatory. Can the church today say the same thing? Nothing He said or did relating to women had any hint of restricting their role in the kingdom. Can the church today say the same thing? Jesus' record, especially against the backdrop of extremely opposite attitudes and practices, should speak clearly and loudly to Christians today. He changed the rules for and about women and left a scriptural witness to prove it and to point the way for others to follow. The One who created women to be equal treated them as if they were equal. And the Bible says, "Whoever claims to live in Him must walk as Jesus did" (1 John 2:6).

Just a sampling of Jesus' treatment of women is adequate to identify the principles that should be guiding the church today. A more thorough study of the Gospels would show that the sampling is indicative of the whole. Though full implementation of these principles may have been premature in the first century,[14] and may be similarly untimely in certain locations in the world today, the right thing to do has been made clear by the Head of the Church, Jesus Christ. May every geographic and denominational branch of His church endeavor to move diligently in the direction that He has dictated by His example to be right in the sight of God.

Equality Established by Jesus' Words

Jesus rewrote the rules regarding women by His words, His actions, and His relationships. Through each of these means, He established their value and potential as being equal to that of men. He departed radically from the perceptions and behaviors of His day in order to demonstrate God's regard for the "other half of humanity" who had been made in His image. In particular, the examples of Jesus' words relating to women cluster into three categories: His references to women, His direct teaching about women, and His conversations with women.

First, Jesus' references to women were so out of the ordinary that they spoke volumes about His position. The Jewish rabbis would not have included any references to women in their teachings except references that criticized or restricted them. With such pressure to do likewise, Jesus did not have to refer to women at all. In His parables, for example, He could have used the everyday situations and examples of men rather than those of women to teach the same truths. But He chose to champion the equal standing of women in God's kingdom by including them in several parables. A woman mixing yeast into flour (Matthew 13:33; Luke 13:20) was paralleled with a man planting a mustard seed (Matthew 13:31–32; Luke 13:18–19). A woman looking for a lost coin was likened to God Himself in His search for lost humanity (Luke 15:8–10), as lofty a reference as can be made. A widow, a member of the class of women who suffered enormously under the scourge of male dominance, was made the model of faithfulness and prayerfulness that the disciples were to follow (Luke 18:1–8). Both women and men were shown to be equally capable of doing right and of doing wrong with the spiritual opportunities and abilities entrusted to them (Matthew 25:1–13; 14–30).

In addition to the parable references, Jesus made other references to women, frequently casting them in a positive light while casting men in a negative light. A poor widow was commended for giving an offering that was far more generous than those of the wealthy, who typically would have been men (Mark 12:41–44; Luke 21:1–4). The religious officials, who were male, were indicted for relishing their lofty positions while abusing widows, the neediest of women (Mark 12:38–40; Luke 20:45–47). They were warned that an ancient, foreign queen would stand in judgment against them because her spiritual perceptiveness had so exceeded theirs (Matthew 12:38–39,42; Luke 11:29–31). They were told that female prostitutes were entering the kingdom ahead of them (Matthew 21:23,31–32).

Second, not only did Jesus refer to women and in so doing repeatedly lift them to a level equal to that of men, He further established their equality through His specific teaching about women. For example, whereas the rabbis put the blame for adultery upon the seductive tendencies of women, Jesus insisted that the blame lie within the lustful hearts of men who were ultimately responsible for controlling themselves (Matthew 5:27–30). This was an extreme departure from the thinking of the day, and it meant that there was no reason to keep women in seclusion.

All of Jesus' teaching regarding marriage depicted the husband and wife as having equal roles, responsibilities, and rights. He affirmed the Old Testament's claim that a father and mother are deserving of equal honor (Matthew 15:3–4; 19:16–19). He denounced the ultimate symbol of male dominance in marriage, the right to divorce a wife at will (Matthew 5:31–32) and identified this wrongdoing against women as being the result of man's spiritual shortcoming (Matthew 19:7–8). He taught that God's desire for marriage is found in the pre-fall account of Adam and Eve rather than in any deviations or accommodations that have occurred as a result of the fall (Matthew 19:3–9). This means that God expects marriage to reflect the husband-wife unity and equality that are described in Genesis 1 and 2 rather than the male-dominance and female-subordination that have come into being since the sin of Genesis 3. The double standard of male privilege in divorce should not exist because neither a husband nor a wife should sin against a one-flesh-for-life marriage partner (Mark 10:4–12). According to Jesus' teaching about marriage, the position of the wife is to be absolutely equal with that of the husband. So, not only did He miss the perfect opportunity to affirm marital or sexual hierarchy, he taught just the opposite.

On one occasion Jesus was given the opportunity to address the belief that a woman's chief role in life is that of being a wife and mother. Or, perhaps it should be said that He *made* an opportunity to correct this erroneous view of women. While He was teaching, a woman in the audience exclaimed, "Blessed is the mother who gave you birth and nursed you" (Luke 11:27). Though this would have struck the crowd as an acceptable comment because it expressed the idea that a woman is defined by her domestic accomplishments, it obviously struck Jesus as unacceptable. He responded, "Blessed *rather* are those who hear the word of God and obey it" (11:28). If there ever were a woman whose domestic responsibilities were of great importance, Mary would have been that woman, but Jesus would not allow her to be restricted to gender-specific roles at the expense of her highest calling, that of hearing and obeying God. This is not to say that a woman who is a wife and/or mother should shirk her family responsibilities. If, however, a husband-father is just as responsible, according to Scripture, to fulfill his family responsibilities as is a wife-mother, then a woman should not be defined by or limited to those assignments any more than a man. For both a man and a woman, spiritual responsibilities must be paramount.

A third cluster of examples of Jesus demonstrating His high regard for women through His use of words can be found in the actual conversations that He had with women. Though commonplace in many modern cultures, conversing directly and publicly with women was such a violation of common practice for a Jewish man and so unheard of for a Jewish rabbi that it had to be deliberate and purposeful on Jesus' part. It was a further demonstration that He viewed and treated women exactly as He did men, with the same regard for their intellectual capacity and their spiritual potential.

Before a large crowd of people Jesus stopped a funeral procession, spoke to the mother of the young man who was dead, raised her son back to life again, and gave him back to her (Luke 7:11–15). He held the hand of a little girl who had died, spoke to her, and raised her to life (Mark 5:21–24,35–42; Luke 8:40–42,49–55). He called a crippled woman out from the audience in a synagogue on the Sabbath, spoke to her, touched her, and made her well (Luke 13:10–13). When a synagogue official voiced criticism, Jesus called him a hypocrite and referred to the woman as a "daughter of Abraham" (13:14–16). "Son of Abraham" was a common title for men, emphasizing their strategic position in the covenant community, but any such reference to a woman was virtually unknown in Judaism, perhaps because women were thought to have relationship with God only indirectly through fathers or husbands.[15] Jesus, however, assigned to the woman this lofty spiritual title and spoke of the man in extremely derogatory terms.

Three women were specifically commended for their faith by Jesus. And to the men of first-century Judaism, the selection of the three would have been particularly offensive. Each one was representative of the lowliest of women: unclean, foreign, and immoral. In contrast, not one male religious leader was ever given such commendation by Jesus. Even the "best of the bunch," Nicodemus, was chided for his lack of perception and his lack of faith (John 3:10,12). But Jesus saw three lowly women as extremely spiritually competent, more so than the male leadership.

The first was a woman who had some type of hemorrhaging condition which would have kept her ceremonially unclean (Matthew 9:20–22; Mark 5:25–34; Luke 8:43–48). Rather than correcting her for touching Him and rendering Him unclean, Jesus spoke to her, even though He was in the midst of a large crowd: "Daughter, your faith has healed you. Go in peace and be freed from your suffering" (Mark 5:34). The second was a foreign woman whose daughter needed deliverance (Matthew 15:21–28; Mark 7:24–30). Jesus engaged in a back-and-forth conversation with her, and she is the only individual recorded in the Gospels as having "won" such a "match of wits" with the Master. She was told, "Woman, you have great faith! Your request is granted" (Matthew 15:28). The third was an immoral woman, probably a prostitute, who afforded Jesus yet another opportunity to criticize a male religious leader while commending a lowly woman (Luke 7:36–50). After allowing her to touch Him and kiss Him and after rebuking the host of the home for failing to pay Him common courtesies, Jesus said to the woman, "Your sins are forgiven. Your faith has saved you; go in peace" (7:48,50).

The most extensive personal conversation that Scripture records Jesus having had with anyone was with a woman (John 4:4–26). And if there was anyone that Jewish men reviled more than an unclean woman, a foreign woman, or an immoral woman, it was a Samaritan woman, the very person with whom Jesus spoke at such length. But He honored her with much more than a lengthy conversation; He singled her out to receive some of the weightiest theological instruction of His ministry and to be the recipient of His first claim to be the Messiah.

Ironically, when Jesus met the Samaritan woman, He had just left Judea because the resentment of religious officials against Him was mounting (John 4:1–3). Those who should have recognized and accepted Him were failing to do so. They would eventually become malicious enough to plot His death, and it was imperative that He time the crucifixion within the perfect plan of the Father. So, once again, a sharp contrast is drawn between the men who saw themselves as intellectually, spiritually, and positionally superior to all women and a lowly woman who proved them to be quite wrong. And what a woman to elevate over the religious leadership of the day. For a woman of Israel or Samaria to have five divorces in her background (4:16–18) would mean that she had been discarded by five husbands, since divorce could not be enacted by a wife. She had, indeed, suffered greatly from the abuse that God had predicted would result from the fall. Perhaps because marriage had lost its meaning and appeal, she was presently living out of wedlock with yet another man.

As Jews, Jesus' disciples would not have spoken with a Samaritan or taken a drink from one of their waterpots (4:9), but what was more startling to them upon joining Jesus was that He was talking with a woman (4:27). He treated her as a person rather than as someone who was in any way different or deficient due to race or gender. Indeed, He obviously thought her capable of processing the most profound of all spiritual truths—that the God-Man stood before her.

One last conversation is worth noting. The setting was extremely public and the crowd was extremely sizable, but Jesus took the occasion to address an entire group of women. Doing so under normal circumstances would have been unthinkable to any other Jewish rabbi; doing so under negative circumstances made the scene even more striking. While being led to Golgotha through the streets of Jerusalem, Jesus called out a prophecy specifically to the women of the crowd who were mourning His death (Luke 23:27–31). It was the last group of people that Jesus addressed before the cross, and it was a group of women.

Equality Established by Jesus' Actions

Other Jewish rabbis would not have had direct dealings with women, but Jesus did so on a number of occasions. The same blessings that He made available to men, He also gave to women—the physical miracles of healing and the spiritual miracles of salvation. Not only did Jesus discharge a considerable amount of His ministry in the direction of women, He also singled out women to be the recipients of some of His most significant and impressive miracles.

Several women received healing from Jesus, sometimes at their request and other times by His initiative. The first person healed on the Sabbath was a woman, Peter's mother-in-law (Matthew 8:14–17; Mark 1:21,29–34; Luke 4:31,38–41). Jesus accomplished the miracle by touching her and by rebuking the sickness, thereby exercising social and spiritual boldness on her behalf. This is also the first record of Jesus delivering and healing a crowd of people, and it began with the delivering of a man (Mark 1:21–27; Luke 4:31–36) and the healing of a woman. (Matthew 4:23–25 is believed to have occurred shortly after this incident.)

Mention has already been made of Jesus healing a woman who suffered twelve years from bleeding (Matthew 9:20–22; Mark 5:25–34; Luke 8:43–48). Her miracle could have been secured without any public notice, but Jesus insisted upon making it known to the disciples and to the crowd. For her to think that just a quick touch of the back of His clothing could cure what money and medicine were unable to relieve is one of the greatest demonstrations of faith in all of Scripture, evidently unusual enough among men and women for Jesus to demand that it be given public attention.

Toward the end of Jesus' earthly ministry, another woman became the recipient of a Sabbath healing, a crippled woman that He chose to call forward from the audience of a synagogue (Luke 13:10–17). As with the first Sabbath healing, Jesus used a combination of His touch and His words. Of course, with this woman, both were displayed before a group of people in a public gathering. This was the woman Jesus called "daughter of Abraham." It is interesting that two of the six Sabbath healings that so incited Jesus' opponents against Him were directed toward women. (The other four were as follows: man with a crippled hand, man with dropsy, invalid man, and man born blind.)

Of all physical miracles, raising someone from the dead strikes the human soul as the most spectacular. And this has solid theological basis. The Father's ability to raise the Son from the grave is one of the great pillars of Christianity (Acts 4:33; 1 Thessalonians 4:14; 1 Peter 1:3). Death is called the last enemy that Christ will conquer (1 Corinthians 15:26; Revelation 21:4). The Gospels record three instances of Jesus raising someone from the dead: a widow's son (Luke 7:11–17), a synagogue official's daughter (Matthew 9:18–19,23–26; Mark 5:21–24,35–43; Luke 8:40–42,49–56), and His own friend Lazarus (John 11:1–45). Each of the three situations had a close link to the female gender. "In one Jesus raised a young girl from the dead; in the other two he raised persons from the dead largely because of women."[16] This gift of gifts, this proclamation that Jesus came to reverse *all* of the consequences of sin, this ultimate embodiment of the message that is to be preached around the world was given as much to women as to men, if not more.

It is clear in Jesus' raising of the widow's son that He was ministering primarily to the boy's needy mother, from inviting her to stop crying to giving the boy back to her. In a totally male-based economy, there could be no needier person than a woman left without her husband and her son. But, in more ways than one, Jesus came to correct the wrongs of such an unjust system.

Jairus, the synagogue official, was obviously desperate for Jesus to heal his daughter. He asked the Master to do something that no Jewish man would have asked another man to do to a daughter, "put your hands on her" (Mark 5:23). As caring as this father obviously was, he actually had very little to offer the girl. He was a representative of Judaism, an advocate of the rabbinical oral teaching that charged this little girl with Adam's death and, consequently, did not count her as part of the congregation or teach God's Word to her or view her testimony as trustworthy. He praised God daily that he was not what this child would grow up to be, a woman. The man who probably would have done almost anything to reverse his daughter's death would not have been equally willing to reverse the discrimination against her, even though these results of sin were identical in their origin. But Jesus came to take away the sin of the world (John 1:29), not part of it, all of it. The proof that He is able to reverse sin's results, all of them, is found in the resurrection which reverses death, the worst result of all. And Jesus chose to demonstrate this truth on behalf of a little girl, the daughter of a synagogue official.

Like the widow's son, Lazarus was raised back to life not so much for his sake as for the sake of the living who mourned his death; and, of course, Mary and Martha grieved for their brother more deeply than anyone else. Interestingly, more is said in the Gospels about Mary and Martha than about Lazarus. They seem to have had a special relationship with Jesus, and it is for them that He performed the third of the three resurrections. The one miracle that was to show more than any other the difference that Jesus can make in someone's life was given very personally to two women.

In addition to the miracles of physical healing received by women, there is also an occasion of a woman seeking and receiving her daughter's deliverance from demonic possession (Matthew 15:21–28; Mark 7:24–30). Some have misunderstood and misrepresented Jesus' response to this foreign woman. During His earthly ministry He was building a base among the Jews for reaching the entire world with redemption, and then the message was to go forth to the ends of the earth (Acts 1:8). Jesus initialized the world-wide phase of the mission by entering Samaritan and Gentile territories, but the bulk of His earthly ministry was spent building the foundation among the Jews. It is possible that Jesus was testing the woman's degree of persistence or was checking the disciples' level of prejudice. Whatever He was doing, the woman demonstrated remarkable theological understanding, more than Peter did as an Early Church apostle (Acts 10:1–16). Even on this occasion Jesus had just reprimanded Peter and the rest of the disciples for their ineptness (Matthew 15:15–16; Mark 7:17–18), then He commended this woman for her insight (Mark 7:29) and the faith that produced it (Matthew 15:28). A woman became the first person Jesus reached on Gentile soil.

Equality Established through Jesus' Relationships

If rabbis did not talk about women, talk to women, or have contact with women, they certainly did not keep company with women. There was virtually no possibility of rabbis welcoming women to become students of their teaching and even less possibility of women joining rabbis in their itinerant travels.[17] But each of these things occurred in Jesus' ministry. There is no explanation of such unrestricted associations other than that Jesus held a very different view of women than did the religious establishment of His day. It should not be surprising that He is still breaking the barriers set by the religious establishment and is still welcoming women to approach His teaching and His service.

Receiving the financial support of women was not extremely unusual for first-century rabbis, but allowing them to participate in the ministry by traveling with the rabbis was something that was not done. According to Scripture, however, there was a band of women who joined Jesus in this way during His travels in Galilee (Luke 8:1–3). The exact wording of the reference is interesting: "The twelve were with him and also some women." It is surprising that at least one of the women is said to be someone's wife. This group of women traveled with Him through Galilee and beyond. They are recorded as having been with Him through His crucifixion (Matthew 27:55–56; Mark 15:40–41; Luke 23:49), something that cannot be said of the twelve disciples (Matthew 26:56).

Obviously, traveling with Jesus gave women many opportunities including the opportunity for daily discipleship. This is not the only way in which Jesus broke the barriers that kept women from receiving training from Him. During His visit to the home of the sisters Mary and Martha (Luke 10:38–42), Martha busied herself with "appropriate" domestic responsibilities while Mary "sat at the Lord's feet listening to what He said" (10:39). Martha protested to Jesus, demanding that He correct Mary. Not only did Jesus refuse Martha's request, He said that Mary was doing the better thing.

Several important details can be drawn from this exchange. First, by visiting their home, Jesus showed these two women the same esteem and intimacy that He had shown men.[18] Other rabbis reserved such regard and access for men only. But Jesus did not treat men one way and women a different way. Second, Jesus dismissed as erroneous the idea that a woman's primary responsibility is domestic. Mention has already been made of the fact that He did the same thing in reference to His own mother (Luke 11:27–28). Some men today would respond to a complaint such as the one brought against Mary by shooing the woman back into her "proper place," away from her intrusion into the activities and privileges of men. But Jesus did just the opposite; He commended her for seeking the spiritual opportunities that were culturally off-limits to women. Third, Jesus allowed and welcomed Mary to learn as only men were permitted to learn. To sit at someone's feet was the position of learning for rabbinical students as well as for students of first-century philosophers. It was associated with high levels of formal education, all of which were restricted exclusively to male students.[19] Not only were women thought incapable of understanding such complexities, there was no reason for them to bother trying since they were also seen as unfit for any possible use of the knowledge. Obviously, Jesus thought differently on both counts. He saw women as worthy recipients of the same training that He made available to men.

It is not known what spiritual truth was imparted to the men and to Mary that day. Whatever it was, it could not have surpassed the revelation that Jesus chose to share with Martha sometime thereafter. And Martha, unlike Mary, did not have to steal her learning opportunity from a man or share it with a man. She was the only person present, and, reminiscent of His dealing with the Samaritan, Jesus entrusted to her one of the most significant teachings of His entire ministry (John 11:17–27). Countless teachers and preachers across the ages have proclaimed Jesus' words: "I am the resurrection and the life. He who believes in me will live, even though he dies; and whoever lives and believes in me will never die" (11:25). These words identify Jesus, explain the way to eternal life, and provide the central focus of apostolic preaching. They were first spoken to a woman. In fact, they are in Scripture today only because they were received, understood, and reported by a woman. How contradictory to the judgment of Christ for anyone to claim that a woman cannot handle and proclaim these very words today.

The ministry so often withheld from women can be said to find its foundation in the profession of faith made by Jesus' "lead disciple" Peter: "You are the Christ (Messiah), the Son of the living God" (Matthew 16:16). To this pronouncement Jesus responded, "Upon this rock I will build my church" (16:18). Unfortunately, many of the same Protestants who argue vehemently that Jesus was promising to build upon Peter's statement rather than upon Peter's person also bar women from ministry because Peter and the other disciples were men and not women. This exclusion, of course, has everything to do with the person and nothing to do with the statement. Is a woman capable of the same insight and declaration as a man? Would Jesus ever elicit from a woman such bedrock, foundational truth? The following is a comparison of Peter's profession, as recorded in three of the Gospels, to the words spoken by Martha during her "resurrection lesson" with Jesus. Each is a word-for-word translation of the Greek text into English:

Peter: You are the Christ, the Son of God the living (Matthew 16:16).
You are the Christ (Mark 8: 29).
The Christ of God (Luke 9:20).

Martha: You are the Christ, the Son of God, the into the world coming (John 11:27).

The similarity between Peter's words in the Gospel of Matthew and Martha's words in the Gospel of John is particularly striking. The core declaration, which is found in the first eight words, is *absolutely identical*. If a woman is capable of realizing and proclaiming the very truth upon which the church is built, why is she not able to serve the church in ministry? If Martha could declare Jesus' identity in first-century Israel, why are women forbidden from declaring Jesus' identity around the world today?

Perhaps no other encounters with women show Jesus' special relationship with them quite like the anointings that He received from them. There were two of these occasions, one anointing by a woman simply identified as a "sinner" (Luke 7:36–50) and a second anointing by Mary, the sister of Martha and Lazarus (Matthew 26:6–13; Mark 14:3–9; John 12:1–11). These two women made a public display of their love for Christ like no man in all of Scripture is found expressing toward his Savior.

The sinful woman, probably a prostitute, acted very boldly in approaching a table of men because Jewish men and women did not mix in this way. She was all the more brazen in entering the home of a Pharisee who would have had no public contact with women and would have felt contaminated by the intrusion of a sinful woman. His attitude of superiority is contrasted with her willingness to humiliate herself. He did not extend to Jesus the courtesies that would have been offered even to an enemy. She, however, loosened her hair, which was never done in public, broke open a stone flask of expensive ointment, and touched Jesus with her tears, her hair, and her kisses. She wiped His feet which only a servant or slave would do. Who "preached" the better message to the guests who were present, the man or the woman?

Jesus used the occasion to teach a fascinating lesson: the person who is forgiven much, loves much. Of course, all sinners are forgiven much, and all of Jesus' followers should realize this and love Him greatly. But with a woman being the instrument through which the lesson was taught, perhaps additional things were being said. After all, according to this Pharisee, women were solely responsible for sin entering the world and for all of sin's consequences, so they must never be allowed to aspire to positions of leadership. Of course, this is not true, even though people still believe it and espouse it today. But if it were true, it would be a large debt indeed. And according to Jesus, this entire debt has "canceled" stamped across it—as if it had never existed in the first place. No wonder this woman was able to be such a great preacher!

The second anointing that Jesus received was from Mary. (The unidentified woman of Matthew's and Mark's accounts is identified by John.) On this occasion, as well, there is a male-female contrast. This time, however, it does not involve just one man but several men, namely, the disciples. With the first anointing it can be said that a religious official should have had the spiritual advantage over a woman, but he didn't respond as perceptively as she did. With the second anointing, surely the disciples should have been more spiritually aware than anyone else. But more than once during Jesus' last days they were found guilty of being unable to see the cross approaching, whereas Jesus said of Mary's anointing, "When she poured this perfume on my body, she did it to prepare me for burial" (Matthew 26:12). How much detail Mary discerned is not known, but this woman sensed in her spirit more than Jesus' closest followers were able to recognize. Their thoughts were financial; her thoughts were spiritual. A woman, Mary, will forever be known for her generous love, and a man, Judas, will forever be known for his greedy betrayal.

Mary, like the sinful woman, was willing to break cultural boundaries by joining a gathering of men and by loosening her hair in their company. She was willing to act on Jesus' behalf in a way that was personally costly, spilling out the equivalent of a year's wages for a common laborer. She was willing to make a spectacle of herself and to receive a harsh public reprimand. The lines that she crossed were not only cultural but were also religious because they had been drawn on the basis of the rabbis' interpretation of Scripture. But Jesus said of her, "She did what she could." Doing what she "could" meant crossing what was to most other men and women some very clear, firm "could not" lines. Surely when Jesus said that her story would be told "wherever the gospel is preached throughout the world," He did not mean that only men would do this telling because women would never again break the cultural and religious "could not" boundaries that Mary was so willing to break.

These glimpses into Jesus' words, actions, and relationships relating to women reveal a Savior who gave them opportunities for instruction and expression that equaled or exceeded what was given to men or at least what was acted upon by men. He seems to have intentionally singled them out to receive some of His most phenomenal miracles and some of His most profound revelations. If religious leaders today are, instead, known for restricting and reprimanding women, it seems rather obvious that they are walking in the wrong direction, in a direction opposite to that of their Lord. He came to earth to redeem from sin and to release from sin. If the gospel that the church is preaching does not offer women both the redeeming *and the releasing* work of Christ, then it is not the full gospel.

Further, Jesus demonstrated the teaching and leading capacity of women by setting them before His disciples as examples on numbers of occasions. Their exemplary lives and their insightful words were subsequently placed in Scripture by God, affording these women the opportunity to teach all other believers throughout history, men and women alike. God is still selecting women whose words and lives are worthy of teaching other believers. The church must never be guilty of prohibiting what God is prescribing. Jesus said, "Whatever the Father does the Son also does" (John 5:19). May the church be able to say, "Whatever the Son and the Father do, the church also does."

Jesus' Family

If Jesus is to be credited with being such an advocate of the spiritual capacities of women, there is one incident involving His mother Mary that probably requires additional explanation (John 2:1–11). Jesus was invited to a wedding which was also attended by His mother. At some point in the celebration the host ran out of wine, an extremely embarrassing occurrence. Mary told Jesus about the need, evidently expecting Him to do something about it. His response was, "Dear woman, why do you involve me? My time has not yet come." Some have misunderstood this exchange as revealing impropriety on Mary's part and a reprimand on Jesus' part.

The address that was used, "woman" or "dear woman," was a perfectly respectful expression. It was, of course, less intimate than a family reference such as "mother" and may have been Jesus' first step away from being her son and toward being her Savior. The question "What have I to do with thee?" (KJV) or "Why do you involve me?" (NIV) is not indicative of disrespect either. Some scholars have suggested that Jesus was testing her faith since she subsequently told the servants, "Do whatever he tells you," a clear signal of her belief that He was somehow able to rectify the situation. Others have concluded that Jesus was, as with the address, distancing Himself from being under her authority as an earthly parent and beginning the phase of His life during which His ear would be tuned exclusively to His Heavenly Father's call.

Jesus' explanation "my time has not yet come" can be understood primarily in two different ways, each of which would have been instructional rather than critical. First, He could have meant that the wedding feast for which He would be responsible was yet to come, namely, the Marriage Supper of the Lamb. Second, He could have been referring to the fact that it was not yet time for Him to fully, publicly reveal His glory because doing so would inevitably result in the cross. This resistance to the beginning of the showing of His glory is similar to His later resistance to the final showing of His glory (Mark 14:35–36). Whatever Jesus meant, there are no grounds for viewing Mary negatively. The very thing she suggested that He do, He proceeded to do. Even though some instruction was evidently necessary for His intervention to be understood, Mary was not spiritually imperceptive to expect the intervention.

If someone in Jesus' earthly family is to be viewed negatively, it should not be Mary who is portrayed as believing in Him; it should be His half-brothers who ridiculed Him and refused to believe in Him (John 7:1–5). Of course, Mary had Gabriel's announcement, the virgin birth, the words of Elizabeth, the visit of the shepherds and magi, and the reception of Simeon and Anna in the temple to nurture her faith; so it is somewhat unfair to compare her with Jesus' earthly brothers. But if any attempt is made to discredit the female gender by citing Mary's supposed deficiencies, then it is the male gender, namely, Jesus' brothers, that this approach must find lacking.

Jesus' Early Evangelists

The New Testament offers a list of ministries that have been given to the church by Christ. "But to each one of us grace has been given as Christ apportioned it.... It was he who gave some to be apostles, some to be prophets, some to be evangelists, and some to be pastors and teachers" (Ephesians 4:7,11). This list should not be seen as exhaustive because the New Testament contains other lists. It is better understood as being representative of various ministries that exist within the church. It may be unwise, as well, to draw sharp lines between ministries. While Timothy was pastoring, he was told by Paul to "do the work of an evangelist" (2 Timothy 4:5). Philip the deacon was also called Philip the evangelist (Acts 21:8). But before Timothy or Philip discharged the ministry of an evangelist (herald of good news), women served Jesus in this capacity.

Returning to the account of the Samaritan woman, attention must be given to what happened after her encounter with Jesus (John 4:27–42). According to Scripture, she proclaimed Him "to the people" (4:28–29, plural of "anthropos" requiring a translation of "people" rather than KJV's "men") which would mean a crowd that definitely included men, and they responded positively (4:30). Specifically, the results of her ministry are described as follows: "Many of the Samaritans from that town believed in him because of the woman's testimony" (4:39). It should be noted that this is the same town that the disciples had just come from (4:8,27), with no indication of having proclaimed Christ to its people.

Jesus' focus was on ministering to the townspeople, as was the woman's focus. When He tried to explain this to the disciples, they failed to understand (4:31–33). He referred to doing the will and work of the Father and identified this as being the harvesting of lost souls (4:34–35). What the disciples struggled to comprehend, a woman was busily doing. Such expressions as "doing the will and work of the Father" and "harvesting ripened fields" are valid, biblical definitions of the ministry. Evangelists and missionaries throughout church history have based their very existence on these lines of Scripture. The passage that provides these definitions of the ministry portrays a woman engaging in that ministry.

It would be difficult to explain how the activity of the Samaritan woman differs in essence from what many denominations prohibit women from doing today. She held a "street service," an impromptu "city crusade." And if it is scripturally acceptable for a woman to do so, it would be most difficult to argue that putting the same activity inside the walls of a sanctuary suddenly makes it scripturally unacceptable. Even though all ministers, men and women, must be careful not to hinder the spread of the gospel by trampling cultural sensitivities, this caution must never become the convenient loophole that arbitrarily and universally banishes women from ministry. What is known about first-century Samaritan culture suggests that a woman would not have been able to do what this woman did, but, thankfully, there was no denominational policy that kept her from doing it.

There is also an interesting similarity between a reference Jesus made to apostolic ministry and what the Samaritan woman did.[20] In His prayer before the crucifixion, Jesus prayed for the disciples who would become the apostles. He then turned His attention to "those who will believe on me through their word" (John 17:20, NIV translates the Greek word for "word" into the English word "message"). He was referring to the converts who would be the direct result of the apostles' ministries. Practically identical wording is used for the results of the Samaritan woman's ministry. The following is a word-for-word translation of the Greek text: "many believed on him...through the word of the woman testifying" (4:39). In addition to the similar use of "logos" ("word") being noteworthy, the Greek word that stands behind "testifying" is used frequently in Acts and throughout the New Testament of the apostles' ministries.

When the various accounts of the four Gospels are compiled into chronological order, one other significant detail surfaces. Not only did the Samaritan woman serve as an evangelist, a ministry that was also assigned to the apostles, she was actually the first evangelist of the New Testament. (John the Baptist did the work of an evangelist; but he is usually thought to be in a category by himself, preceding Jesus' earthly ministry and distinct from Jesus' actual converts. Of course, if someone insists upon counting him as first, the woman Anna would have to be counted before him.) Hopefully no modern evangelist or foreign missionary, who is basically an evangelist, would ever teach that a woman cannot serve as an evangelist in light of the fact that the first evangelist was a woman.

In a desperate attempt to minimize the ministry of the Samaritan, it has been argued that her "sermon" was not long enough to qualify as preaching. It is faulty, however, to assume that the biblical account includes her words in their entirety. The text indicates that additional converts were made by Jesus during the course of a two-day visit (4:41), but none of His words were recorded. Later, when the twelve and the seventy were sent out as evangelists, not one word of their preaching was recorded. It simply cannot be disputed; this woman did the work of an evangelist, heralding the good news of having found the Messiah and Savior, and an entire city was impacted by her ministry.

The Samaritan was not Jesus' only early evangelist. The faithful women who traveled and trained with Him are seen in Scripture as serving in this capacity as well. Their devotion compelled them to be present at the crucifixion. Of the twelve disciples, one betrayed Jesus, one denied Him, three disappointed Him, and all of them deserted Him (Matthew 26:56); but the women are reported in all four Gospels as being at the cross, several of them cited by name (Matthew 27:55–56; Mark 15:40–41; Luke 23:49; John 19:25). The one woman whose name appears in all four accounts would be judged by some to be an especially unworthy individual, Mary Magdalene, out of whom Jesus had cast seven demons.

At what point John approached the cross is unknown beyond the fact that he was available to be assigned the care of Jesus' mother (John 19:26–27). The number of crucifixion details included by Matthew, Mark, and Luke but excluded by John has led many scholars to conclude that John was not present for all of the crucifixion. If true, then many details of Jesus' death are known today through the testimony of the faithful women who did not leave their Lord during His hour of greatest need. If they qualified to be the channel through which truth was preserved for the world, it seems odd that they do not qualify to be the channel through which truth is preached to the world.

Certain of these same women were present at Jesus' burial, though nothing is said of the disciples being there (Matthew 27:61; Mark 15:47; Luke 23:55–56). The two men who oversaw Jesus' burial, Joseph of Arimathea and Nicodemus, were members of the Sanhedrin Council which had initiated Jesus' arrest (Matthew 27:57–60; Mark 15:43–46; Luke 23:50–54; John 3:1; 19:38–42). Joseph and presumably Nicodemus also were followers of Jesus (Matthew 27:57) who had not agreed with the Sanhedrin's decisions (Luke 23:51). These two men perhaps faced less danger from their colleagues than the eleven disciples would have faced in requesting the body for proper disposal. It should be noted, however, that John the Baptist's disciples buried him (Matthew 14:12; Mark 6:29) despite the likely threat of personal danger.[21] So the contrast still stands; the eleven disciples did not associate themselves with Jesus' burial, but the women did (Mark 16:1–3; Luke 23:56–24:1). In fact, many hours after the entombing, the men were still fearfully hiding behind locked doors (John 20:19). This picture does not say much in favor of men having instinctive leadership capacities that women fail to possess.

The biblical account of resurrection morning opens with several women approaching the burial site to perform additional anointing. This is the only event of the day recorded in all four Gospels. Even though it can be said that they were first to witness the empty tomb simply because they were first to visit the tomb, the fact that they were first to hear about the resurrection and first to see the risen Christ cannot be dismissed quite so easily. An angel announced the resurrection to the women; no such announcement was given to Peter and John. Jesus chose to show Himself to the women before showing Himself to the eleven disciples or to any other men (Matthew 28:8–10; John 20:14–18). And not only were the women given these high honors, they were commissioned by the angel (Matthew 28:5–7; Mark 16:5–7) and by Jesus Himself (Matthew 28:10; John 20:17) to deliver the good news of the resurrection to the men. They were appointed to serve as evangelists ("heralds of good news"), the *first* evangelists of the resurrection. They ministered in this capacity to the eleven disciples "and to all the others" (Luke 24:9).

Jesus was familiar with the tradition of Judaism that rejected the testimony of women. By appearing to them first and by assigning to them the role of informing the other followers, He, once again, overturned their second-class status and made His view of their reliability quite clear.[22] His church was meant to view women differently than the world. His church was meant to view them as fully capable of conveying a message entrusted to them by Him.[23] When the disciples resisted this change that Jesus so clearly inaugurated, He rebuked them (Mark 16:14; John 20:29). Unfortunately, some men still regard women as incapable of proclaiming the gospel. It escapes their notice that Jesus thought differently and signaled them to think differently.

That Jesus chose to commission women to announce the resurrection, in particular, is of great significance. There are many claims of gods who live, minister, and die; but there is only one God who is alive *again* and *always*. The news, "He is risen!" is the greatest news of human history. It became the central truth of apostolic preaching (Acts 4:33; 17:2–3). It was the key

point of Peter's first sermon to the Jews (Acts 2:32) and of his
first sermon to the Gentiles (Acts 10:39–41). It was the recur-
ring theme of Paul's ministry throughout the world (2 Timothy
2:8). Salvation rests upon it (Romans 10:9), doctrine rests upon
it (1 Corinthians 15:17), and eternity rests upon it (John 14:19–
20; 2 Corinthians 4:14; 1 Thessalonians 4:14). The resurrection
was seen by early Christians as so fundamental to the gospel
that being a witness to the event was an early qualification for
apostleship (Acts 1:21–22).

This most important truth about Jesus, this truth upon
which the church is built, was first entrusted to women. They
were first to witness it and to proclaim it. They were actually
assigned to act as apostles ("sent ones") to the apostles. They
could not have been given any greater affirmation or elevation
by Jesus. They could not have been granted a more foundational
or a more prominent role in the kingdom than to serve as the
first evangelists of the resurrection. Because Jesus was so
deliberate and conspicuous in this positioning of the women, to
reduce and restrict their "front and center" role to secondary
subservience is to act in violation of His explicit will.[25]

Jesus commissioned women to proclaim the good news, and
He is still commissioning them to do so. How can His church
refuse to do likewise? According to the Apostle Paul, three
truths comprise the gospel—the death, the burial, and the
resurrection of Jesus (1 Corinthians 15:1–4). Jesus' faithful
female followers possessed a first-hand, complete knowledge of
these three tenets of the gospel beyond that of any of the eleven
disciples. Only they were present for all three of these events.
How can it be that women are unqualified to proclaim this very
gospel? It may be that women must join the Apostle Paul in
saying that they are sent "not from men nor by man, but by
Jesus Christ" (Galatians 1:1). If this alone is their commissioning, then they have the highest commissioning possible.

The Great Commission

After Jesus' post-resurrection appearances to the women, He
gave considerable attention to the eleven disciples. He said such
things to them as, "As the Father has sent me, I am sending you"
(John 20:21); "If you forgive anyone his sins, they are forgiven"
(20:23); and "Feed my sheep" (21:17). Whether before His death
or after His resurrection, if Jesus explained or assigned some

aspect of ministry to the disciples that today's clergy wishes to withhold from women, this is usually done by making much of the fact that the original recipients were men and not women. Of course, nothing is made of the fact that the original recipients were members of a specific group of first-century Jews which no clergyman today can claim to be.

There is an additional inconsistency in claiming such activities to be off-limits to women simply because they were first opened to the disciples. A number of attitudes and behaviors that were mentioned only to the disciples are never interpreted as applying to that audience alone or even to a male, ministerial audience alone. A study of the Gospel of Matthew produces several examples. "Ask the Lord of the harvest...to send out workers into his harvest field" (9:38). Are male ministers the only ones who are to pray this prayer? "Whoever acknowledges me before men, I will also acknowledge him before my Father in heaven. But whoever disowns me before men, I will disown him before my Father in heaven" (10:32–33). "If anyone would come after me, he must deny himself and take up his cross and follow me" (16:24, KJV inserts "man" for Greek "anyone"). "If you have faith as small as a mustard seed, you can say to this mountain, 'Move from here to there,' and it will move" (17:19–21). "I tell you the truth, unless you change and become like little children, you will never enter the kingdom of heaven" (18:1–4). Are these attitudes and behaviors restricted to the twelve simply because they were first revealed to them? Jesus' teaching on correcting wrongs (18:15–17) and on forgiving others (18:21–35) was given only to the disciples. Are these activities limited to them? Of course not!

One of the most well-known of all of Jesus' commands, the Great Commission, was voiced only to the eleven disciples who were left after the resurrection: "Go and make disciples of all nations, baptizing them in the name of the Father and of the Son and of the Holy Spirit, and teaching them to obey everything I have commanded you" (Matthew 28:16–20). As has been made clear, the fact that the audience was limited does not necessarily mean that the assignment was to be restricted to that audience alone. And it is doubtful that today's clergy would ever present the Great Commission as applying to ministers alone. Indeed, after telling sinners to become converts, the church is quick to tell all converts to witness to others, and the Great Commission is used as the primary basis for this exhortation.

But the point that is oftentimes overlooked is this: the same individual who is told to go and to disciple others is also told to baptize and to teach the converts who are discipled as a result of the going. If someone wishes to bar women from baptizing and from teaching, then biblically, he must bar women from witnessing as well. And it is highly unlikely that Jesus was describing in the Great Commission the witnessing that occurs in a sanctuary church service, since very little of His ministry took place in any type of a religious building or service. Banning women from witnessing would mean banning them from the "everyday witnessing" that occurs in homes and in workplaces and along the roadways of life. Of course, any such absolute stifling of women would align well with a strict interpretation of the "be silent" passages, but the silencing would have to extend outside the sanctuary service into all Christian witnessing. Women would not be able to open their mouths about Jesus, but of course they would be free to talk about absolutely everything else. How ludicrous!

The Great Commission, though first spoken to the eleven disciples, was recorded in Scripture to be read and obeyed by all of Jesus' followers, men and women alike, clergy and laity alike. According to the closing verse (28:20), Jesus will be with the individual who obeys this commission—going, discipling, baptizing, and teaching. Religious opinion may not be with the individual. Denominational policy may not be with the individual. But Jesus will be with him *or* her.

As the "case" favoring women ministers becomes more firm and more forceful with every turn of the pages of Scripture, perhaps a gentle caution is worth inserting in an effort to strike the proper balance. No amount of biblical evidence favoring the entry of women into spiritual leadership should be perceived as encouraging women to mount an aggressive, abrasive fight for their ministerial rights. First, this would be exchanging the central cause of advancing the gospel for a side cause of advancing a person. Second, to attempt to accomplish the work of Christ without exemplifying the Spirit of Christ would be one of the most serious mistakes any minister could make. Jesus' righteousness and anointing blended with humble servanthood made room for His message to go forth. The same qualities must be present in ministers today, male or female, in order to see the same result—*His* message going forth.

8

Women in the Early Church

It is not surprising that male leadership dominated the Early Church. Just as it would have been self-defeating for a woman to serve as one of the twelve disciples whose task was to reach people who were virtually unreachable by women, the viability of women ministers continued to face great challenges. In His last instructions before the ascension, Jesus made it clear that the Jews were to remain the starting point for world evangelization (Acts 1:8), and the apostles were faithful to follow this strategy. A woman would not have been able to address a synagogue audience or most other gatherings of Jews and would, thereby, have been severely limited in reaching them. Jewish men who praised God daily for not making them a Gentile, a slave, or a woman were not likely to accept female leadership, certainly not before conversion and probably not immediately after conversion.

Jewish resistance was not the only obstacle. Most men in the surrounding Roman Empire did not view women as having serious leadership capacity. They were likely to associate female religious leadership with the emotional frenzies and extreme feminism that oftentimes characterized women of the fertility cults. Jewish and Gentile women alike were typically denied access to the levels of education that would have given them the appearance of being knowledgeable individuals. They were certainly kept from learning Old Testament Scripture which was so foundational to an understanding of Jesus and the gospel.

These circumstances that made it difficult for women to serve as ministers during the first century were cultural and educational, not theological. They were situational and temporary, not universal and permanent. The same daily prayer that left Israel more reachable by male apostles than by female apostles simultaneously resulted in all of the original apostles being Jewish rather than Gentile. Neither qualification, however, has any theological basis for continuing across the centuries and across the continents. It may be that because men have a tendency to view women as inferior and/or subordinate, women will never be as prevalent or as prominent in the ministry as men. But the fact that men dominated the ministry in the first century is no reason to conclude that the ministry is in any way the exclusive domain of men.

What is absolutely amazing is that women were as visible in first-century ministry as they were. As the gospel went forth, women were typically numbered among the converts and were sometimes notable enough to be named and detailed in the biblical record. As the church developed its own identity separate from Judaism and matured in its following of Jesus' teachings, women slowly but surely began to rise to positions of responsibility and leadership. If first-century women could be as significantly involved in the ministry as they were, despite extremely adverse conditions, then women today should be able to engage in ministry to an even greater extent, at least in many parts of the world.

Women at Pentecost

Before ascending to Heaven, Jesus told His followers to wait in Jerusalem to be baptized with the Holy Spirit (Acts 1:4–5). This experience was to give them power to be His witnesses to the ends of the earth (1:8). It occurred on the Feast of Weeks or Day of Pentecost, an Old Testament feast day which fell fifty days after Passover. Very much in line with its initiating of the spreading of the gospel around the world, the day was also known as the feast of harvest (Exodus 23:16) and the day of firstfruits (Numbers 28:26). This outpouring of the Holy Spirit and birthing of worldwide evangelization inaugurated the New Testament church.

Pentecost in the Old Testament was one of three feasts that every Israelite man was required to attend (Deuteronomy 16:16). The law made provision for women to attend as well (Deuteronomy 16:11); consequently, they probably did so. The New Testament account of Pentecost, however, specifically indicates their presence (Acts 1:13–14). In fact, of the 120 people in attendance (Acts 1:15), only three groups are given special mention: the eleven disciples, Jesus' earthly brothers, and the women. The text says, *"All* of them were filled with the Holy

Spirit and began to speak in other tongues as the Spirit enabled them" (Acts 2:4).

There can be no doubt that "all" includes the women. When Peter rose to explain the event to the crowd that gathered, he quoted an Old Testament prophecy which said God's Spirit would be poured out upon sons and daughters, upon male servants and female servants (Acts 2:17–18). The KJV translation of verse 15 is more reflective of the original than the NIV translation. The Greek text says "these" rather than "these men." Because the word "these" is in the masculine form, the NIV translators rendered it "these men." In Greek, however, demonstrative pronouns such as "these" must be masculine, feminine, or neuter (referring to things). If a group is all male, the masculine "these" may be translated "these men." In the case of a mixed group, however, it must be translated "these people" or simply "these" because there is no other way to refer to a mixed group but to use the masculine form.

Just as women were noticeably present in Jesus' ministry, being saved by Him, they were noticeably present in His Early Church, being empowered by Him. And they certainly spoke out in this first public meeting! They were not any more silent than the men; men and women alike burst forth in other tongues. This same experience that was given equally to men and women on the Day of Pentecost continues to be available to all believers, male and female alike. Peter said to the crowd, "Repent and be baptized, every one of you, in the name of Jesus Christ so that your sins may be forgiven. And you will receive the gift of the Holy Spirit" (2:38). Then he said, "The promise is for you and your children and for all who are far off—for all whom the Lord our God will call" (2:39). The "all who are far off" and the "all whom the Lord our God will call" extends the experience to every Christian. A great gift had become available and would continue to be available to *all* believers.

The Holy Spirit had been poured out in the Old Testament but only upon select individuals (usually ministers) to assist them in accomplishing specific tasks for God. The prophecy that Peter quoted promised a widespread outpouring for the future: "'In the last days,' God says, 'I will pour out my Spirit on all people'" (2:17). The "last days" is the time period between Christ's ascension and Christ's return, the era of the church. During this period all believers are to do God's work; therefore, all believers are to be empowered by God's Spirit. The same

Spirit who rested upon Moses and Aaron and Joshua, the same Spirit who rested upon Elijah and Elisha and Isaiah is to rest upon every male *and every female* believer! He provides an empowering for ministry, certainly not an empowering for silence. He provides an empowering to do the teaching and preaching assigned to the church in the Great Commission (Matthew 28:18–20; Mark 16:15).

The Old Testament prophecy quoted by Peter is exceptionally clear as to the universal availability of the Holy Spirit (Acts 2:17–18). Specifically, the three distinctions that were most significant within Judaism and are most significant within any culture — gender, age, and class — are made irrelevant. The Spirit has been made available to sons and daughters, to young and old, and even to servants. There is to be no distinction. Whatever is available to a son is equally available to a daughter; whatever prophecy flows forth through a son may flow forth through a daughter. Ministering the gospel of Jesus Christ is as open to one as it is to the other.

Just as Jesus' ministry was inaugurated by the quoting of an Old Testament prophecy (Luke 4:16–21), the church's ministry was inaugurated in the same way. What was Jesus' ministry all about? He was anointed by the Spirit to preach good news and to set prisoners free. What is the church's ministry all about? The church has been empowered by the Spirit to witness about Jesus to the ends of the earth, and this empowering has been enacted in such a way as to eliminate all divisive, enslaving distinctions within the church. Men and women, young and old, and all classes are to do this witnessing. None is to be silent.

If there is any one passage of the New Testament that deserves to act as the yardstick against which all other texts about women are measured, it is this Acts 2 passage. Because it births the church into existence and indicates so clearly God's disregard for gender, age, and class in the equipping of the church for ministry, it holds a scriptural position that no other text comes close to holding. If some other passage seems to deviate from the principles established by Acts 2:17–18, that passage must be seen as pertaining to a unique local situation; it cannot be seen as contradicting and reversing the truths that God positioned so strategically at the very outset of the church's existence.

The Significance of Women

Not only did women play a significant part in the first church service, they continued to be among the new converts (Acts 5:14; 8:12; 17:4; 17:12). Whether it was Jews, Samaritans, or Gentiles being evangelized, women responded. By the time the last reference was made (17:12), they were mentioned before the men, typically indicative of a position of prominence. This mentioning of women is unusual enough for first-century writing; it is even more striking that some female converts were acknowledged by name (16:13–14; 17:16–17,34). One of only two individuals recorded as being raised from the dead through the ministry of the Early Church was a woman, Tabitha or Dorcas (9:36–42). It is somewhat humorous that the man raised from the dead is depicted as falling asleep during a sermon and plunging to his death from a third floor window ledge; whereas, the woman is described as possessing what seems to be one of the gifts of the Spirit, the gift of helps.

The Bible is specific in identifying women as being included in the believers who were seized, imprisoned, and executed by Saul (8:1–3; 9:1–2; 22:4) in an effort to stop the spread of the gospel. If they had been silent during meetings, simply learning from the teaching and preaching of the men, they would not have posed the threat to Judaism that caused Saul to arrest them. He was not attempting a wholesale purging as God frequently administered in the Old Testament because there is no mention of children being involved. He was trying to stop the advancement of this new faith by snatching everyone who was propagating it. Because he arrested women as well as men, it must be concluded that women and men were equally involved in spreading the news of Jesus.

This same man, after his own conversion to Christ, was still willing to recognize the potential of women in the building of the church. He was willing to plant a local church starting with a core of women (16:12–13) and with the household of a woman (16:14–15). This contrasted sharply with Judaism which would not count women in determining a quorum sizable enough to establish a worship community. In Christianity, however, women and men are of equal significance and standing. Saul knew this when he was trying to destroy the church, and he knew it when he was trying to build the church. It seems that if women qualify to constitute the core of a church, then they qualify to constitute the eventual leadership of that church.

Women as Coworkers in the Ministry

The Apostle Paul used a specific term over and over again to identify the ministers who joined him in his pioneer missionary work. It was, in fact, the expression that he used more often than any other to refer to his church planting colleagues. The Greek word "sunergos" is typically translated "fellow worker" or "coworker" in English. It means "one who works side-by-side with." Paul used the term to refer to himself (1 Corinthians 3:9), Aquila (Romans 16:3), Urbanus (Romans 16:9), Timothy (Romans 16:21; 1 Thessalonians 3:2), Apollos (1 Corinthians 3:5,9), Titus (2 Corinthians 8:23), Epaphroditus (Philippians 2:25), Clement (Philippians 4:3), Aristarchus (Colossians 4:10–11; Philemon 24), Mark (Colossians 4:10–11; Philemon 24), Justus (Colossians 4:11), Philemon (Philemon 1), Demas (Philemon 24), and Luke (Philemon 24). It is noteworthy that Paul never used this word to designate believers in general, but reserved it for references to his associates in the ministry.[1] Four of these men were also identified as apostles: Paul (Romans 1:1), Timothy (1 Thessalonians 1:1; 2:6–7), Apollos (1 Corinthians 4:6,9), and Epaphroditus (Philippians 2:25, "apostolos" translated "messenger"); therefore, being a "sunergos" was not a small or casual designation.

In addition to calling these 14 men "sunergos," Paul also called three women the very same thing: Priscilla (Romans 16:3), Euodia (Philippians 4:2–3), and Syntyche (Philippians 4:2–3). Priscilla was assigned the title in the same breath and in exactly the same way as her husband Aquila. Much more will be said about her in a subsequent section as one of the teachers of the Early Church. Euodia and Syntyche were not only referred to as being "sunergos" but were also described as having "struggled/contended" side-by-side with Paul "in the gospel." The verb that was used for "struggled/contended" ("sunethlesan") was a very strong word, denoting the type of grueling athletic combat that was found in gladiator matches.[2] The image is far from one of two ladies serving refreshments or assisting in some other quiet, behind-the-scenes fashion. They were front and center alongside one of the greatest ministers the world has ever known. They were doing what he was doing, fighting aggressively to spread the gospel.

Euodia and Syntyche were individuals of such prominence that the disagreement that they had could not remain a small, private matter.[3] It was evidently capable of affecting the church as a whole, causing Paul to intervene with a personal appeal. It is interesting, however, that they were not told to be silent or submissive as the solution, nor were they put under the jurisdiction of the male leadership of the church.[4] In fact, the only man who was mentioned was told to begin offering his help to these two workers. And lest the fact that they were disagreeing with each other be thought to lessen their credibility in some way, it should be noted that two men who were coworkers, Paul and Barnabas, had an even more serious dispute which rendered them unable to stay together (Acts 15:36–40). It must be recognized that these two women were very much ministers in the first-century church, as much as any of the men that Paul designated as his "sunergos." Surely they were the equivalent of any modern minister and probably exceeded most modern ministers in the rigor of their work, and yet they would not be acknowledged as ministers in many churches today.

In the same Romans 16 list of greetings in which Paul identified Priscilla as a ministerial coworker ("sunergos"), he mentioned a number of other women as well. Several of them were referred to using the Greek verb "kopiao" which is translated "labor" or "work very hard" in English. This and its noun counterpart "kopos" were used frequently by Paul of the ministerial endeavors of himself and others, sometimes even of apostolic efforts (1 Corinthians 3:5–8; 15:9–11; 15:58; 2 Corinthians 10:15–16; 11:23; 11:27; Galatians 4:11; Philippians 2:16; Colossians 1:28–29; 1 Timothy 5:17). This being the case, it is reasonable to conclude that he identified four other women as ministers in Romans 16 because he referred to them, using this ministerial terminology: Mary (16:6), Tryphena and Tryphosa, who were probably sisters (16:12), and Persis (16:12). The last three are specifically said to have labored very hard "in the Lord," increasing the likelihood of their labors being ministerial rather than menial in nature.

Elsewhere in Paul's writings he says that believers are to submit to those who "kopiao" (1 Corinthians 16:16), and he refers to those who "kopiao" as admonishing believers and as being over them (1 Thessalonians 5:12). Actually, in both passages, it is "brothers" or "brethren" who are addressed. This term "adelphos" ("brothers, brethren") is frequently used in a collective sense and can usually be assumed to include all believers, both men and women. It would, however, never be used in reference to a group of women only, so the use of such an address makes it certain that men are very much targeted by the instructions given in these two passages.

A further note of explanation might be helpful regarding the word "such" in 1 Corinthians 16:18. The Greek text does not read "such men" as do some English translations. It simply reads "such." The word is in the plural masculine form, so the word "men" has been inserted by some translators. As has been clarified earlier, Greek demonstrative pronouns have only three options: masculine, feminine, or neuter (referring to things). If a group of people is comprised of men and women, the masculine form functions generically rather than indicating men only. If verse 18 refers back to the list of three men named in verse 17, then no harm is done by inserting the word "men." However, the idea of "men only" should not be read back into verse 16. Not only does verse 15 refer to an entire household of people which is likely to include men and women, but verse 16 says "everyone" (without indication of gender).

The 1 Corinthians 16:16 and 1 Thessalonians 5:12 uses of "kopiao" support two conclusions. First, if a ministerial laborer admonished believers, stood in a position over believers, and deserved the submission of believers, then it is all the more likely that the term "kopiao," especially when applied to a specific individual, identified that person as a spiritual leader in the Early Church. Second, the four women who are associated with this ministerial terminology in Romans 16 can be assumed to have admonished (instructed, warned) men and to have been in a position of authority and leadership over men. So Paul affirmed women for doing the very things that some would propose women are forever forbidden from doing. "The evidence seems incontrovertible that women worked alongside men in the Pauline churches, and there is absolutely nothing in the text which would suggest that the work was of a subordinate character."[5]

Paul's citations in Romans 16, then, identified Priscilla, Mary, Tryphena, Tryphosa, and Persis as ministers on a level equal to that of men. In addition, he spoke of Phoebe as a "diakonos" ("minister" or "deacon") (16:1) and referred to Junia as an "apostle" (16:7). Phoebe and Junia ministered with Paul as well and will be dealt with at length in subsequent sections. In addition to acknowledging these seven women, he also mentioned three others: the mother of Rufus (16:13), Julia (16:15), and the sister of Nereus (16:15). All together 29 people are cited by name in this passage (16:1–16), and ten of them are women, fully one third. It was a woman, Phoebe (16:1), who was introduced and commended to the entire church in Rome, and it was a woman, Priscilla (16:3), who led off the list of noteworthy individuals within that church. "Historians know of no comparable list of greetings in antiquity that gives such a prominent place to women."[6] Indeed, it is worth asking, if the church today compiled a list of ministers and other prominent individuals, would one third of the names on that list be those of women, or would church policies prevent such a possibility?

Women as Deacons and/or Ministers

Without question, Romans is one of the most significant books in the New Testament. As a theological document, its value is beyond calculation. It was probably written during Paul's third missionary journey, specifically while he was in Corinth (Romans 16:23; 1 Corinthians 1:14). It was evidently delivered to Rome by Phoebe (Romans 16:1) of Cenchrea, a seaport community about six miles outside Corinth. How interesting that such an important letter would be entrusted to the care of a woman. This may not be something that the Jewish Saul would have done, but it is something that the Christian Paul was willing to do.

In introducing and commending "Sister Phoebe" to the Christians of Rome, Paul referred to her as a "diakonos" of the Cenchrean church (Romans 16:1). This Greek word is likely to be translated "servant" in an English Bible, but it is questionable whether this is the best option available. The word "diakonos" appears a total of 30 times in the New Testament, eight times in the Gospels and 22 times in Paul's writings. It can refer to domestic attendants as it does in three of the Gospels' locations (Matthew 22:13; John 2:5,9), even though these individuals are usually designated using various other Greek words. The other five Gospels' locations are instances of Jesus speaking of His followers in a way that emphasized their lowliness (Matthew 20:26; 23:11; Mark 9:35; 10:43; John 12:26). All eight of these passages are best rendered "servant" because of how the word "diakonos" is used in them.

The translations of Paul's uses of the word are much more revealing. Of the 22 occurrences, the KJV renders 18 "minister," three "deacon," and only the reference to Phoebe "servant." These 22 words are identical in the Greek text (sometimes singular, sometimes plural); there is absolutely no reason to render only one reference "servant" other than the fact that it was a woman who bore the title. Unfortunately, this reflects blatant gender bias on the part of the translation team. Modern versions such as the NIV and NASB translate three passages "deacon" (the same ones as KJV: Philippians 1:1; 1 Timothy 3:8,12; these being the instances that do not involve proper names); use an assortment of "minister," "servant," and one instance of "fellow worker" for the other 18; and refer to Phoebe as "servant."

What was this woman Phoebe? As a "diakonos," was she a minister, a deacon, or simply a follower of Jesus characterized by a lowly spirit? Perhaps the answer cannot be determined with absolute certainty, but surely some indications can be drawn from 22 uses of the word, at least if these references are handled with care and consistency. Rather than reading the 22 passages according to the choice of English words and grouping them accordingly, all 22 should be read inserting the word "diakonos" and should be grouped according to how the word is used.

Four of the 22 may fall outside the realm of relevance for this study: two are used of divinely appointed governing authorities (Romans 13:4, two occurrences) with the context indicating that secular officials (Romans 13:1) were at least partially if not primarily in view, and two are used of Jesus (Romans 15:8; Galatians 2:17). Three other references are to false apostles (2 Corinthians 11:15, two occurrences; 11:23), at least signifying recognizable positions rather than general service, even though the doctrine being spread was false. The remaining 15 uses can be categorized as follows: one of Phoebe (Romans 16:1), one of Paul and Apollos (1 Corinthians 3:5), two of Paul and others (2 Corinthians 3:6; 6:4), three of Paul (Ephesians 3:7; Colossians 1:23,25), two of Tychicus (Ephesians 6:21; Colossians 4:7), one of Epaphras (Colossians 1:7), two of Timothy (1 Thessalonians 3:2; 1 Timothy 4:6), and three of a distinguishable position in the church known today as "deacon" (Philippians 1:1; 1 Timothy 3:8,12).

There is no question about the ministerial status of Paul. On more than one occasion he claimed the highest possible level of New Testament ministry, that of an apostle. Apollos was a teacher and preacher (Acts 18:24–28), a spiritual leader with "followings" similar to Peter's and Paul's (1 Corinthians 1:12), and an apostle (1 Corinthians 4:6,9). Timothy was Paul's missionary colleague (Acts 16:1–5), a teacher (1 Timothy 4:11), a preacher (2 Corinthians 1:19; 2 Timothy 4:2), and an apostle (1 Thessalonians 1:1; 2:6–7). Tychicus and Epaphras were also Paul's missionary colleagues (Acts 20:4; Colossians 1:7). Tychicus was sent by Paul to more than one congregation to "parakaleo" ("exhort, encourage") them (Ephesians 6:21–22; Colossians 4:7–8). The same Greek word is used on many occasions for the ministry of Paul as well as of Peter (1 Peter 2:11; 5:1; 5:12) and Jude's (Jude 3) ministries. Timothy is told to "parakaleo" in connection with preaching the Word (2 Timothy 4:2), and Titus is told to do so in connection with teaching and with exercising authority (Titus 2:15). Epaphras was responsible for evangelizing the city of Colosse and for founding its church (Colossians 1:6–7).

Other than the references to divinely appointed secular officials and to Jesus, then, three uses of "diakonos" point to false ministers; and the other 15 divide between 11 references to specific individuals known to have been true ministers in the Early Church (Paul, Apollos, Timothy, Tychicus, and Epaphras), three references to a clearly distinguishable position in the Early Church known today as "deacon," and one reference to Phoebe. This means that the weight of evidence leans very heavily toward concluding that Phoebe was a minister to the same degree as the five men who carried the title. If she is not viewed in this way, then the passage naming her would stand in sharp contrast to the 11 other passages naming specific individuals. It is perfectly acceptable for the sake of honoring Jesus' emphasis upon lowliness to translate all 12 citations (one of Phoebe and 11 of men) as "servant," but for the sake of clarity it must be understood that five of the six individuals named in this way were "official Early Church ministers," and there is no reason to view Phoebe otherwise except to exercise a bias against her gender.

Is there any possibility that Phoebe was, instead, what is referred to today as a deacon? Out of Paul's 22 uses of "diakonos," three passages do designate this position (Philippians 1:1; 1 Timothy 3:8,12). First, it must be said again that the weight of evidence does not point in this direction. Second, this solution to the "problem" of having to concede that she was a minister may not solve much of anything for those wishing to diminish the role of women in the church. If Phoebe were a deacon rather than a minister, then it follows that women today should be permitted to serve as deacons. But most churches that do not allow women ministers also do not allow women deacons. And the version of a deacon that would have to be open to women would have to reflect an Early Church version of the position.

It is frequently assumed that the office of deacon originated with the Acts 6 choosing of the seven. According to the brief sketch that is given (6:1–6), the twelve apostles needed to be freed from the administrative task of charitable food distribution in order to give themselves more wholly to praying and ministering the Word of God. Seven men were chosen for the assignment. It cannot be known for sure if these men were the first deacons because the word "diakonos" that is translated "deacon" in the list of qualifications found in 1 Timothy 3 is not used in the Acts 6 passage. Further, the Acts account does designate these men but does so using the expression "the seven" rather than the term "deacon" (Acts 21:8). If they were the original deacons, however, and if Phoebe is understood to have been a deacon, then the Early Church, obviously, proceeded to open the Acts 6 office to women.

According to Acts 6, the line between deacon and minister that is so clear in many churches today was not nearly so clear in the Early Church. The candidates had to be full of the Holy Spirit (6:3), an unusual requirement for serving food, and they were installed with the laying on of hands (6:6), clearly a spiritual ritual. The only individuals from the list of seven who are detailed in Scripture resemble ministers more than laymen. Stephen performed mighty miracles (6:8), preached the longest sermon recorded in the New Testament (7:2–53), and posed enough of a threat to Judaism that he became the first Christian martyr (7:54–60). Philip preached (8:4–5,12,40), performed miracles and healings and deliverances (8:6–7), taught Scripture (8:26–35), and baptized (8:36–38). If these two men were representative of the entire group, then the office of deacon was not in the least bit confined to practical concerns or administrative tasks. It extended into what is identified today as ministerial activities and was actually better known for the ministry of preaching than for the ministry of tables.[7] If Phoebe served as a deacon as described in Acts 6–8, then women today should be given the opportunity to serve as local church deacons who engage in administrative leadership, teaching, preaching, baptizing, and other ministerial responsibilities.

If Acts 6–8 is actually reporting on some office other than that of deacon, then 1 Timothy 3:8–13 offers the only description of a New Testament deacon available because it offers the only use of "diakonos" (along with the Philippians 1:1 allusion) that is not referring by name to individuals known to be ministers. Evidently, various activities of early itinerant ministers eventually formalized, at least in certain cities, into local church offices. This would explain a reference to the position of deacon in Philippians, a Prison Epistle written in Paul's late years, and in 1 Timothy, a Pastoral Epistle written even later. Of course, the reference to Phoebe as a "diakonos" appears in Romans, a letter written during Paul's earlier years when itinerant ministerial activities were probably not yet formalized into local offices. This, along with the fact that the reference to her is like that of the references to known ministers, makes it unlikely that Phoebe served in the position described in 1 Timothy 3:8–13. But if she did, if the Romans 16:1 designation of her should be translated "deacon" and should be aligned with the 1 Timothy 3 passage, then what can be concluded about her and, more generally, about women?

Actually, the 1 Timothy passage provides less information than may be expected or desired. Its focus is more upon qualifications for the position than upon activities of the position. But if Phoebe met these qualifications, then obviously the office of deacon should be viewed as being open to women. A quick argument against this conclusion might be based upon the NIV wording of 3:8, "Deacons, likewise, are to be men," or upon the provision listed in 3:12, "A deacon must be the husband of but one wife." But neither argument is valid.

In the Greek text the word "men" does not appear in 3:8; it has been added by the NIV translation team. It is true that the word "diakonos" is masculine, but this results from the fact that Greek nouns have a masculine, feminine, or neuter gender built into their spelling. The gender of nouns that name abstract or physical things can be quite interesting. For example, "death" is masculine, and "life" is feminine; "feet" is masculine, and "head" is feminine. Designations for people, however, do not feature such a mix; almost all of them carry a masculine ending, except those that relate specifically to women ("mother," "daughter") or counterpart words ("goddess," "priestess"). This means that titles with positive connotations as well as titles with negative connotations typically carry the masculine gender. Both "friend" and "enemy" are masculine, although, obviously, not all friends and enemies are male. The word "sinner" is masculine, even when referring to a woman. What all of this means is that the gender of "diakonos" does not mean that men and only men were in focus. The male version of the word was the only version available in first-century Greek, whether the reference was to a man or a woman. This is evident in the titling of Phoebe as a "diakonos" in Romans 16:1.

It is not accurate to insert the word "deaconess" for an occurrence of "diakonos" that refers to a woman because the Greek word that properly translates "deaconess" ("diakonissa") was not in use until the late third or early fourth century, over 200 years after the writing of Paul's letters. By that time it designated an order of women whose role was different from that of male deacons.[8] Using a different word for a woman than is used for a man, when the Bible does not do so, invites considerable misunderstanding. In this case, it invites the impression that the position was different when held by a woman. Just the opposite conclusion should be drawn from the fact that Paul used exactly the same title for Phoebe (Romans 16:1) as he used for himself, for other men, and for the 1 Timothy 3:8 office.

In the 1 Timothy 3 passage, then, the position of deacon should be viewed as being equally open to both genders, even though the Greek word is masculine in its spelling. Nowhere in the New Testament is there any indication that the work of a female deacon differed in any way from that of a male deacon. In the Early Church a woman was neither denied the office nor restricted in her function within it. It follows, of course, that the same should be the case in the church today.

What can be said about the 1 Timothy 3:12 stipulation that a deacon should have only one wife? In light of the fact the Jewish and Gentile societies of the first century were extremely patriarchal in orientation, it is likely that the Early Church had far more male deacons than female deacons. Consequently, it is understandable that a list of qualifications for a position would make special stipulations pertaining to men. It would be easier to answer this question if it were certain what is being said about men in verse 12 as well as in verse 2. If the issue is the prohibition of polygamy, then a woman would not have had that possibility open to her within the culture. If it is the prohibition of divorce and remarriage or marital infidelity, then these too would have been practiced primarily if not exclusively by men. It is odd that the necessity to check the sinfulness of male candidates more than female candidates is today interpreted as welcoming men to the position over women.

Whatever "husband of but one wife" means, it results from an assumption; it does not reflect the setting of a qualification. Just as the first-century world was male-based, it was equally marriage-based. An adult male candidate for deacon was very likely to be married, so Paul simply said that his marital status, which was assumed, must involve only one wife. It was similarly assumed that a married man would have children, so the same verse reads, "must manage his children and his household well." If deacons must be male, then a consistent application of the passage requires them to be married and to have children and a household. But this is not what Paul was saying, nor is it what churches practice today, because assuming and requiring are two different things. As a matter of fact, requiring marriage and children would have disqualified Paul as much as requiring maleness would have disqualified Phoebe. The truth is, the passage is not meant to exclude women any more than it is meant to exclude the unmarried or the childless. A correct understanding of the text would be as follows: If a man is married, his marital status must involve only one wife; and if a married man has children, then those children must be managed well.

Several translations, including the KJV and the NIV, take the liberty of rendering 1 Timothy 3:11 as if setting qualifications for the deacon's *wife*, thereby furthering the impression that deacons must be men. The Greek word being translated in 3:11 is a form of "gune." It was the primary designation for a woman or a wife. It meant one as much as it meant the other because in a marriage-based culture, the two were usually the same. (If not, other words like virgin, unmarried, widow, or harlot, were available.) If Paul meant "wives," then the passage does lean heavily toward male deacons. If he meant "women," however, then a specific inclusion of "women deacons" was built right into the apostle's only detailed handling of the office.

Anytime a determination of "woman" or "wife" must be made, the context offers the only means of deciding which designation to favor. Probably the major claim to verse 11 translating "wives" is its location in the middle of the deacon material of verses 8–10 and 12–13. This, however, is just as likely to explain a natural reference to women deacons as it is to defend the insertion of material about wives of deacons. The evidence in favor of translating the word "women" rather than "wives," on the other hand, is quite strong. First, it is unlikely that Paul would specify qualifications for deacons' wives and omit similar requirements for the higher position of overseer detailed in verses 1–7. If the "wife material" is said to cover both the overseer and the deacon, then inserting it right in the middle of the deacon section would be extremely strange placement. Second, the natural way to refer to deacons' wives would have been to structure the very wording of the phrase to indicate possessiveness, which Paul did not do.

The third indication comes from the structure of the 1 Timothy passage as a whole. The verb "must be" occurs in verse 2 but not in verses 8 or 11. In fact, verses 8 and 11 are without a verb. The word "likewise" ("hosautos") that follows "deacons" in verse 8 and "women/wives" in verse 11 signals a connection to the material in verses 1–7 and allows a borrowing of its verb "must be" from that material. This means that three groups of people are being marked off by the structure of the passage: overseers, male deacons, and female deacons. Not surprisingly, the positives that are stipulated for male and female deacons are similar. The negatives for each probably forbid behaviors that were associated with each gender: men not indulging excessively in alcohol or pursuing dishonest gain (3:8) and women not engaging in malicious talk (3:11). So, just as verse 8 introduces a group of church officials, male deacons, verse 11 does the same thing, introduces a group of church officials, female deacons. It does so in exactly the same way, using the word "hosautos" ("likewise"). This would not have been done if verse 11 were focusing upon the same individuals as verses 8–10.

In all of this discussing of female deacons, something about the nature of deacons in general should not be obscured. Most churches today place a significant demarcation between overseers and deacons: one is a member of the clergy, the other a member of the laity. According to the use of "diakonos" in the New Testament, the work of ministers in Acts and in the early epistles seems to have institutionalized into the office of deacon in later materials such as 1 Timothy. So, historically, there was a close link and probably an overlap between the two. Even the 1 Timothy 3 passage links the office of overseer with that of deacon in the grammatical structuring of the material. It is very likely, then, that the position of deacon was more "ministerial" in nature even after its formalization into an office than it is expected and allowed to be today, more an order of minister than an order of layman. If the Early Church patterned itself after synagogue structure, then the overseer probably represented the principal spiritual leader and the deacon the assistant.[9] All of these considerations press the modern view of the deacon beyond its common boundaries.

Returning to the Romans 16:1 designation of Phoebe as a "diakonos," it must be concluded that she was probably a minister like Paul, Apollos, Timothy, and others who carried the same title. At the very least she was a deacon, not according to today's definitions but as defined by Acts 6–8, 1 Timothy 3, or both. Therefore, Phoebe was a spiritual leader in the Early Church, either of high ministerial stature or of official local church stature. Either position would have necessitated her being vocal and authoritative. And whether a minister or a deacon, she served the entire Cenchrean church in that capacity, not just a group of women (Romans 16:1).

One other title is used of Phoebe in Romans 16:2, "prostatis." It is translated in a variety of ways in English Bibles, probably the weakest being "help" in the NIV. Unfortunately for the sake of deciphering the meaning of the word, it is not used elsewhere in the New Testament. Its verb form, "proistemi," which literally means "to stand before or over," is used eight times: six times with the idea of directing, managing, leading, or ruling some*one* (Romans 12:8; 1 Thessalonians 5:12; 1 Timothy 3:4,5,12; 5:17) and two times with the idea of being devoted to some*thing* (Titus 3:8,14).

Assistance is also available from occurrences of the word in other first-century writings. According to Liddell and Scott's *A Greek-English Lexicon*, the word carried the meaning "leader, chief, presiding officer, or one who stands before to protect."[10] According to Thayer's *Greek-English Lexicon of the New Testa-*

ment, it meant "a woman set over others."[11] *The New Analytical Greek Lexicon* lists "one who stands in front or before; a leader; a protector, champion, patron."[12] The first-century historian Josephus consistently used the word "to refer to the leader of a nation, a tribe, and a region."[13]

These possibilities certainly connote power and authority, not mere assistance, supportiveness, or helpfulness. Two factors, however, cause some scholars to pull away from concluding that Phoebe was being called a leader. First, whatever is being said of her, she functioned in that capacity toward "many people" (16:2) rather than in a specific location. But in light of the loose structure of the Early Church and the exchange of people between certain congregations, this may not be a compelling point. Second, whatever Phoebe was to many, she was to Paul as well (16:2). Rather than viewing her as ever having exercised authority over Paul, she is viewed, instead, as having had financial or political means which assisted him and others on various occasions. If this were the case, then translations such as "patroness" or "protectress" would be preferable to "leader." But odd as it may seem for Paul to refer to an individual as exercising authority over him, his use of the expression "including me" or "even me" (16:2) seems to allow and even invite the possibility that he was, indeed, saying something unusual or surprising.

It is not possible to determine the meaning of "prostatis" with certainty. Whether Phoebe was a leader or a helper to Paul and to others, however, the assistance of the entire church of Rome was put at her disposal (16:2). This included men and women alike. It included the local church leaders as well. An entire congregation of believers was to assist this woman in any way that she thought necessary. How very different from the male-female arrangement of men being dominant and women being subordinate that Paul is represented (misrepresented) as establishing as universal principles for all churches to follow.

Women as Pastors

It is not at all unusual to meet someone who simplistically and categorically announces, "A woman can do anything in the church except serve as senior pastor." In light of all that women are depicted as doing and are commended for doing across the pages of the New Testament, this position would be difficult to defend. But the question is, nonetheless, well worth asking, "What does the Bible say specifically about women pastoring churches?"

Much of the challenge of answering this question stems from the fact that only sketchy glimpses of Early Church leadership are visible in Scripture, and many of these predate the fullest development of local structure. Patterns were extremely varied from congregation to congregation, with positions existing in some churches that seemingly did not exist in others. Flexibility is also apparent in the overlap that existed between the responsibilities of different offices, particularly obvious in the way that "position gifts" such as apostle and "function gifts" such as leadership are both found in the listings of ministries (Romans 12:6–8; 1 Corinthians 12:28–31; Ephesians 4:11–13). In the same lists, there is a mixing of what was probably done primarily by the "clergy" and what was open to the "laity," reminiscent of the uncertain line between deacon and overseer. Frequently, titles were used without any clear indication of the responsibilities of the office. A number of leaders were given several rather different titles, and it was not unusual for any one of these individuals to be itinerant at times and local at other times depending upon the need. Further, authoritative apostolic letters were usually addressed to congregations rather than to leaders, leaving the overall role of leadership rather unclear.

In addition to the diversity and fluidity that characterized the organizational structure of the Early Church, a unique challenge confronts any discussion of the office of pastor. The position certainly existed in the first century because it is listed as ordained by Christ (Ephesians 4:11–13), but no one in all of the New Testament is called a pastor ("poimen" meaning "shepherd" in Greek) except Jesus. So, yes, it can be said that no woman was titled "pastor" in the Early Church, but neither was any man except the Savior. The only avenue available for pursuing a scriptural study of the position is to investigate any leaders who seem to have functioned like today's pastor functions.

The need to approach the topic indirectly should act as a constant reminder that set patterns for local church leadership cannot be found in the New Testament. If the Early Church determined the titles and functions of its ministerial positions according to the immediate needs and opportunities of its situation, then perhaps the church today should be equally adaptable.[14] None of this is proposing any culturally driven determination of qualifications or any lowering of spiritual standards. But rather than rigidly following traditional or denominational patterns that, for example, exclude women from the pastorate, Christians should realize that the time is especially right for opening doors to women to the fullest extent that is biblically endorsed.

One conspicuous appearance of women in the Early Church that may overlap with today's understanding of the role of a pastor has to do with the house churches of the first century. Probably every Christian congregation that is portrayed in the New Testament met in someone's home, simply because other facilities were generally not available. This seems to have involved more than simply opening a large living room for a Sunday service. Some type of spiritual leadership seems to have been present because the congregations were identified with the hosts in a way that resembles today's associating of local churches with pastors. If some other official were pastoring these congregations, it is quite odd that no mention of that individual is ever made. A pastor certainly would have been more prominent than a host and seemingly would have been included, at the very least, in an address to the body of believers, but this was never the case.

There are six congregations specifically referred to as meeting in the homes of the following people: Mary, the mother of John Mark (Acts 12:12); Lydia (Acts 16:40); Aquila and Priscilla while in Ephesus (1 Corinthians 16:19), Aquila and Priscilla while in Rome (Romans 16:3–5); Nympha (Colossians 4:15); and Philemon (Philemon 1–2). (According to manuscript evidence, the KJV is inaccurate in rendering the Colossians passage "him" rather than "her," and Nympha is undeniably a female name.) There are a few less definitive references to house churches (Acts 17:5–9; 21:8–12; 28:30–31; Romans 16:15) and numerous "household of" references which could indicate either relatives or congregations (1 Corinthians 1:11 being an example of referring to a woman's household). But of the six certain citations, three are of women, two are of a woman and man together, and the sixth which is of a man includes a closely connected greeting to an additional woman (wife? sister?) and man (son? brother?). If a congregation were founded upon the conversion of a woman, as was the case with Lydia (Acts 16:12–15), or if a woman were exceptionally knowledgeable in Scripture, as was the case with Priscilla (Acts 18:24–26) and probably with John Mark's mother Mary, then it is entirely plausible that such a woman cared for the body of believers that subsequently met in her home.

The New Testament title that is most often associated with today's pastor is that of "elder/presbyter" ("presbuteros") or "bishop" ("episkopos"), either or both of which might be translated as "overseer," perhaps in an effort to suggest the function of the office. Some scholars attempt to differentiate between the two offices, but two passages use them interchangeably (Acts 20:17,28; Titus 1:5,7), suggesting that the two words meant the same thing. Although these titles are surprisingly missing from the various lists of ministries (Romans 12:6–8; 1 Corinthians 12:28–31; Ephesians 4:11–13), the Bible indicates that Paul and Barnabas appointed these individuals for each church (Acts 14:23). Further, Paul instructed his ministerial associate Titus to do likewise (Titus 1:5).

There is good reason to associate the office of overseer ("presbuteros" and/or "episkopos") with the role of pastor ("poimen" which is the noun shepherd, "poimaino" which is the verb "to shepherd"). 1 Peter 5:1–2 links "presbuteros" with shepherding, and Acts 20:28 links "episkopos" with shepherding. There are some difficulties, however, indications that the position of overseer in the Early Church may have been different in some ways from the modern concept of pastor. First, multiple overseers served each church (Acts 14:23; 15:2; 20:17; Philippians 1:1; Titus 1:5; James 5:14), with every indication being that all of them had equal, identical standing. This is certainly different from today's arrangement of only one pastor or of one senior pastor and a support staff. Second, not every overseer engaged in teaching and preaching (1 Timothy 5:17) which would contrast considerably with today's understanding of a pastor. Third, in addition to "presbuteros" referring to the position of elder, the same Greek word was used to refer to older men and women. A clear example of this is found in Acts 2:17. 1 Peter 5 seems to mix the two meanings, with verses 1–4 evidently referring to local church officials (consequently the NIV rendering of "elder") but verse 5 making a sudden switch to what sounds more like an age issue (consequently the NIV rendering of "older"). There is enough overlap between the "elder" and "older" uses that translators are unsure how to translate certain passages. 1 Timothy 5:1–2 and Titus 2:2–3, for example, either put men and women alike into positions of local church leadership, or these two passages simply make stipulations regarding old age. The overlap suggests the possibility that "elders" (remember, multiple) may have been chosen from "older" members of the congregation, resulting in a considerable contrast with today's idea of the qualifications of a pastor.

In light of these considerable differences, it is difficult to conclude that the Early Church elder/bishop/overseer was the counterpart of today's pastor. If it was, then three objections are typically raised against women serving in this capacity. First, the KJV reads, "If a *man* desire the office..." (1 Timothy 3:1). The Greek text, however, reads, "If *anyone*..." The word that is used is "tis" which is a pronoun with no gender designation implied, not "aner" or "arsen" which mean "man" as in "male." If Paul wished to limit the office to men, he missed an easy opportunity to do so.

Second, the 1 Timothy 3 and Titus 1 passages both stipulate that the overseer is to be the husband of but one wife. But, as with the parallel qualification for "diakonos" ("deacon") (3:12), this stipulation does not disqualify women. In such a patriarchal society there were probably more male leaders than female leaders, so it is understandable that special provisions for men were included. In such a marriage-based society it is equally likely that many if not most of the male church officials were married and had children, so special provisions were made in these directions as well. But provisions do not translate into requirements. Deacons did not have to be married or have children; likewise, it follows that they did not have to be male. The fact that Phoebe was a "diakonos," makes it clear that women could serve in this capacity. There is no reason to conclude, then, that the "husband of one wife" stipulation affected the openness of either office to women.

It should be noted that the 1 Timothy 3 passage features a specific inclusion of female deacons (3:11) that is missing from the overseer section. Even though the verse does not say "female *deacons*" but only "women likewise," it is unlikely that it refers to female overseers as well as female deacons because of its location in the middle of the deacon material. Perhaps the explanation is found in the fact that overseers were assigned a teaching function (3:2), something that was not being assigned to deacons. As will be discussed in a subsequent chapter, the Ephesian women did not yet qualify to fulfill this function.[15]

Third, no woman is identified in the New Testament as an elder or bishop. This is true, but neither are men identified in such ways with the exception of the designations that the elderly Peter and John used of themselves (1 Peter 5:1; 2 John 1; 3 John 1:1). In light of the close relationship between apostles and elders in the Jerusalem church (Acts 15:2,4,6,22–23; 16:4), it is possible that all twelve of the original apostles became elders. And of course, these three self-designations must be balanced with the several references to women in association with house churches and with the address to a woman found in 2 John.

The Apostle John's second letter, one of the two that refer to him as an elder, is addressed to a "chosen lady and her children" (v. 1). The Greek word behind the English word "lady" is "kuria," the female version of the word "kurios" which means "master" or "lord." Though "kuria" is not found elsewhere in the New Testament, its connotation in first-century Greek was definitely that of power and authority, as in a person of position.[16] The letter closes with the children of a second woman sending their greetings, this second woman being the sister of the chosen lady (v. 13).

These children to whom John wrote were members of a house church (v. 10). It follows that the children sending greetings (v. 13) were members of a second house church. This aligns well with John's repeated references in his first letter to his own children, clearly indicating the believers who were under his care (1 John 2:1,18,28; 3:7,18; 4:4; 5:21). If the children were the members of churches, then who was the "chosen lady" and who was her "sister"? Who were these two women to whom the children are said to belong? If the address had been to a man and if reference had been made to his brother, the interpretation would be instant and undisputed. They would be viewed as congregational leaders, namely, as pastors. But for no reason other than the fact that the two individuals involved were women, scholars look for other explanations. If women were foundational in planting churches (see earlier "Coworkers" section), is it so hard to believe that they pastored churches?

Understanding "children" as referring to a congregation and "chosen lady" as referring to their pastor is the most natural, straightforward reading of the text. The children were hers in the same way that the children addressed in 1 John were his,[17] like sheep entrusted to the care of a shepherd. And, of course, this was a term of endearment, not a literal reference to chronological age. A reading of 1 & 2 John makes it clear that "adult-like" requests were made of the recipients. Any other interpretation would only be sought because the most obvious conclusion is being rejected, probably due to a personal bias against female pastors.

The replacement explanation that is most frequently proposed is that "children" and "lady" both refer to the same body of believers. This is extremely unlikely because the two expressions have opposite connotations, "lady" connoting a position of authority ("kuria" being the female form or "kurios" meaning "master, lord") and "children" connoting a position of dependency and subordination. If a masterful writer such as John had used redundancy at all (v. 1), he would not have done so in such a confusing manner. Also, "children" is used throughout the Old Testament and the New Testament as a metaphor for God's people, but "lady" is never used in this way.

What is not evident in most modern English translations is that John switched from the singular "you" or "your" in verses 4 and 5 to the plural in verses 6–12 and back again to the singular in verse 13. This would make sense if he were addressing his opening and closing remarks to an individual and the body of his message to a group of people, as would be done in writing to a pastor and a congregation or in writing to a congregation via a pastor. The mix of singular and plural is hard to explain otherwise. Again, the obvious interpretation of the language found throughout 2 John is that a female pastor and her congregation were the original recipients of the apostle's letter and were the recipients of greetings sent from a second congregation pastored by a woman.

Those who exempt women particularly from the senior pastorate do so because holding this office would so clearly involve women being in authority over men, an arrangement they claim is unbiblical. Pressing their thinking to its logical conclusion, however, surfaces an intolerable position, one that is *truly* unbiblical. If a woman cannot be in authority over the men of a local congregation, this must be because these men are to be, instead, over her. After all, there are no other arrangements available except everyone having equal standing, which this perspective never prescribes. So, every woman who might aspire to be a pastor is barred from doing so because the position would put her over the men that she is supposed to be under. This means that *all women* are under the authority of *all men*. Such a fallacy invites a quick renouncement by women, by husbands, and most importantly by Scripture.

Women as Teachers

Much has been made of the fact that the Greek structure of Ephesians 4:11 does not list pastor and teacher separately, but combines the two positions and designates pastor-teacher as one of the gifts that Christ has given the church. This being the case, any pastors who are identified in the pages of the New Testament can be assumed to have served as teachers. This would include the women who seem to have pastored house churches and the two women cited as pastors in 2 John. These women pastors must have engaged in teaching ministries, and they must have taught entire congregations, not just women and children. Conversely, because the two offices are presented as one, many scholars claim that if the New Testament portrays someone as a teacher, that individual can be assumed to have served in a pastoral capacity as well. Whether or not this is true, whatever is said of the men who served as teachers must be said of women who served as teachers. The evidence continues to mount that women did in the Early Church the two things that are commonly withheld from them today—pastor and teach.

Priscilla was just such a woman, a pastor-teacher. It is true that she never appears without mention of her husband, but what is much more significant is that he never appears without mention of her. A number of other wives traveled with their husbands in ministry (1 Corinthians 9:5), but no mention is ever made of these women. What a ministry Priscilla must have had that her husband Aquila could not be named without her. In fact, with the exception of the initial introduction of the couple by Luke (Acts 18:2) and the first, early greeting sent from them by Paul (1 Corinthians 16:19), Priscilla's name repeatedly appears before Aquila's. (KJV reverses the order of the Greek text in Acts 18:26.) This highly unusual deviation from the cultural norm clearly suggests that her prominence exceeded his. With the name reversal appearing in both Luke's and Paul's writings, her prominence must have been commonly recognized throughout the Early Church.

Paul first met the couple in Corinth as his second missionary trip was turning homeward (Acts 18:1–3). They had been expelled from Rome along with other Jews. Like Paul, they were tentmakers by trade, and the language of the text seems to indicate that he stayed in their home. It is not known whether they were Christians before meeting Paul or if he was responsible for their conversion. Whichever was the case, after a lengthy stay at Corinth, founding the church (Acts 18:11), Paul took the couple with him for his first visit to Ephesus and left them there (Acts 18:18–19). It was at Ephesus that Priscilla and Aquila met and trained Apollos (Acts 18:24–28). They were evidently still in the city during Paul's third missionary trip when he spent a lengthy period of time there. It was from Ephesus during this third journey that he wrote 1 Corinthians (16:8) and sent the couple's greetings to the Christians of Corinth along with greetings from the members of their house church (16:19). The emperor's edict against Jews evidently lifted enough for them to return to Rome because they were there hosting a house church when Paul sent a letter and greetings to that location (Romans 16:3). For unknown reasons they must have returned to Ephesus during Paul's final years because he greeted them there in his second letter to Timothy, thought to be his last letter (2 Timothy 4:19).

As has been noted in a previous section, Paul called Priscilla, along with other women, a "sunergos" or "coworker" (Romans 16:3), a word that he used exclusively to refer to himself and to other ministers who joined him in pioneer missionary, church-planting work. And what extensive ministry she and Aquila had. They were present with Paul for the founding of the church at Corinth and the church at Ephesus, two extremely strategic works. They hosted/pastored congregations in Ephesus and Rome. At some time they risked their lives for Paul (Romans 16:4) and were so important to him that greetings mentioning them by name appear in three of his letters.[18] This is more often than he includes greetings involving any other colleague except Timothy, more often than Luke, Silas, or John Mark. In all of this, Priscilla was *at least* Aquila's equal. They are the scriptural example of a couple ministering as a team, just as Stephanas' family serves as an example of an entire family ministering together (1 Corinthians 16:15–16).

In all of Paul's references to this couple there is no indication that Priscilla's work was essentially different from Aquila's.

Everything that is said of one is said of the other. This treatment of them as a couple, however, should not be misconstrued as opening the ministry only to married women, a position typically taken by those who require a wife to minister under the "covering" of her husband. According to Paul, the more desirable state for both male and female ministers is singleness because it affords greater concentration and commitment (1 Corinthians 7:32–35). So, if the ministry is open to married women, it is all the more open to single women. Also, there is no indication that Priscilla ministered in some special way "under" Aquila's leadership. The name reversal negates this possibility and suggests that she became the lead minister. It is particularly significant that there is no depicting of the couple in a negative or semi-supportive manner. Both Luke and Paul refer to their work completely positively and without the slightest qualification, in the very passages in which they place her name before his. In other words, though Priscilla seems to have surpassed Aquila in the exercising of certain leadership gifts, there is no check or correction offered, only affirmation of them and of their ministry.[19]

In addition to their many other accomplishments, Priscilla and Aquila are remembered perhaps most of all for having taught one of the greatest ministers of the first century, Apollos (Acts 18:23–28). At the time he was already a "learned man with a thorough knowledge of scripture" (18:24), and he was already ministering fervently and accurately (1:25). What they imparted to him, then, were the more advanced theological truths that he was still lacking (18:26). In essence, they acted as seminary professors[20] for this minister-in-training who was destined by God to become a strategic leader of the Early Church. He developed "followings" comparable to those of Peter and Paul (1 Corinthians 1:12). Paul himself viewed Apollos as his equal in the ministry (1 Corinthians 3:6,8–9) and regarded him as a fellow apostle (1 Corinthians 4:6,9).

Priscilla engaged in the teaching of Apollos right alongside Aquila. In fact, this is one of the times that her name precedes his, indicating that she probably took the lead. This rectifying of the inadequacies in Apollos' theological understanding (Acts 18:26) undoubtedly put Priscilla in a position of authority over him. And all of this occurred after Paul had just spent 18 months in Corinth with Priscilla and Aquila (Acts 18:1–3,11). It would seem that if he had a firm policy that all women should remain silent, that no women should ever teach men or exercise authority over men, then Priscilla and Aquila would have been aware of that position and, since they were working with Paul (Acts 18:18–19), would have complied.[21] Furthermore, this authoritative teaching of Apollos by Priscilla was done in the very city, Ephesus, in which Timothy was later pastoring when he received Paul's letter supposedly forbidding all authoritative teaching of men by women. Isn't it clear that Paul is being misunderstood and misrepresented today by those wishing to silence and subordinate women?

In an effort to explain away Priscilla's ministry to Apollos, some have claimed that the fact that she taught him privately makes it entirely different from what is done, for instance, during a sanctuary service. How can this be? How can a mere change in buildings, from a house to a church, have any bearing on the matter? This proposal is especially shaky in light of the fact that *houses were churches* during the first century and have served likewise at various times and in various locations throughout history. Likewise, how can a change from one man to two men or several men or many men have any bearing on the matter? At what number of men do the prohibitions suddenly apply, and how is that number significantly different from all of the other lower numbers? No, if all women are to be silent and are to avoid the authoritative teaching of men, there would have to be essential theological reasons for such prohibitions.[22] These reasons would not bend to minor physical details such as the location or size of the audience. Neither would they conveniently bend to the modern tendency to let women do whatever men want and need women to do.

It is sometimes claimed, as well, that even though Priscilla taught Apollos, she was not a teacher. This would have to be the fine line of all fine lines. Following the logic, though, does this mean that women may pastor as long as they are not pastors, that they may lead as long as they are not leaders? Worse than a fine line, this proposal seems to rest upon a foolish line. Furthermore, it fails to acknowledge the fact that "formal positions" were not a characteristic of the Early Church,[23] especially not as early as Acts 18. Doing something and being something were basically the same because ministries flowed forth from people's gifts rather than from official offices (Galatians 1:1).

It is an undeniable fact that Priscilla was the primary teacher and the primary leader in authoritatively training the great man Apollos after having been left on ministry location by Paul. In one of his listings of ministries, he ranks what she did amongst the three highest privileges available in the church: "God has appointed first of all apostles, second prophets, third teachers" (1 Corinthians 12:28). This third highest ministry was obviously open to qualified women in the Early Church, and it should be open to qualified women today.

Priscilla is not the only woman in the New Testament credited with a teaching ministry, a *significant* teaching ministry. Paul's most valuable colleague Timothy, being the son of a man who was evidently an unbeliever (Acts 16:1–3), was taught not by his father but by his mother and grandmother, Eunice and Lois (2 Timothy 1:5; 3:14–15). Of course, this is an example of parental teaching rather than an example of pastoral/ministerial teaching per se, but it should not be relegated to the sphere of women and children. It should be noted that Paul told the *man*, the *minister* Timothy to continue in his knowledge of Scripture "because you know those from whom you learned it " (3:14–15). This was a direct reference to the continuing reliability of the women in his life and an injunction to extend their instruction into his adulthood. It is most unlikely that this same Pastor Timothy interpreted any instructions penned by Paul as universally barring all women from any and all teaching that could possibly influence men.

With the examples of women being behind the spiritual training of such men as Apollos and Timothy, it should come as no surprise that Paul wrote the following: "The things you have heard me say in the presence of many witnesses entrust to reliable 'anthropois' who will also be qualified to teach others" (2 Timothy 2:2). The Greek word that Paul used (the indirect object version of the word "anthropos") is the word that usually means "human being" in the New Testament. He did not use "aner" or "arsen" which are the words for a "male." The English language uses the word "man" to refer specifically to an adult male and generically to humanity, so most English translations use the word "man" in this passage without indicating that the generic use of the word should be understood. A translation that would better reflect Paul's choice of words would be, "entrust to reliable persons who will also be qualified to teach others."

The Greek word "anthropos" rather than "aner" or "arsen" is used in other New Testament passages that refer to teaching and to ministry gifts. "All Scripture is God-breathed and is useful for teaching, rebuking, correcting and training in righteousness, so that the 'anthropos' of God may be thoroughly equipped for every good work" (2 Timothy 3:16–17). It is the *person* of God, not just the man of God, who is to be prepared by Scripture for *every* good work. And who is to do this preparing of all persons? "When Christ ascended on high, he led captives in his train and gave gifts to 'anthropois.' It was he who gave some to be apostles, some to be prophets, some to be evangelists, and some to be pastors and teachers to prepare God's people for works of service" (Ephesians 4:11–12). Christ gives gifts to *persons*, not just to men, and then He gives these *persons* to the church in the form of apostles, prophets, evangelists, and pastors-teachers to prepare all *persons* for service. In these and other passages, if it were Paul's intent to exclude women from the ministry, it is doubtful that he would have used the generic, inclusive word "anthropos" over the word "aner" or "arsen."

How frustrating that the man of God who repeatedly welcomed and affirmed women ministers, including women teachers, is misrepresented today as prohibiting their very existence. How frustrating that such a glaring contradiction is not recognized. It would have been impossible for the women identified in Scripture as Paul's ministerial colleagues to engage in ministry without engaging in teaching. This includes not just Priscilla but Euodia, Syntyche, Mary, Tryphena, Tryphosa, Persis, Phoebe, and Junia. As has been made clear, the titles given to them *by Paul* place them on equal footing with any and all of his male associates, including the men who were trained by women, Apollos and Timothy. It would have been impossible for them to have served in front-line missions work, in church-planting work, in the spreading of the gospel without teaching. And it was Paul who welcomed and affirmed their valuable contributions, unusual behavior indeed for a man who supposedly did not believe that their ministries should even exist.

Women as Prophets

Mention has already been made of the list of ministries that ranks apostles as first, prophets as second, and teachers as third (1 Corinthians 12:28). Though other ministry lists differ in

various ways from this list and from each other, there is a
consistency in the handling of these three ministries. All of the
New Testament references to apostles and prophets identify
apostles before prophets, and all of the references to prophecy
and teaching identify prophecy before teaching.[24] It should
probably be assumed, then, that these three ministries are the
three highest gifts that Christ has given the church with the
apostle being highest, the prophet second, and the teacher
third.

The fact that Scripture identifies women as being prophets
and as prophesying lends further support to the claim that
teaching and all other "lower" ministries were generally open to
women in the first century and should remain open to women
today. The female prophets of the Old Testament and the
prophet Anna who proclaimed the birth of Jesus have already
been detailed. In addition to these, women were included in the
prophecy that inaugurated the New Testament church: "'In the
last days,' God says, 'I will pour out my Spirit on all people. Your
sons and daughters will prophesy'" (Acts 2:17). Several years
after the eventful outpouring of the Spirit on the Day of Pentecost, the evangelist Philip is said to have had four single
daughters who prophesied (Acts 21:8–9). In his letter to the
charismatic Corinthian church, Paul made deliberate provision
for women to prophesy in a way that would be culturally and
scripturally proper (1 Corinthians 11:3–16), and he set their
doing so within the confines of acceptable activity (1 Corinthians
11:2).

Those who bar women from authoritative ministries seem to
overlook the extremely authoritative nature of this ministry of
prophecy which was obviously open to women in the Old Testament and the New Testament. Throughout Scripture, the prophet
is consistently portrayed as speaking for God. Whether the
prophecy involves foretelling or forthtelling, predicting or preaching, the message is received directly from God and rings with a
note of "thus saith the Lord." It could not carry much more
authority. It is more authoritative than teaching or administrating or leading, ministries commonly withheld from women
today. Yet if women are to obey the first half of 1 Corinthians
14:1, then they are to obey the second half as well and are to
desire even greater gifts than teaching or administrating or
leading; they are to desire the extremely authoritative gift of
prophecy.[25]

All New Testament Christians, even those who reject the ministries of women, have been "built" upon the foundation of the prophets (Ephesians 2:19–20), some of those prophets being women. How foolish and futile to deny one's own foundation. According to 1 Corinthians 14, prophecy strengthens (v. 3), teaches (v. 31), edifies the entire church (v. 4), speaks to men as well as women (v. 3, "anthropos" meaning "humanity" or "people" but never referring to women only), benefits believers (v. 22), benefits unbelievers (v. 24–25), and is spoken in public gatherings (v. 29). This is the authoritative ministry that is equally open to the church's sons and daughters (Acts 2:17).

Even if someone insists that the charismatic gift of prophecy is no longer operative in the New Testament church, the scriptural support for women ministers is not diminished in the least. The point that bears on the issue of women ministers is simply this: if women served in the very highest, most authoritative levels of spiritual leadership that were available *in the Early Church*, then they should be able to do likewise *today*. Whether or not prophets still function, if women served as prophets in the apostolic age, then today's comparable or less strategic positions of ministry should be wide open to them.

Women as Apostles

Was the very highest, most authoritative position of first-century ministry, that of apostle, open to women? Obviously they were not numbered among the original twelve apostles, for which a reasonable explanation is available. The plan of God was for the gospel to go forth to the Jews first and then to the Gentiles. The initial phase of this plan, building a base among receptive Jews, dictated both the ethnicity and the gender of the messengers—they would be Jewish, and they would be male. If they were anything other than Jewish and male, their message would not have been received by the target audience.

The title "apostle," however, was not reserved exclusively for reference to the original twelve whose role was uniquely foundational. According to the New Testament, other ministers who engaged in apostolic work were called apostles as well. The word that was used, "apostolos," means "messenger sent forth on a mission." Though the rendering in a particular English translation may obscure the presence of the word, "apostolos" is found in the Greek text referring to the following individuals: Paul

(Acts 14:1–4,14; Romans 1:1 and in several other letters), Barnabas (Acts 14:1–4,14; 1 Corinthians 9:5–6), Silas (1 Thessalonians 1:1; 2:6–7), Timothy (1 Thessalonians 1:1; 2:6–7), Apollos (1 Corinthians 4:6,9), Epaphroditus (Philippians 2:25), and other unnamed individuals (2 Corinthians 8:23). The spiritual leadership of these ministers was evidently commensurate with that of the original apostles in spreading the gospel, establishing sound doctrine, and planting churches.

There is one other citation that must be added to the list. In the Romans 16 greetings that Paul sent to friends and associates in Rome, he not only identified Andronicus and Junia as apostles but referred to them as "outstanding apostles" (16:7). What is especially noteworthy about this citation is that Junia is the name of a woman. This means that a woman served as an apostle in the Early Church, just as Paul and others did, and she did so in some way that caused her to be labeled as outstanding. Paul, a man of God who knew full well what it meant to be an apostle and what it meant to fight for recognition as an apostle, did not identify Junia as disqualified or misdirected; he identified her as outstanding among all other apostles.

In an effort to eliminate this woman from the picture, some scholars and translators have refused to let the text say what it says most naturally. First, there is the claim that Junia is not a woman's name but a man's name. Specifically, it is argued that what appears in the Greek text is a contraction (abbreviation) for the male name Junianus. This is a difficult point to prove and is obviously being forced upon the text because neither Junianus[26] nor its contraction[27] can be found anywhere in ancient literature. The very existence of either version of the male name is nothing but speculation. Junia, on the other hand, was a relatively common female name that was sometimes adopted by Jewish women who operated in Roman society.[28] The likelihood of Junia being a woman is so solid that a male identity was not even suggested until the late 13th or early 14th century; all earlier commentators viewed Junia as female.[29]

If Junia must be a woman, then the second attempt to diminish her position is to claim a different rendering for "outstanding among the apostles." Instead, the idea of "highly regarded by the apostles" is proposed, eliminating Andronicus and Junia from being apostles. Without going into cumbersome details, this is an unnatural and unlikely reading of the Greek text. The word "episemos" behind the word "outstanding" implies selection from a group as in the inscribing of certain coins.[30] These two individuals were "stamped" or "marked" as special, prominent apostles.[31] Further, the use of "en" as the Greek preposition is better read "among" than "by."[32] All of this aligns well with the fact that Paul would not have needed or used the endorsement of other apostles for anyone he knew as well as he did two people with whom he had been imprisoned.[33]

The relationship between Andronicus and Junia is not known. Because a male-female team other than brother and sister or husband and wife would have been questionable, one of these two relationships is probable. As with Priscilla, however, there is no indication of Junia working in some secondary way under the authority covering of Andronicus. Neither is there any reason to jump to the conclusion that only married women qualify to serve as apostles. With virtually no information about the relationship between Andronicus and Junia, such specifics about the arrangement should not be invented and imposed upon the text. Also, as with Priscilla, Paul viewed the ministry as being in some ways more fitted to the single person than to the married person (1 Corinthians 7:32–35), so any discrimination to the contrary is totally unfounded. What is certain about these two individuals is that the same title of apostle was applied identically to each of them. This fact stands, and no attempt should be made to reverse or minimize it simply because someone wishes to bar women from the ministry.

Paul's reference to them as "relatives" could mean actual earthly relatives or fellow Jews. The occasion behind the imprisonment of the three of them is not known, but it can be assumed that Junia was not arrested for baking cookies and staffing the nursery. She must have been vocal and forceful in the spreading of the gospel, as was Paul. As an apostle, she was a spiritual leader of the Early Church. She undoubtedly engaged in authoritative teaching and preaching, establishing the first-century believers in sound doctrine.

Whatever view one holds regarding the availability of spiritual gifts or the existence of the office/gift of apostle today, early Christians were told to desire the greater gifts (1 Corinthians 12:31). Paul said this after identifying apostles as the greatest of the gifts (12:28). If this gift was to be desired, it had to have been available. He also said to desire the gifts that "build up the church" (14:12), which would definitely include if not feature the "position gifts" such as apostle (Ephesians 4:11–12). These admonitions were given to the Early Church as a whole, not just to its men. If some chose to deny the gifting of certain individuals, Paul was not one to determine gifts and offices according to human decision or consensus. He said to the Corinthians, "Even though I may not be an apostle to others, surely I am to you! For you are the seal of my apostleship in the Lord" (1 Corinthians 9:2). In other words, the fruit of one's ministry, not the acceptance and approval of others, provides the definitive evidence of calling and gifting

These truths of Scripture support the conclusion that first-century ministry was equally open to all qualified believers, with the will of God determining the appointments (1 Corinthians 12:18). It follows, then, that whatever ministry gifts are available today should be seen as being available to all believers, men and women alike. If a woman, Junia, was an apostle in the Early Church, then qualified women can be ministers at any and all levels of spiritual leadership today. It also follows that the same criterion that proved the godly origin of Paul's ministry should be used to settle the question of whether a given woman is called and anointed by God to teach and preach the Word.[34] The policies of a denomination are not the final authority; the selection of God is the final and only authority.

It is true that male ministers outnumber female ministers across the pages of the New Testament. This, however, does not establish God's design for the ministry any more than the predominance of any other situation automatically indicates God's favor toward that situation. As has been shown, God does not impose gender restrictions upon the ministry; therefore, any barriers that limited the women of the first century must have resulted from the world in which they lived. If women were generally uneducated, it would have been difficult for them to qualify. If women were generally disrespected, it would have been difficult for them to function. The point that matters is that several did qualify and several did function, usually with exceptionally impressive results. If male dominance in the ministry continues until the Second Coming, may it be due to obstacles erected by the world, not by the church.

9

The New Testament View of Ministry

Regardless of the many examples of women who clearly served as spiritual leaders in the Old Testament and the New Testament, the ministry is oftentimes defined by Protestants and Catholics alike in ways that prohibit women from entering its ranks. If the ancient priests are used as the defining model, the absence of women is said to permanently disqualify them from becoming ministers today. A similar conclusion is drawn if the twelve disciples are used as a model. If all else fails, Jesus Himself is thrust forward along with the argument that He was male so His representatives must be male. It is interesting that the ministers of the Early Church who align most obviously and closely with today's clergy are seldom used as the defining model. Doing so, of course, would immediately open the door of ministry to women because of the number of women who were Early Church ministers.

In addition to a host of biblical examples of women ministers that should be enough to settle the question of whether women qualify for the ministry, a definition or "theology" of ministry can be drawn from Scripture that includes women rather than excludes them. It is not based upon the gender of the priests, the disciples, or Jesus, all of whom were male for specific reasons that have nothing to do with the gender of other ministers found throughout Scripture. It is based upon what the Bible reveals about the nature and role of New Testament ministry, whether that ministry is exercised in the first century or the twenty-first century.

Servanthood Versus Rulership

It is undeniable that the exercise of authority is present in the New Testament's portrayal of spiritual leadership. The churches were asked to obey the decision of the apostles and elders of Jerusalem regarding Jewish-Gentile difficulties (Acts 16:4), Paul referred to using his God-given authority over an individual congregation (2 Corinthians 13:10), and believers were asked to submit to the authority of local leaders (1 Corinthians 16:15–16; Hebrews 13:17). (It should be noted that "they" and not "men" is present in the Greek text of Hebrews 13:17. Though the word is in the plural masculine form, there was no other form of "they" available to refer to a group of men and women.) Authority was and still is a necessary dimension of leadership, including spiritual leadership.

What is much more striking than the necessary presence of authority in New Testament leadership, however, is the deliberate deemphasis of it. Jesus was adamant that the exercising of authority should not characterize spiritual leaders (Matthew 20:20–28; Mark 10:35–45). Though it characterizes leadership in the world, things are to be markedly different in the church. In fact, Jesus completely reversed the world's view of leadership. It is out of sacrifice *for* others, not out of standing or status *over* others, that any influence is to arise (Matthew 20:22; Mark 10:38). It is an opportunity for eager service and giving oneself as an example (1 Peter 5:2–3). The leader is to be at the disposal of others, seeking and promoting their good rather than his rule. Later Paul would echo this same principle in his discussion of the "head" of the home (Ephesians 5:25). It is through being in low standing and through serving others that anyone is seen by God as being in high standing and as leading others (Matthew 20:26–27; Mark 10:43–44; Luke 22:26). Jesus modeled this during His earthly ministry, and He expected His disciples to follow His example (Luke 22:27; John 13:13–15).

To insist upon a hierarchical arrangement that positions men authoritatively at the top and women subordinately at the bottom could not be any more diametrically opposed to the explicit teachings of Jesus. The male-female or husband-wife hierarchy that operates in the world is a direct result of the entrance and reign of sin (Genesis 3). Jesus identified hierarchical authority as just that, the way of the world (Matthew 20:20–28; Mark 10:35–45). He made it quite clear that no such arrangement is appropriate in the community of those who are redeemed from sin. If an individual is not to conduct himself in this way, certainly no class of individuals is to do so either. Believers are not to be ruled any longer by sin but are to be ruled by righteousness (Romans 6:17–18). Those who argue that "boss in the marriage results in boss in society and boss in the church" are actually saying that "wrongdoing in the marriage results in wrongdoing in society and wrongdoing in the church."

If authority must be present in leadership and yet it is not to characterize leadership, how are these two "opposites" united in the New Testament's description of spiritual leaders? First and foremost, decision-making rests upon determining the will of God. This can be done by all believers by virtue of being transformed into godliness (Romans 12:2; Ephesians 5:8–10). It can also be done by leaders who are then, in turn, recognized and supported by others as being right (Acts 15:6–7,27–28,31–34; 1 Corinthians 14:29; 1 John 4:1). Leadership, by this definition, is discovering or helping others discover God's will, rather than exerting one's own will. In fact, the leader's interests are frequently sacrificed for the good of the whole community (Philippians 2:3–4).

Subsequently, a strong emphasis is put upon the role of the body of believers. Not only is their welfare sought, but their collective judgment and voluntary agreement are valued. This explains why most of the apostles' letters were addressed not to local officials but to entire congregations. It also explains why local officials were not extremely prominent in the Early Church. A leader is not so much mediating God's grace to the people as most Catholics think or exercising God's authority over the people as most Protestants think as he is standing alongside the whole group enabling and strengthening them in their recognition and following of God's will.[1] If this view of leadership differs from what is understood and practiced in the church today, then differing perspectives must be rejected as being semi-worldly rather than wholly biblical.

Westerners may value representative government, but at the same time they view themselves primarily as independent individuals. They have little understanding of the community identity and unity that is emphasized not only in the Old Testament but also in the New Testament. According to Scripture, individual leaders are given "to prepare God's people for works of service, so that the body of Christ may be built up until we all reach unity in the faith and in the knowledge of the Son of God and become mature" (Ephesians 4:12–13). The focus is clearly upon helping the body of believers collectively become what God intends them to become rather than upon individuals ruling over other individuals in any way.

Because the collective goals of maturing in Christlikeness and of evangelizing a lost world need facilitating, God "gifts" certain individuals with special abilities in order to help the body of believers accomplish these common purposes as effectively as possible.[2] These special abilities enable these individuals to function as "servant leaders," a concept that is rather foreign to the world's understanding of leadership. It is a servant leader, however, who is most able to "prepare God's people for works of *service*" (Ephesians 4:12). A ruler would prepare God's people for ruling others, but a servant prepares God's people for serving others. A ruler would lead God's people into valuing and exercising power, but a servant leads God's people into valuing and exercising sacrifice.

If for once, the creation of woman and her traditional social standing could be used favorably rather than injuriously, it would become obvious that she is a strong candidate for church leadership as defined by God's Word. Her original creation was marked with the word "helpmeet." She is seen by society as being especially capable of serving the good of others.[3] If the church would define and position its leaders as the helping servants that the Bible describes rather than as the ruling authorities that the world inspires, the nature and the image of a woman would suddenly align quite well with the demands of leadership. Who better could lead God's people into "works of service" (Ephesians 4:12), the core calling of all ministers, than a woman who is typically very well acquainted with this realm?

The Priesthood of Believers

The first official ministers, the Old Testament priests, were members of a select group of men whose primary task was to offer sacrifices unto God on behalf of the people, including both sacrifices of repentance and sacrifices of worship. A young woman could not serve in this capacity, but neither could the vast majority of young men. God had good reasons for instituting such an exclusive office, reasons that do not extend into the New Testament. Under the new covenant, the same two sacrifices are present, that of repentance and that of worship, but they are no longer presented to God by a select group of clergymen.

The priestly role of offering sacrifices of repentance to atone for the people's sins foreshadowed the ministry of the great high priest Jesus. This role was fulfilled and consequently abolished with Christ's once-for-all, perfect sacrifice on the cross (Hebrews 7:23–28). To extend this ministry in any way to today's clergy is absolutely wrong because it is eternally complete in the work of Jesus Christ. What was once done by a select group of men is today and forever done by God's Son.

The other priestly role, offering sacrifices of worship, has been reassigned as well. Under the new covenant, every believer becomes a priest unto God (1 Peter 2:4–5,9; Revelation 1:6) and serves in this capacity throughout eternity (Revelation 5:10; 20:6). This new "priesthood of believers" includes clergy and laity alike, men and women alike, because it includes all believers. They are to offer sacrifices of praise directly unto God because they are the recipients of salvation (1 Peter 2:5,9). What was done only by men and only by select men under the old covenant is to be done by all under the new covenant. To use this office as a means of excluding women or anyone else from anything runs contrary to everything the New Testament teaches about it.

The Gifting of Believers

Spiritual gifts, including leadership gifts, are bestowed upon the priesthood of believers in order to benefit the entire body. All members of this priesthood, men and women alike, are recipients of these gifts and participate in ministry by using their gifts. In the several listings and discussions of spiritual gifts that are found in the New Testament, there is never any indication that certain gifts, such as leadership gifts or teaching gifts, are restricted to the male members of the priesthood of believers. In fact, the tone and the point of these passages are always just the opposite. The emphasis is clearly upon the scattering of the gifts, not according to human determination, but according to the sovereign will of God the Father (Hebrews 2:4), God the Son (Ephesians 4:8,11), and God the Spirit (1 Corinthians 12:11). Because men and women alike comprise the general "pool" of those receiving gifts, every indication is that both men and women will be recipients of each gift, including gifts such as leadership and teaching.

Of course, this aligns perfectly with the point that has been made in the preceding chapter, that men *and women* are seen in the Early Church exercising these gifts. No, women cannot be found exercising every spiritual gift; neither are there examples of men exercising every gift. However, a woman can be found serving as an apostle, a prophet, and a teacher; and because these are the greatest of all of the spiritual gifts (1 Corinthians 12:28), it can be assumed that women exercised every other gift as well. And because each gift is given for the good of the entire body of believers (1 Corinthians 12:7), there is no reason to think that women are to exercise their gifts privately and individually and only men are to exercise their gifts publicly and collectively.[4]

Unfortunately, the universal availability of spiritual gifts is sometimes obscured in translating the Greek text. The NIV inserts "man" into Romans 12:6, and the KJV does the same in 1 Corinthians 12:7 and 1 Peter 4:10. The word "man" is not present in the Greek text of these passages. The most that is present is a masculine version of "each" in the Corinthians and Peter verses, but this word has two possible meanings. Of course, it can be used to say "each *male*," but it is also the only generic version of "each" available in the Greek language to say "each *person*." The New Testament is full of passages that use this word to refer to all Christians, starting with its first use in Matthew 16:27 and ending with its last use in Revelation 22:12. The word "man" *is* present in Ephesians 4:8 (plural "men"), but it is "anthropos" rather than "aner" or "arsen." The Greek word "anthropos" can mean "adult male," but it is much more likely to carry the meaning of "person" or "humanity." Throughout the New Testament it is used repeatedly and almost exclusively in the generic sense. One of the common Greek words for "male" ("aner" or "arsen") could have been used in Ephesians 4:8 but was not.

Both Romans 12 and 1 Corinthians 12 open with an address to "brethren" or "brothers," sometimes said to mean that men are being targeted with the instruction about gifts that follows. The Greek word "adelphos," however, is used over and over again throughout the New Testament in passages that clearly target all Christians. For example, it is not only men who are to live lives free from sin (Galatians 5:13), be strong in the Lord (Ephesians 6:10), live lives of rejoicing (Philippians 3:1), think properly (Philippians 4:8), and respect leaders (1 Thessalonians

5:12–13); it is, obviously, all Christians. Unless women are to be excluded from these texts, they should not be excluded from the Romans 12 and 1 Corinthians 12 material. These two chapters stipulate a discussion of the body of believers, of which women are as much members as men; so the very thrust of both passages requires that women be included in what is said about gifts, unless a specific statement is made to exclude them, which Paul does not even come close to doing.

In Romans 12, the gift of teaching is listed in between the gifts of serving and encouraging (12:7–8). In such a passage that discusses the whole body of believers (12:4–5), there is no reason to think that Paul switches from a gift that is open to all believers to a gift that is unavailable to half of the believers and then back again to a gift that is open to all believers. The same is true of 1 Corinthians 12 which lists the gift of helping right alongside the gift of administrating (12:28), after an extensive discussion of the entire body of believers and immediately after saying, "You are the body of Christ, and each one of you is a part of it" (12:27). To the contrary, every member of the body of believers receives spiritual gifts, and all indications are that every member is a candidate to receive any of the gifts. Whatever factors determine distribution, to say that gender is one of them can only be done by forcing the qualification of gender into these key texts.

Ministry, then, extends out from the body of believers. This means that ministers are not essentially different from or separate from the body of believers. Actually, according to the New Testament, all members of the body engage in ministry. Certain members are simply chosen and gifted by God to teach or preach or lead; whereas, other members are marked for other ministries. The same noun "diakonia" which means "service, ministry" was used by Paul of his own apostolic activities (Romans 15:31; 1 Timothy 1:12), as well as for the role of charitable offerings given by congregations (2 Corinthians 8:4; 9:1,12) and for the works of all of God's people (Ephesians 4:12). The same verb "diakoneo" which means "serve, minister" was applied by Paul to himself (Romans 15:25) and was applied by Peter to all Christians (1 Peter 4:10).

It is true that there are distinctions, even in the Early Church, between the clergy and the laity. Paul reserved certain titles, including "diakonos" (which is from the diakonia-diakoneo family) and "sunergos" ("fellow worker") for references to those who served in positions of spiritual leadership. As a clergyman himself, he referred to carrying the burden of the churches upon himself (2 Corinthians 11:28), something that exceeds the responsibility level of the laity. The clergy are said to serve as shepherds; whereas, the laity are likened to sheep (Acts 20:28; 1 Peter 5:3). There is even biblical basis for the ministry being someone's profession in the sense of providing an income (1 Corinthians 9:7–10,13–14; 1 Timothy 5:17–18). However, the exceedingly wide gap that has been cut between the laity and the clergy is a human invention, not a reflection of New Testament teaching and practice. It has resulted in an unhealthy church in many ways, including fostering the contradiction that women can be members of the body but cannot be ministers of the body. If church ministry flows forth from church membership, as it certainly does, then disqualifying women from ministry brings into question the full legitimacy of their membership.

So unlike today's approach, ministerial positions in the Early Church were not determined by denominational approval or appointment, either favoring or disfavoring someone. Offices resulted from gifts, which came directly from God. If God gave someone the gift of apostleship, then that individual served as an apostle, *period*. Just ask Paul! He was an apostle because he was gifted and called by God to be an apostle (Galatians 1:1,11–24). The same was true for every other position whether it was prophet, teacher, leader, or any other. A genuine gift qualified and obligated an individual to exercise that gift, including the gifts that put certain people into the "clergy category." This is exactly what Scripture commands in reference to honoring gifts: "If it is serving, let him (generic in each instance, not male only) serve; if it is teaching, let him teach; if it is encouraging, let him encourage...if it is leadership, let him lead diligently" (Romans 12:7–8). The "if, then let" language of this passage is crystal clear. It must be heard and obeyed.

There *is* precedent in Scripture for gifts to be acknowledged by other believers such as in the sending of Paul and Barnabus (Acts 13:1–3). Even in this instance, however, the gifts were present (13:1) before the sending occurred (13:3), and the sending was not the church's bidding but God's (13:2). Unfortunately, Paul did have to defend his apostleship on numerous occasions, but he nonetheless spent his entire life serving as an apostle. So, even with such an unlikely ministerial candidate as he was, God's gifts did not *require* credentials from others to function; God's gifts *were* Paul's credentials. With Timothy, some gift or gifts were bestowed upon him through the laying on of hands by the elders (1 Timothy 4:14) and by Paul (2 Timothy 1:6). The nature of this gifting, however, is not clear. What is clear is that Timothy was told to be affirmed and strengthened in ministry not by the recognition of others but by the gift of God.

God obviously values the contributions that can be made by every member of the body of believers, likely and unlikely. Because of this, He gifts every member, including both men and women. There is more to gender differences than procreative organs. Though many of the specifics may remain uncertain in the continuing debate of nature versus nurture, men and women do tend to bring into the church different perspectives and approaches. Welcoming the gifts, including the leadership gifts, of both genders results in a wider complement of strengths and skills. In turn, then, a world comprised of needy men and women can best be reached by a clergy comprised of born-again men and women as they represent a God who is without favoritism (Acts 10:34), a God who makes all things new and right, including male-female relationships.

The Importance of Evangelism

Evangelizing a lost world held the attention of New Testament ministers. Following Jesus' example, Paul and others concentrated on reaching sinners rather than on revamping society. They must have known that collective sin can only be made right by first dealing with its source—individual sin. Consequently, in a world teaming with social ills, they were first and foremost evangelists of salvation, missionaries of salvation, proclaimers of salvation. Spreading the gospel was primary; all other compelling causes had to be secondary and subsequent to this effort, because there was no hope apart from this effort.

This approach, whether practiced in the first century or in the twenty-first century, must not be misunderstood. Those who suffer from one or more of the social ills that are not given "top agenda item" attention must never conclude that their plight is being ignored or, worse yet, condoned by Christ and His church. This is far from the truth. The truth is, no matter how awful social crimes may be, spiritual corruption screams even more loudly for the touch of the Savior because it lies at the root of all other evil. Those who support or inflict social wrongdoing must be equally careful not to misunderstand. Because Jesus did not abolish all abusive human activity and because His first ministers did not do so either, its advocates should never conclude that they enjoy the support of the Righteous One. Everyone—victims, perpetrators, and even casual bystanders—should realize that there are few sins that God hates more than the wrongful oppression, the selfish abuse of *His* creation!

In order to see redemption made available to the entire world, then, first-century ministers did not spend themselves on other crusades. For example, a nation such as Israel should not have been held under Rome's imperial rule, but Jesus simply said "Give to Caesar what is Caesar's and to God what is God's" (Matthew 22:21). Similarly, Paul advocated prayer and peacefulness rather than resistance so that the gospel would go forth (1 Timothy 2:1–3). This must have been a challenging assignment for Jewish Christians who were seemingly quite nationalistic by nature. The same principle that applied to national injustices was applied to personal injustices. Paul had rights in the church as an apostle and rights in the empire as a citizen, but he repeatedly exercised or forfeited them solely on the basis of which approach advanced the gospel.

One of the worst injustices that existed in the first-century world was that of slavery. It was present during Jesus' ministry as well as during Paul's ministry, but neither one overthrew it. Instead, Jesus allowed himself to be sold by one man to other men (Matthew 26:14–16,47–50) in order that He might offer total freedom to all slaves, specifically, slaves of sin. Paul returned a runaway slave to his master (Philemon) and told other believing slaves to obey their masters, again, for the sake of furthering the gospel (Titus 2:9–10). This was their approach even though the New Testament identifies slave trading as being contrary to the very gospel that they were endeavoring to advance, right alongside such sins as murder and adultery (1 Timothy 1:8–11).

It is hard to believe but tragically true that many "Christians" throughout church history have misunderstood and misrepresented the Bible's view of slavery. Because Jesus, Paul, and others did not specifically and aggressively fight against it, slavery has been said to be part of God's design for humanity. Even biblical scholars failed to see that wrestling with something as a current reality is not the same as condoning it as right. With the same breath that slaves were told to obey masters, masters were told to treat slaves properly. The very letter (Philemon) that accompanied the runaway slave who was returned to his master told the believing master in no uncertain terms that he should release the slave. The New Testament strategy was to regulate slavery until the Christlikeness in individual masters and in society as a whole would eventually abolish the evil entirely. The gospel would work its own overthrow of the system, but first the gospel had to be allowed to spread.

The problem is not that this strategy has been confusing to people who read the New Testament with minds and hearts that are open to see the wisdom of God. Instead, people with pre-set conclusions have searched the Bible to find support for their selfish, sinful ways. It is they who have refused to see that God's provisions regarding slavery were "culturally conditioned," in other words, temporary, localized accommodations of specific situations. To represent these provisions as permanent, universal principles of righteousness is contrary to the whole tenor of New Testament teaching. The status quo of the first century was tolerated long enough for the gospel to have its own natural, powerful effect; the status quo was certainly not meant to become the norm or the standard for all future Christians.[5]

Not only were social concerns not allowed to hinder the spread of the gospel by distracting ministers' attention and effort, these matters were not allowed to hinder evangelism by overly offending the society into which the gospel was to spread. Had Christianity been perceived as an attempt to overthrow Roman imperialism or as an attempt to abolish something as culturally and economically ingrained as slavery, the very doors that had taken centuries to open would have slammed shut. The gospel would not have gone forth, and the greatest hope of righting these wrongs would have been lost.

There are striking similarities between the slavery issue and yet another social injustice of the first century—the sexual hierarchy issue. How interesting that the Bible has been used, actually, *misused*, to defend both of these wrongs. Both are attempts to subordinate one class of people to another class of people and walk away calling the arrangement "the divine order of things." Both take passages of Scripture that were clearly intended to "negotiate" or "referee" specific, first-century situations and, instead, apply the stipulations to all times and all places. Precisely because of the tight similarities, it is not possible to say, "I'm too smart or too sensitive to advocate slavery, but I will continue to advocate sexual hierarchy." To be hermeneutically consistent, anyone who defends one of these positions as scriptural must be ready to embrace the other as well.

Proponents of sexual hierarchy will be quick to claim that their position differs from slavery in that it has the prior support of the creation account. They need to recheck Genesis. Yes, the origin of sexual hierarchy is found there, but it is found in chapter 3 as a result of sin rather than in chapters 1 & 2 as a result of the creation order.

Next, they will complain that if certain New Testament passages are read as culturally conditioned, then all passages will be open to this reading. For example, children will be able to disregard their parents, and homosexuals will be allowed to continue their sexual wrongdoing. This is an unnecessary scare tactic. One of the major things that safely signals the reader that a passage is to be read as pertaining to temporary, localized situations is that its contents, if read without this understanding, would contradict the rest of Scripture. In the case of certain New Testament passages about women, if a permanent, universal reading is given, then women are put in subordination to men and are kept from entering the ministry, conclusions which clearly contradict everything else that is established throughout the Bible about God's view of women and God's use of women ministers. However, this is not the case with issues such as respect for parents, which is established in the Ten Commandments as solidly as marital fidelity (Exodus 20:12) and undergirded in mosaic law with the threat of death (Exodus 21:17), or homosexual activity, which is said to be sinful enough to exclude participants from the kingdom of God (1 Corinthians 6:9–10). These examples stand in sharp contrast to the questionable texts regarding women.

In summary, rather than trying to overthrow Roman imperialism, slave trading, sexual hierarchy, or any other societal practice, first-century ministers such as Paul threw themselves into spreading the gospel. And rather than allowing the threat of civil, economic, or cultural upheaval to stop the effective spread of the good news, Christians were commanded to sacrifice personal rights to the overall cause of evangelism. Paul practiced this himself and was not hesitant in asking others to practice it as well.

How, then, did Paul treat the "woman issue" of his day? He treated it as less important than evangelizing the world. He treated it as subservient to evangelizing the world. If the new-found liberty that women had in Christianity was exercised too quickly or too extremely, and if this became an obstacle to anyone's perception and acceptance of the gospel, then Paul told women to refrain from exercising their freedom. Anytime personal freedom and obligation to others clashed, obligation to others always won out. No practice was permissible if it overly offended the prevailing custom; if it associated the church with paganism; or if it in any other way generated unnecessary controversy, confusion, or criticism. Nothing was to hinder the task of evangelizing the world.

However, to apply these restraints permanently and universally is to mishandle the Bible, and doing so might even result in reversing the good effect that Paul was intending to produce. In a world that allows women to rise to positions of leadership in almost every sphere of living, to silence or restrict them in the church would cause the very offense that Paul was trying to avoid. This is not allowing culture to set doctrine; it is simply checking if culture is ready to receive the full application of a doctrine. If so, fine; if not, personal freedoms must be patiently and sacrificially forfeited. This is also not to say that sins such as fornication or idolatry should be temporarily permitted until a culture is ready to hear otherwise. Asking Christians to forego personal rights in sensitivity to the demands of a surrounding culture is a far cry from practicing or promoting gross sins.

This understanding of the importance of evangelism and the way its preeminence is to decide certain lifestyle details is extremely helpful in placing certain New Testament passages alongside the rest of Scripture. There is actually no other way to explain the Bible's overall teaching regarding women, versus a handful of passages that seem to say otherwise. Nor is there any other way to explain the fact that Paul repeatedly commended women for doing the very things that he asked certain women to refrain from doing. Paul walked a fine line between advancing the gospel and protecting the gospel; sometimes women assisted in the one task, and sometimes they assisted with the other.

10

The New Testament View of Marriage

The most *intimate* human relationship, marriage, was damaged severely by the entry of sin into the world. In the process the most *fundamental* human relationship, the male-female dynamic, was damaged as well. It is not surprising that extreme levels of sin in society inevitably produce high levels of sin in these two relationships of life, evidenced by such things as sexual promiscuity, marital infidelity, and sexual perversion. Men and women who are not right with God have great difficulty living in right relationship with each other sexually or maritally.

Redemption has been made available through Jesus Christ to not only make right a person's relationship with God but to also make right that person's relationship with others, very much including gender and marriage relationships. A church that cannot show the world these relationships made right is failing to testify to the full scope of redemption's power and blessing. Gender was proclaimed by God at creation to be very good (Genesis 1:27,31). Marriage was instituted by God in the garden (Genesis 2:24); in fact, it has been said that He conducted the first ceremony. What were male-female relationships within the bond of marriage originally meant to be? Is there any evidence in the New Testament that this magnificent arrangement can be everything it was originally designed to be as a couple allows redemption to make *all* things new (2 Corinthians 5:17)?

Absolute Equality

In original creation Adam and Eve were absolutely equal, certainly not identical but nonetheless equal. If God were to restore that absolute equality within the marriage of a redeemed couple, what one area, if made right, would strike at the very center of their relationship? What one area, if made equal, would be so strategic it would mean that the marriage in its entirety had to stand on level footing? In 1 Corinthians 7:3–4, Paul instructs the Christian couple regarding their sexual relationship, and he gives the husband and wife equal say in the matter. Because the issue of authority is such a focal point in the discussion of marriage, it is unfortunate that the NIV obscures the fact that verse 4 is one of only three times that any Greek word for authority appears in the New Testament regarding male-female relationships (also 1 Corinthians 11:10 and 1 Timothy 2:12), and it indicates that the wife and husband "exousiazo" ("exercise authority") over a partner's body in an absolutely equal way. The same word is used in both parts of the verse; the wife's authority is equal and identical to the husband's authority.

It would be hard, indeed, to convince a man of the world that he is absolute ruler in his marriage except in this one exceedingly important area. He would immediately interpret such a stipulation as meaning that he is not ruler at all. In doing so, he would be understanding Scripture better than some Christians understand it. Because of the strategic and symbolic role that sex plays in marriage, to assign both partners equal authority in this of all areas is to assign them equal authority in the entire marriage. Paul's statement reverses the "male rules female" arrangement that resulted from the fall of humanity and replaces it with the same mutual authority and mutual submission that characterized pre-fall marriage.[1] In the community of the redeemed, marriage no longer has to be crippled by male dominance and female subordination; it can be a reflection of the same equality and mutuality that is meant to permeate the entire body of believers.

Equality in Declining Marriage

If Paul's assigning of equality in the opening verses of 1 Corinthians 7 is not striking enough, he continues throughout the chapter to parallel the rights and responsibilities of men and women as pertaining to other major aspects of marriage. It would be an interesting study to count the number of times he specifically refers to both genders in some equal way. For an ancient document to address men and women in such parallel fashion was simply unheard of, but to propose identical provisions for men and women in such areas as are cited in this chapter was *"beyond* unheard of."

The chapter opens with Paul acknowledging a specific question that the Corinthians had raised regarding celibacy. Whether the statement quoted in 7:1 is theirs or his is unknown; either way, he proceeds to speak in favor of it (7:7–8,25–26) but adds considerable clarification along with certain exceptions. Jesus had spoken in favor of voluntary ministerial celibacy with an indication that it was not meant for everyone (Matthew 19:10–12). Basically, Paul says the same thing throughout this chapter. Renouncing marriage for the sake of the ministry is a practical decision (7:32–35). It may fit certain situations more than others (7:26), and it definitely fits certain individuals more than others (7:7).

A reading of everything the Bible says about marriage would generate the conclusion that it is, by God's design, the overall norm for humanity. Consequently, advocating singleness over marriage must not be mistaken as a negative reflection upon marriage. Paul warned against a blanket, forceful application of celibacy teaching (1 Timothy 4:1–5). However, voluntary ministerial celibacy is treated by Jesus and by Paul as honorable, even preferable; therefore, any views of the ministry that *require* marriage for a man *or a women* are nonscriptural views of the ministry. In some Christian circles women are encouraged to marry in order to secure the *only* possible access to ministry, but in Scripture they are encouraged to stay single in order to secure the *best* possible access to it. They are encouraged to marry for entirely different reasons.

What is striking about 1 Corinthians 7 is not Paul's defense of celibacy; it is the fact that he offers voluntary *ministerial* celibacy to men and women alike. The words for "man" and "men" that are used in verse 7 are forms of "anthropos," the Greek word that the New Testament uses generically for "person" or "humanity." The Greek word "agamos" that is behind the word "unmarried" in verse 8 is completely without indication of gender. He says the same thing for both genders in the verses that speak most clearly about celibacy being for the purpose of *ministry* (7:32–35). In his concluding remarks, he, again, offers a male-female parallel address, referring to the situations most likely to affect each gender (7:36–38,39–40). Actually, it is a form of "temporary celibacy within marriage" for spiritual purposes that introduced this whole discussion, and it too is described in collective language (7:5).

The only portion of the chapter that may not discuss celibacy as pertaining to men and women alike gives the extra treatment not to men but to women. The Greek word translated "virgins" in verse 25 was usually used of women; and if this is the case here, then extra sensitivity is being employed in encouraging women toward celibacy, probably because of the extra challenge they would face in opting for it in such a male-based culture. Even so, they are urged toward remaining single. This word is used once in Scripture of men (Revelation 14:4); so if men are being included with women here in a generic version of "virgins," then verse 25 becomes yet another instance in which gender has no bearing on remaining celibate.

Handing the decision regarding celibacy to both genders topples the cultural norm of fathers or eldest brothers determining the marital future of the women of their household. Thus, one form of male rulership is overthrown. Presenting celibacy to both genders as optional and preferable, furthermore, displaces the cultural notion that a woman's primary or best role is that of wife and mother. If this is based on and/or results in the rulership of a husband, then yet another form of male rulership is overthrown. In the community of the redeemed, women are not to be dominated by men in one of the most important decisions of their lives; so it is very likely that they are not to be dominated by men in the other decisions and details of their lives.

Equality in Dissolving Marriage

It could be said that renouncing marriage is a decision that primarily or only affects the individual making the decision. Divorcing a marriage partner, however, affects both members of the marriage; consequently, the equality that Paul stipulates in this area is even more shocking than what was made available relating to remaining single. Again, Paul is simply following the teaching of Jesus who said, "Anyone who divorces his wife and marries another woman commits adultery against her. And if she divorces her husband and marries another man, she commits adultery" (Mark 10:11–12). Such equality was so unknown in the ancient world that there are virtually no words to adequately describe its uniqueness and its significance.

The point of Jesus' and Paul's teaching is not to encourage men or women to disregard their marriages. To the contrary, the Bible is quite clear in commanding that no one separate what God joins together (Matthew 19:6). Divorce is only permissible in the case of the other partner being sexually unfaithful (Matthew 5:32), and the same is true for remarriage after divorce (Matthew 19:9). Not even the spiritual unevenness that is present when a believer is married to an unbeliever is grounds for ending a marriage (1 Corinthians 7:10–16). The point is that both partners are equally involved in the marriage, so their "rights" regarding divorce and their responsibilities for avoiding divorce are very much equal.[2] According to Scripture, both the husband and the wife are to be equally committed to the health of the marriage, and that commitment is to be great.

1 Corinthians 7 is, by far, the lengthiest treatment of marriage found in the New Testament, in the entire Bible for that matter. If a hierarchical arrangement were God's design for this extremely important relationship, it is hard to believe that no hint of it is found in this key passage. There is not the slightest indication of male dominance or female subordination to be found anywhere in the text. Instead, the chapter is literally shouting with equality—equal options, equal rights, equal responsibilities, equal authority. The parallelism that establishes this equality is so exacting that it is nothing less than deliberate. It would be virtually impossible to paint a picture of marriage that is any more opposite to the man "ruling the roost" than this passage paints.

Some have complained that someone must be in charge of any marriage. They liken the relationship to a business, a government, or an army and insist that a chief executive or ruler or commanding officer is necessary. Their conclusion is wrong, however, because their initial premise is wrong. A marriage is not like these other earthly "relationships," if businesses and governments and armies can be called relationships at all. In no other human relationship except marriage are two people designed to become one. And this oneness far exceeds the uniting of two bodies in a sexual act; it is the joining of two entire persons into unity. The more friendship, intimacy, love, and unity that are mutually present between a husband and wife, the less need there is for *any* form of power or authority in their dealings with each other. Games and competitions require tiebreakers; if a marriage is not a game or a competition, then it does not require a tie-breaker. What the church needs to show the world in its marriages is not a hierarchy that makes unity impossible but a unity that makes hierarchy unnecessary.

Submission Passages

How can the teachings of 1 Corinthians 7 be squared with the teachings of the "submission passages" in the New Testament? Even people who cannot quote one verse of Scripture seem to know that something about wives submitting to husbands is in the Bible. Some people even assume that the wife's wedding vow to "love, honor, and *obey*" her husband is a direct quote from Scripture. Doesn't all of this mean that the husband is essentially the boss over the wife?

Before anything else is said, a few clarifications and explanations would be in order. Whatever the Bible says about husbands and wives, it is not necessarily saying these things about men and women in general. Unfortunately, the line between the two is not always as obvious as one might assume. In the Greek language the words "aner" and "arsen" are the words for a male or husband, and the word "gune" is the word for a woman or wife. If possessive language is used such as "your man" or "your woman," then marital identity can usually be assumed. Otherwise, the immediate context and/or the teaching of the rest of Scripture must help determine the more likely meaning of either of these words.

Regardless of the challenges sometimes posed by the language, there seems to be a tendency toward a quick, easy jump from what is commanded for husbands and wives to what is applied to men and women in general, at least if the jump strengthens the case for a male-female hierarchy. The following thinking is very common: whatever God says about husband-wife relationships, He intends to extend into male-female relationships in society and in the church. So, if a woman is told to submit to her husband, then she is thereby assumed to be positioned in submission to men in general. Not only does this line of reasoning fail to address the questionable ramifications of a man's wife being under the authority of all other men, it also fails to apply the rest of the passages in question in a consistent manner. For example, if a woman is to somehow submit to all men, then is a man to somehow love all women?

Not all but most of the "submission passages" are found within larger portions of material that are known as the household code or domestic code passages. Some understanding of the role of these portions of Scripture would be helpful. These types of writings typically outlined a man's relationship to his wife, children, and slaves. They appeared quite often in Greek and Roman literature, dating back as far as Aristotle (4th century B.C.). Paul adopted the format to present Christian principles in Ephesians 5:21–6:9 and in Colossians 3:18–4:1, and Peter did the same in 1 Peter 2:18–3:7. Some overlapping material is found in 1 Timothy 5:1–6:2 and Titus 2:1–10, but these passages differ in format and focus from the household code approach.

The fact that people recognized the form and function of these codes was probably not the only reason or even the primary reason that Paul and Peter chose to arrange their teaching in this way. Throughout the Roman Empire "foreign religions" were basically suspect, particularly by the elite members of society who viewed themselves as the guardians of traditional lifestyles. Many of these religions were seen as encouraging social instability by advocating the liberation and advancement of classes of people thought to be "rightfully low" in their standing, such as women or slaves. If the religion was gaining converts rapidly, it was perceived as being all the more dangerous. Christianity fit each of these descriptions. It is very likely that Paul and Peter were encouraging Christians to present themselves to the world as stable members of society in order to ward off as much hostility and resistance as possible.[3]

One social issue that was extremely sensitive throughout the empire during the first century was the standing of women. In large cities and within aristocratic circles, women had made impressive gains and were threatening to continue their upward climb. In today's feminist writings, it is not unusual for this era to be tagged "the first major sexual revolution" because the changes were of such significant proportion. The fight against these changes, however, was of equal proportion. If Christianity seemed to be a mechanism in disguise for liberating women beyond the tolerance level of Roman culture, the spread of the gospel would have been sorely hampered.

In their constant reminders to wives, Paul's and Peter's words were reminiscent of Jesus' wisdom when He said, "Give to Caesar what is Caesar's and to God what is God's" (Matthew

22:21). Christianity was not meant to be a civil or sexual revolution; it was meant to be a spiritual revolution which, if allowed to progress, would affect civil and sexual matters for the rest of human history. Paul and Peter told wives to submit to their husbands, but they also told slaves to submit to their masters. They cannot be accused by this of advocating marital or sexual hierarchy any more than they can be accused of advocating slavery. They simply instructed Christians to comply with the authority structures of the day, without condoning the structures that were clearly unbiblical and certainly without mandating unbiblical structures for all time.[4]

Upon closer scrutiny, what these passages actually accomplished is quite ingenious. Society's concerns were acknowledged and addressed by telling wives and slaves to be submissive. At the same time, *all* believers were told to be submissive, and husbands and masters were challenged to live in ways that further matched and even neutralized what was asked of wives and slaves. In other words, Paul and Peter turned a potentially threatening situation into an opportunity to decrease the world's resistance while simultaneously increasing the church's righteousness. May this careful balance and great accomplishment not be overlooked or overturned by believers today.

Wives in Ephesians 5

The most extensive of the apostles' household codes is found in Ephesians 5:21–6:9. Other texts that address relationships are sometimes even said to be abbreviations of this material. Many scholars think that Paul's letter to the Ephesians was a circular letter that was meant to be read to all of the churches of Asia Minor. If this were the case, it is understandable that he would insert such a thorough treatment of household relationships in this document. Regardless, as with other topics in the Bible, conclusions are usually better drawn from lengthy coverage of an issue than from a brief handling of it. No one would build a doctrine of end times events from the three verses found in 1 Thessalonians 4:15–17 while ignoring the entire book of Revelation. Even though this is an extreme example, the point is nonetheless legitimate. Ephesians 5:21–6:9, the most extensive of the household codes, should stand rather authoritatively as an explanation of how Christians are to relate to each other.

The passage does not begin with 5:22 as many translations may indicate with a section heading or paragraph break; it begins with 5:21. This point is crucial to a proper understanding of the text, but it is also an undeniable fact of the text. Verse 22 cannot begin the section because it is an incomplete sentence, actually, an incomplete thought if it is separated from verse 21. Verse 22 has no verb; it is dependent upon verse 21 to supply its verb. Though the original manuscript did not contain verse numbers or paragraph indicators, Paul built right into its very structure a tie between these two verses by leaving verse 22 dependent upon verse 21 for its completion. Verse 22 literally reads, "wives to your own husbands as to the Lord." It's funny that the "big 'S' word" that commands all of the attention anytime this passage is read, actually doesn't even exist in the original text of verse 22! This verse must borrow its verb "submit" from the preceding verse in which all believers are told to submit to each other.

This grammatical arrangement that Paul locked into the material places verse 21 into the position of an opening topic sentence for the entire household code. Every instruction that is given is to be interpreted against the backdrop of this verse.[5] The "household of faith" is first and foremost to be ruled by the mutual submission of its members, and every instruction that follows is simply a way of fleshing out this mutual submission. Everyone is to bend in thoughtfulness and honor toward others. Ironically, the wife is the only individual in a lineup of six groups of people who is told nothing more than to do this submitting. For everyone else, submitting will require some rather taxing assignments. But the one role in life, about which the most fuss is made regarding submitting, is actually charged with the lightest version that's possible—that of simply submitting. And the irony continues, as will be seen below. The one person, the husband, who oftentimes walks away from this passage the least affected, is actually given the heaviest submission assignment of them all.

The word "submit" ("hupotasso") has a wide array of meanings in the secular literature of the first century as well as throughout the New Testament. Uses range from very commanding images such as the submission of demons (Luke 10:17), to less forceful images, such as Jesus' relationship to His earthly parents (Luke 2:51), or the relationship between a prophecy and the one giving the prophecy (1 Corinthians 14:32).

Sometimes submission is to God (James 4:7), other times to earthly officials (Romans 13:1), and still other times between fellow believers (Ephesians 5:21; 1 Peter 5:5).

In Ephesians 5:21, the fact that the submission is mutual along with the fact that the verb is used in the middle voice (the subject acting on himself) results in the connotation of willingly deferring to others, voluntarily cooperating with others, yielding one's personal preferences for the sake of others. Because of the middle voice, the image is not one of demanding or forcing the compliance; this would require the active voice and would read "put under subjection." Nowhere in Scripture is a believer ever told to put another believer under subjection. The image is of a self-yielding individual in a community of other self-yielding individuals. Mutual submission of this nature is absolutely opposite from any notion of hierarchical order in which a higher level gives orders and a lower level receives orders. If mutual submission is functioning, then hierarchical levels either do not exist or do not matter.

According to verse 21, all believers are to practice this mutual submission. Perhaps the phrase "out of reference for Christ" acts as a reminder that there is actually only one individual in a community of Christians who possesses inherent authority over others, Christ the Lord. Just before He laid down His life to redeem them, He prayed for one thing for them—unity. And He said that through this display of unity, the world would take notice (John 17:20–23). Grammatically it is not possible to say that anything more than or different from this community submissiveness is being assigned to wives in verse 22. Whatever all believers are to practice, wives are to practice because verse 22 borrows its verb from verse 21.

Why are all believers told to be submissive and then wives, in particular, are told again about submissiveness? As previously noted, not just wives but six groups of people are addressed beyond the general statement of verse 21. Everyone *except the wife* is told one or more ways to implement the general statement according to what would fit his/her "station" in life, and these assignments or applications extend verse 21 considerably. The wife is not unique because she is singled out to extend verse 21; to the contrary, she is only unique because she alone is not asked to extend verse 21 in any way other than to remember that it applies to her husband. She is simply told to practice toward her husband what she practices toward all other believers.

It is possible that first-century wives were experiencing such exhilaration from their new-found freedom in Christ that they were forgetting their responsibilities to their husbands. The marriage of two believers is no longer bound to the reign of sin which had put them in hierarchical relationship to each other, but the marriage is nonetheless bound to a master, a *new* master, the reign of righteousness. This puts them into an equal relationship of mutual submissiveness. But just because the husband is to be submissive toward his wife as detailed in verses 25–32, this does not lessen the wife's responsibility to be submissive toward her husband. In her submitting to all believers, the one believer that a wife is not to overlook is her husband.

In addition to noticing what Paul says to wives, it is important to notice what he does not say. Believers are not called to "mutual obedience" which is, of course, an impossibility. Likewise, a wife is not told to obey her husband, not here and not anywhere else in Scripture, although the KJV does incorrectly translate the Greek word for "submit" ("hupotasso") into the English word "obey" in more than one location. The word for "obey" ("hupakouo") was known to Paul and was available to him, as is obvious by his use of it only verses away in his instructions to children and to slaves (6:1,5). Actually, his culture would have left him inclined toward using the word in reference to wives because the ideal wife of the first century was one who was obedient to her husband, even slavishly so.[6] But Paul, evidently deliberately, chose not to use this word in regards to the marital relationship. He used it for two of the three relationships detailed in the household code, child-parent and slave-master. He did not use it, however, for the one relationship that was originally designed by God to be equal.

It should be noted, as well, that possessive wording is found in the Greek text of verse 22, meaning that husband-wife relationships are in view, not male-female relationships. Whatever interpretation anyone proposes for this section of material, then, it must apply only to marriage, not to society in general and certainly not to anything pertaining to local church leadership. The Bible presents Deborah as the highest ranking civil and spiritual leader in all of Israel even though she was married. God's desire for a proper marital relationship for her and her husband Lappidoth was obviously not in any way jeopardized or impeded by the corporate leadership position into which He placed her.

The wife is told to submit to her husband "as to the Lord." Since her culture already demanded submission and much more, Paul is adding a spiritual motivation to what is already socially and legally required of her. Perhaps because submission was culturally mandated, some wives had difficulty exercising it, especially with a right spirit. Paul is not saying that a husband acts in some way as the Lord's replacement or representative, thereby wielding the Lord's authority and deserving the same respect. He is simply inviting a wife to view any sacrificial behavior toward her husband as "counting" as behavior done directly unto the Lord.

Headship in Ephesians 5

In Ephesians 5:23–24, Paul gives a reason for the wife-to-husband submission that he specifies in the preceding verse. These two verses open with the word "hoti" which means "for, since, because." Verses 23–24, then, supply the foundation upon which verse 22 is to be properly built. A wife is to submit to her husband *because* "the husband is the head of the wife as Christ is the head of the church." Next, the passage moves into considerable detail about the husband's responsibilities to his wife by further extending this headship analogy. Obviously, much insight about the marriage relationship, both in the direction of the wife and in the direction of the husband, can be unlocked through an accurate understanding of what Paul meant by his use of the word "head" ("kephale").

Those who "think in English" must receive a quick, firm caution against drawing premature and faulty conclusions. Paul is obviously not using the word "head" literally because he is not saying that a husband is the uppermost part of a physical body containing the cerebrum (brain). He is obviously and unquestionably using the word figuratively. Anytime a word is used figuratively, however, the same meaning or meanings are not necessarily triggered as would be triggered if the same word were used figuratively in a different language. For example, even though "head" can mean "boss, ruler, leader, authority" in English as in "head of the corporation," this collection of possible meanings is totally nonexistent in such languages as French and Spanish. When the word "head" is used in one of these two languages, the meaning of "ruler, leader" cannot be transferred from a totally different language such as English and imposed upon languages that do not have the meaning available.

Of course, the meaning of "head" in any of these modern languages has no bearing on its meaning in Ephesians 5:23. This sentence was written in first-century Greek, and it was written to first-century, Greek-speaking people. The only thing that matters is what the word "kephale" meant in that language at that time. Unfortunately, biblical scholarship is split as to the figurative meanings of "head" ("kephale") that were present and prevalent in first-century Greek, basically split between two camps. Some scholars say it meant "ruler, leader" which would position the husband in authority over the wife. Others say it meant "source, origin," as in the fountainhead or headwaters of a stream or river, which would indicate a very different husband-wife relationship that has nothing to do with authority.

One resource that is commonly used in deciding such matters is the Greek lexicon which reports word use in ancient literature. Several Greek lexicons favor "source, origin" as a likely meaning of "kephale," as does the extremely comprehensive work by Liddell, Scott, Jones, & McKenzie, A Greek-English Lexicon. This lexicon's findings are the result of examining thousands of writings in classical and common Greek from several hundred years before to several years after the New Testament era. It lists numerous meanings for "kephale," including "source" and "origin" and other similar words. It does not include a single listing that even approximates "ruler" or "leader." Apparently, ordinary Greek-speaking people of the first century, not to mention the centuries before and after, did not register images of position and authority as common meanings for the word "head."[7]

A second resource for studying such matters is the Septuagint, the translation of the Hebrew Old Testament into Greek, which dates between 250 and 150 B.C. Even though this important ancient document is represented in lexicons, it can also be analyzed by itself. The value of doing so stems from the fact that the known meaning of a Hebrew word sheds considerable light on the meaning of the Greek word that was chosen to translate it. In this case, most of the uses of the Hebrew word for "head" ("ro'sh") in the Old Testament are literal, and the vast majority of these were translated with the Greek word "kephale." So, there is no doubt that "kephale" was the Greek "word of choice" to convey the meaning of a literal, physical head.

Conveniently, the Hebrew word "ro'sh" also carried the figurative meaning of "ruler, leader," and this use occurs approximately 180 times in the Old Testament. So, the question is, when these 180 passages were translated into Greek, was the word "kephale" chosen to convey the figurative meaning of "ruler, leader"? It would seem that if it was the overwhelming choice when the meaning of head was literal, then it would be the choice when the meaning was figurative. But, of course, this would only be possible if the Greek language defined "kephale" as having the figurative meaning of "ruler, leader."

What is actually found in the Septuagint , is not the *prevalence* of "kephale" in these passages that require a word that conveys the idea of "ruler, leader" but the *absence* of it, as is shown in the following chart:[8]

180 Septuagint Translations of the Figurative Word "Ro'sh"			
Greek "archon" = ruler, leader		109 times	61%
Other Greek words (not including "kephale")		47 times	26%
Hebrew "ro'sh" (no translation)		6 times	3%
Greek "kephale"		18 times	10%
—in head-tail metaphors	4 times		
—with other alternatives suggested	6 times		
—probably as Hebraisms	8 times		100%

Rather than seeing 180 figurative uses of the Hebrew "ro'sh" translated into the Greek "kephale," most of the occurrences (109 or 61%) are translated into the Greek word "archon" which clearly means "ruler, leader." Obviously, the translators perceived "archon" rather than "kephale" as conveying the image of an authority figure. An additional 47 of the 180 are translated into 12 other Greek words, bringing the total to 156 or 87% of the occurrences. This indicates a considerable resistance to translating "ro'sh" into "kephale" when the meaning is "ruler, leader." The obvious explanation for this resistance is that "kephale" does not convey this meaning explicitly enough.[9]

What is done with the other 24 occurrences? Six times "ro'sh" is not translated at all; it simply appears as "ro'sh." The remaining 18 times it is translated "kephale," but these instances are not entirely what they seem. Four of the 18 times, the word is half of a "head-tail" metaphor which would make no sense if the Greek word for "head" were not used. Six times the Septuagint offers alternative readings alongside its use of "kephale," indicating an uncertainty about "kephale" being the reliable translation. The only true, "clean" instances of "ro'sh" translating "kephale" out of a total of 180 possibilities are the following eight: Judges 11:11; 2 Samuel 22:44; Psalms 18:43; Isaiah 7:8–9 (4 times); and Lamentations 1:5.[10] These obscure passages collectively represent 4% of the 180 opportunities to use "kephale." Precisely because these instances are so rare, it is very likely that the translators were simply inventing "Hebraisms," which are found throughout the Septuagint. These are occasional translations of figurative Hebrew words into literal Greek equivalents with little or no regard for the fact that the meaning would be lost in the translation if it were not for the context supplying additional assistance or the audience knowing some Hebrew.[11]

Tedious as this explanation may seem, all of it can now be summarized very simply and decisively. The Old Testament uses the Hebrew word for "head" ("ro'sh") in a figurative way a total of 180 times. In each of these occurrences, the intended meaning is some version of "ruler, leader." When these passages were translated into Greek in the Septuagint, if the normal, natural meaning of "kephale" had been "ruler, leader" then many if not most of the 180 occurrences of "ro'sh" would have been translated into "kephale." Since this is far from what was done, it is very unlikely that "kephale" was commonly understood to mean "ruler, leader" in first-century Greek. This conclusion, of course, is in agreement with the total absence of any "ruler, leader" definition of "kephale" in A Greek-English Lexicon.

It is true that lexicons can be found that list "ruler, leader" as an optional definition for "kephale," although their evidence is lacking and questionable. They usually rely heavily upon the Septuagint occurrences that have just been described and dismissed. A computer search of ancient documents has generated additional claims to the word carrying the "ruler, leader" meaning, but the examples that are given as evidence and the interpretation of the data are so disputable any claim that "kephale" tended to mean "ruler, leader" in first-century Greek remains extremely doubtful.[12] Even if the word is shown to have had this meaning available, it becomes one optional definition among several better possibilities. Other scholars offer strong evidence that "source, origin" is the figurative meaning of "kephale" in enough ancient documents to give this definition greater credibility.

To read "head" ("kephale") in Ephesians 5:23 as meaning some type of authority figure is not legitimate since this figurative meaning for "kephale" probably did not exist in first-century Greek. Even if it did exist, which is yet to be proven, unless it was the *commonly* understood meaning of the word, which it was not, this definition cannot be automatically imposed upon any and all New Testament passages that use the word. It simply would not have been the understanding that people of the first century had. Instead, the passages must be allowed to define the word for themselves whenever they seem to do so, and if this does not occur, other more likely definitions of "kephale" must be given consideration.

"Kephale" appears in the Greek New Testament a total of 76 times, the vast majority being in reference to a literal, physical head. The exceptions to this fall into four categories. First, there is one reference that uses "head" as representative of a whole person which is only slightly different from using it literally (Acts 18:6). Second, there are five passages which refer to Jesus as the "head of the corner," typically translated cornerstone or capstone (Matthew 21:42; Mark 12:10; Luke 20:17; Acts 4:11; 1 Peter 2:7). This use does not suggest the idea of one stone being the "boss" of a wall or corner but of it being the most prominent stone, and "prominent" is one of the documented figurative meanings of "kephale." Third, there are five references to Jesus being the "head" of something or someone (Ephesians 1:22; 4:15; Colossians 1:18; 2:10,19), and, fourth, there are two other references to Jesus being the "head" in conjunction with the "aner" ("man" or "husband") being the "head" of the "gune" ("woman" or "wife") (1 Corinthians 11:3; Ephesians 5:23).

Obviously, the 1 Corinthians 11 and Ephesians 5 passages have the most if not the only bearing on the marital relationship because they are the only ones that liken the role of the husband to that of Jesus. It would be possible for Jesus to serve as a "head" in various ways, as detailed in the five other passages, but it can only be said with certainty that a husband's role mirrors Jesus' role as described in 1 Corinthians 11 and Ephesians 5 because only these two passages make the comparison. In other words, figurative language in Scripture never acts as a "blank check" invitation to draw any and all conclusions that are possible, carelessly mixing and matching passages. This would be blatantly bad hermeneutics. Conclusions must be limited to the connections that are specifically indicated as existing.

If 1 Corinthians 11 and Ephesians 5 are allowed to speak for themselves, they are clearly reaching for the "source, origin" meaning of the word "head." 1 Corinthians 11:3 can only be understood as referring to authority if the notion of authority is imposed upon the verse. Otherwise, it is simply listing in chronological order the coming into flesh of man, woman, and the incarnate Christ, a reference to each one's "source, origin." There is a way in which Adam came from Christ (John 1:3; Colossians 1:16), a different way in which Eve came from Adam (Genesis 2:21–22), and a different way yet in which God the Incarnate Son came from God the Heavenly Father (Matthew 1:20; John 1:14; 8:42; 16:27–28). References to creation (source, origin) continue throughout the passage (1 Corinthians 11:8,12), but there is absolutely no reference to authority other than to the authority *of* the woman (11:10).

Likewise, in Ephesians 5:23 and the verses that follow, the focus is upon Christ giving of Himself to birth the church into existence and then continuing to be the means through which that spiritual life is nurtured. This is "source, origin" imagery, not authority language. It is difficult to get an accurate impression, however, because verse 24 begins with "therefore" in the KJV and with "now" in the NIV. The Greek word that actually opens the verse is "alla" which demands a translation of "but" or "nevertheless" or some other word that indicates contrast. If headship in verse 23 refers to authority and consequently to submission, then it makes no sense for verse 24 to say, "*but* submit." However, if verse 23 is speaking of the husband being a giving, nurturing source for the wife, then it makes perfect sense for the wife to be reminded again, *in contrast*, in verse 24 to exercise her half of mutual submission toward her husband.

Without extending the discussion into undue length and detail, it is worth noting that none of the other five figurative uses of "head" in the New Testament involve a "leader, ruler" definition of the word. (1) Ephesians 1:22 offers two different metaphors. The first one regarding feet that is detailed in verse 21 does pertain to authority over all things. The second one *regarding the head* that is detailed in verse 23, however, has nothing to do with authority but with Christ filling the church with His fullness, clearly depicting His giving and nurturing.[13] (2) Ephesians 4:15 pictures Jesus as the source of the church's gifts (4:11–13), steadiness (4:14), growth (4:15), and unity (4:16). Obviously, the issue is not His authority but, again, His giving and nurturing. (3) Just preceding Colossians 1:18, Christ is identified as the creator (1:16) and the sustainer (1:17) of all things, and then "head" is defined as "the beginning and firstborn from among the dead." So, just as He is the originator and sustainer of natural life, He is the originator and sustainer of resurrection life, and verses 19–20 describe how He accomplishes this. The word translated "supremacy" or "preeminence" ("proteuo") is not a reference to rulership because the passage says nothing about this aspect of His position; it is a reference to His "firstness." Because He is first in every way, which the opening verse indicates (1:15), all things, whether natural or spiritual, flow forth from Him. This is yet a third use of "head" as "origin, source." (4) Colossians 2:10 is part of an overall discussion of the new life that Christ provides, as is made clear by the opening verses of the section (2:6–7). In line with this, verse 10 clearly signals that the "life-giving source" definition of "head" is intended with the statement, "you have been given fullness in Christ who is the head." Perhaps this meaning is obscured by the phrase "head *over* every power and authority," but it should be noted that the preposition "over" (NIV) is not present in the Greek text. A preposition must be supplied, and "of" (KJV) would fit the context more accurately. What is being said is that Christians receive fullness from Christ because He is the "head" or "origin, source" *of* all mightiness. (5) Colossians 2:19 is part of the same section of material and is obviously continuing the use of "head" to indicate Christ's life-giving function, warning believers not to disconnect from this supply. (No other passages contain a figurative use of "kephale." If a figurative use of "head" appears in an English version, a different Greek word or phrase is being translated.)

Nothing, then, supports the claim that a husband is in authority over his wife because he serves as "head"—not the meanings of "head" that are found in secular Greek literature, not the meanings of "head" that are evident in the translating of the Hebrew Old Testament in Greek, and not the use of "head" in a single New Testament passage. This meaning cannot be imposed upon the Greek language from a language that predates it such as Hebrew or from a language that postdates it such as English. The idea of "ruler, leader" simply wasn't the clear, common understanding of the Greek word "kephale." There are, of course, many references to authority figures in secular and in biblical Greek literature, but "kephale" or "head" is not the word that is used in these many instances. This is probably because in Greek thinking, it was the heart, *not the head*, that was the seat of intelligence and decision-making. The head was thought to be the source of life because the body was viewed as growing forth from it.

The fact that Christ is the supreme authority over the church, indeed, over all of creation, is not to be minimized; but this is a function of His lordship, not a function of His headship.[14] As has been shown, the passages that refer to Christ as "head" focus upon His loving, cherishing, giving, providing, nurturing, fulfilling, completing role. This emphasis is particularly present in the Ephesians 5 passage that makes the most of likening a husband's role to Christ's role. To misrepresent this portion of Scripture as positioning the husband as the wife's commander rather than as her enabler is to do a great injustice to the passage and to marriage. As Christ is the church's resource, the husband is to be the wife's resource, which is quite different from being her ruler. The wife, in turn, can fulfill her portion of mutual submission toward her husband (5:22) *because* (5:23) he is her resource.

Husbands in Ephesians 5

The portion of Ephesians 5 that addresses wives states that the husband is to be head of the wife in the same way that Christ serves as Head of the Church (5:23), and then the wife's response is to mirror the church's response of embracing that role in her life (5:24). The portion that addresses husbands focuses upon a description of this role of headship (5:25–32). Noticeably missing from the description is any suggestion of exercising rulership, leadership, or authority over the wife. If this is a primary function, perhaps, *the* primary function of a husband, then it is odd that he is nowhere in all of Scripture instructed to exercise it. The only responsibility that is assigned to him in Ephesians 5 is that of loving his wife in a totally self-giving, self-sacrificing way (5:25–27). Her well-being is to be his consuming passion,[15] even to the point of putting her needs before his very life.

According to this description, the husband's task has nothing to do with ruling but everything to do with caring and serving, nothing to do with bossing but everything to do with bending over backwards to benefit. In fact, the husband's *authority over* his wife could not be any further from the point that is being made; instead, *assisting* his wife is the focus. He is not to use his wife to strengthen himself; he is to use himself to strengthen his wife. Jesus is his example, and Jesus described this aspect of Himself with the following words: "The Son of Man did not come to be served, but to serve, and to give his life as a ransom for many" (Matthew 20:28). Just as Jesus seeks the full potential/fulfillment/completion of the church (5:26–27), the husband is to seek the same for his wife, though it requires the outpouring of himself (5:25). This is far from the limiting and hindering of women that is frequently defended with a misreading of this passage.

Men and women must stop reading Ephesians 5 as if the wife is given the hard sentence and the husband is to be the fortunate recipient of her servitude. Both wives and husbands are to be mutually submissive as are all believers (5:21). A marriage is not truly Christian unless both partners practice this mutual submission.[16] The wife, already terribly overburdened by the demands of a patriarchal culture, is simply told to fulfill this assignment (5:22–24). The husband, however, is given profoundly more challenging responsibilities. His duties require a level of giving and sacrificing that uses Jesus Himself as the standard, a level of loving someone else that can only be explained on the basis of being one with that someone (5:28–31). He is to join everything that he is to everything that she is, not vice versa (5:31), and the result is to be unity, not hierarchy (5:31). Even the summary of the passage (5:33) indicates that the wife's assignment merely requires respect (5:33), whereas the husband's requires love and a degree of love that equals his love for himself.

A scriptural view of marriage, then, does not eliminate the idea of a husband serving as its head. After all, it is Scripture that assigns this role to him. In turn, he can probably be said to serve as head of the family and head of the home, as well, since these entities derive from marriage. His headship, however, does not supply his wife and children with their commander-in-chief; it supplies them with their source of strength, particularly with their source of spiritual strength. He is to do everything within his power to ensure their well-being. He is to serve as a source of enablement, meeting their needs and nurturing their development. None of this is an exercise of his power; all of it is an exercise of his love.

Of course, neither side of these husband-wife descriptions is to be pushed beyond the intent of the text, but, instead, both sides are to be understood against the backdrop of the mutual submission commanded in the opening verse of the passage (5:21). On the one hand, a husband must not read his instructions as saying too much. Likening his role to Christ's role is not to be understood as making him the wife's savior or spiritual superior because comparing him with Christ is not the same as identifying or equating him with Christ. The analogy is not to be pressed beyond its designated points of contact, namely, the giving of himself in love on behalf of his wife.[17] If a woman can be a minister of the gospel without the help of a husband (Acts 21:8–9; 1 Corinthians 7:34), then she can certainly be a full recipient of the gospel without the help of a husband. On the other hand, a wife must not read her instructions as saying too little. Even though more material and more demanding material is addressed to her husband than to her, this portion of Scripture must not be understood as overly easing her marital responsibilities. More than likely, the intent is to balance the age-old imbalance that favors the husband, not establish a new imbalance favoring the wife. It is difficult to imagine that God's ideal design for marriage, the oneness which was originally described in Genesis 2:24 and which is reaffirmed in this passage (5:31), could be possible without the husband and wife feeling and acting in complete mutuality.

One other detail is worth noting. When Jesus and Paul spoke about marriage, both reached for a pre-fall passage of Scripture. In fact, Jesus in Matthew 19:4–6 and Paul here in Ephesians 5:31 reach for the very same passage to serve as God's *defining standard* for this most intimate male-female relationship. They quoted Genesis 2:24 which speaks of unity rather than hierarchy. They said nothing about Genesis 3:16, nothing about male dominance and female subservience, because this post-fall passage reflects the results of sin rather than the original, perfect design of God.

Parenting in Ephesians 6

In light of the mutuality that is assigned to both marriage partners in Ephesians 5, it is not surprising that fathers and mothers are given equal, identical standing in the words that are spoken to children in Ephesians 6:1–3. If God's desire for marriage were a hierarchical relationship, then one of two arrangements for children would result: either they would be focused directly upon the father since the "boss" of the marriage would thereby be the "boss" of the children, or they would be instructed to follow their mother's lead as she conveys her husband's lead since she serves as his agent. However, neither of these arrangements is described in Ephesians 6, but, instead, something quite different is commanded. The children are to relate to both parents in exactly the same way. This can only be because these two individuals are positioned at the very same level of leadership, both in the marriage and in the family.

The only "special attention" that is given to the father is actually corrective in nature (6:4). This is probably due to the fact that ancient culture was not very different from many modern cultures, in that the bulk of the burden of child-rearing was typically relegated to women, leaving men relatively uninvolved. To rectify this tendency and to restore the dual participation that God desires, the father is given two directives. First, he is told to avoid exasperating his children. This could result from either extreme of underusing or overusing his fatherly authority. He is not to remain in the one extreme, nor is he to reach for the other extreme. Second, and *instead*, he is told to involve himself in the proper spiritual influencing of his children.

Ephesians 6:4 cannot be interpreted as including the father but excluding the mother from exercising authority over the children because both parents are given the same standing in the passage's opening (6:1–2). Rather than establishing unevenness in parental leadership, the intent of the provisions is to reestablish evenness. This positioning of both parents equally over their children dates from the Old Testament. When God laid the foundation of His relationship with Israel in Deuteronomy 6, the same individuals who were told to recognize Him as the only true God (6:4), to obey Him (6:3), and to love Him (6:5) were told to transmit these commands to their children (6:6–9). This would include men and women, fathers and mothers. Consequently, for a child to disregard either of them was and is a serious sin (Exodus 20:12; 21:17).

Because of this even positioning of both parents over their children, children are told in Ephesians 6 to obey both of them. The same stipulation is made in one of the other household codes (Colossians 3:20). Nowhere in Scripture, however, is the wife told to obey her husband. The difference is obvious and significant: the parent-child relationship is hierarchical, but the husband-wife relationship is egalitarian.

The Household Code of Colossians

An abbreviated version of the Ephesians household code is found in Colossians 3:18–4:1. Although the overall provisions do not change in any significant way, there is a noticeable difference in emphasis. Whereas the largest amount of material in Ephesians is directed toward the husband, slaves are given the lengthiest treatment here. The other household code, 1 Peter 2:18–3:7, features an emphasis upon two categories, slaves and wives. These differences suggest that the locations to which these letters were originally addressed each had a specific imbalance that needed to be counteracted with an overemphasis upon one or more areas.

This means that caution must be taken in reading meaning into the absence of a detail in one of the accounts if that detail is present in one of the other three passages. The understanding of domestic roles that is most reflective of Scripture is an understanding that is drawn from a combining of all three passages. Even if someone insists upon one of the household codes carrying the most weight and being the standard by which conclusions are judged, as has already been noted, the choice would have to be Ephesians, the lengthiest and most extensive of the three. Of course, to the dismay of anyone wishing to establish marital hierarchy from Colossians or 1 Peter, the Ephesians account establishes quite the opposite; and there is no proper way of handling these other two codes that would change this fact.

The Greek text of the Colossians code contains possessive language that limits its focus to the husband-wife relationship.

As with the Ephesians code, then, whatever is being said is not to be extended into general male-female relationships in the community or the church. The issue is husband-wife dynamics and nothing more. There are a few details added to the Ephesians code by this passage, but scholars differ as to whether these details are of any significance. The wife's submission is described as being "as is fitting in the Lord" (3:18) which could be synonymous with "as to the Lord" (Ephesians) but could also be offering a restriction against having to allow any abuse by her husband. The husband is not only told to love his wife but is warned against any harsh treatment of her (3:19). It is possible that these types of additional stipulations were inserted in order to address specific wrongdoing that was prevalent among the Colossians.

The Household Code of 1 Peter

Peter attached an unusual section to his household code, a section addressing the responsibility of citizens to submit to civil authorities (2:13–17). This is undoubtedly a reflection of the state of the church when his letter was written. Generally, the later a New Testament document was authored, the worse was the persecution being experienced by believers. Peter's letters are two of the latest writings of Scripture, and not surprisingly the first is all about suffering for the cause of Jesus Christ. As societal and governmental scrutiny of Christianity increased throughout the Roman Empire, it became extremely important for Christians to avoid all unnecessary suspicion and offense. Not only were their lives in jeopardy, but their ability to spread the gospel was also at stake. Attaching this unusual section to his household code served two purposes: it reminded believers of the need to be perceived as compliant citizens, and it provided an official description of Christianity that emphasized civilian cooperation.

So, the code that appears in 1 Peter 2:18–3:7 is prefaced with a special section (2:13–17) that is not normally a part of these codes, but it is incorporated into the whole of Peter's presentation in a very intentional way. He uses the word "submit" ("hupotasso") of citizens (2:13), and then he uses the same word of slaves (2:18); next, he describes the ultimate example of submission that Jesus demonstrated (2:21–25); and finally, he ties his comments to wives and husbands into the rest of the code by using the word "likewise" ("homoios") for each group (3:1,7). In chain-like fashion, each section is deliberately linked to the other sections.

The word for "submit" here (2:13,18) is identical to the word used in Ephesians 5:21 for what is required of all believers toward each other. Citizens are to submit; slaves are to submit; Jesus exemplified submissiveness; and wives and husbands are to function "likewise." Peter, like Paul in the Ephesians code, writes a passage that is all about submission. Regardless of the category into which someone falls and regardless of the various twists that submission may take according to someone's station in life, everyone Peter addresses is being included in a code that is all about submission.

The progression of Peter's presentation is interesting. He begins with submission to government officials which was an especially challenging assignment for the Christians of his day. Next, he moves to an even more difficult application of submission, slave to master, emphasizing the worst case scenario of a harsh master. Then, lest any believers think that the apostle is asking too much, he recalls the supreme display of submission exhibited by their Savior. Once his presentation reaches this obvious climax, Peter connects what he asks of wives and husbands with what was lived by Jesus through the use of the word "likewise." Any husband who objects to the idea of mutual submission within marriage because the word "submit" is not in his section must be silenced by the fact that "submit" does not appear in Jesus' section. Nonetheless, the description of Jesus is as much about submission as are the descriptions of citizens and of slaves. In fact, it is as much about submission as it can be. *"Likewise,"* the description of the husband is all about submission, with or without the word "submit" appearing in the text.

Obviously, "submit" is not synonymous with "obey." Early Christians were to have a submissive spirit toward civil authorities though they were not always able to obey their dictates. The version of submission that is required of parents and of masters in the Ephesians code certainly doesn't involve obedience. And, of course, Jesus is not depicted by Paul's code or by Peter's code as obeying the people He came to earth to redeem. Submission involves respecting and regarding others above oneself and bending in thoughtfulness toward others, regardless of one's own rank or rights. With the mutual submission that Paul and Peter build into their treatment of marriage by virtue of the very structure of their household codes, this respecting, regarding, and bending is clearly to be done by both husbands and wives.

There is an interesting difference between Paul's and Peter's codes. Whether Paul's treatment is lengthy as in Ephesians or brief as in Colossians, he addresses six categories of people. He includes the three that are commonly included in secular versions of these codes: wives, children, and slaves. In a distinctly Christian fashion, he also inserts their counterparts: husbands, parents, and masters. Peter, however, did not reverse his words to citizens and slaves by including comments to government officials and slave owners. The wisdom of this is obvious. The atmosphere of his day was so tense that any allegation against Christianity was capable of unleashing extreme persecution in an instant. Probably nothing could have invited more animosity on the part of the wealthy, powerful aristocracy than viewing Christianity as a religion that brought correction to the institution of government or the institution of slavery. Consequently, nothing is said about the proper treatment of citizens or slaves; the focus is upon their obligation to be submissive.

There is one relationship that Peter does handle in both directions, however, and that is marriage. He follows his lengthy treatment of wives with a brief but extremely challenging address to husbands. How crucial it must have been to this apostle to make right *both* sides of this extremely important relationship.

In looking at what Peter says to wives, it must be pointed out that he, like Paul, uses possessive wording in referring to both the woman and the man which reveals that his focus is definitely upon wives and husbands, not upon men and women in general. He also reveals his primary reason for mentioning the submission of wives (3:1–2). This alone could explain why the word "submit" appears in this section and not in the husband's section. As with the citizen and slave sections, what concerns Peter most is the perception that sinners have of the gospel as they observe believers' lives. Evidently wives were converting to Christianity without their husbands doing so. In a culture in which the wife was expected to follow the religion of her husband,[18] this could invite considerable misunderstanding and opposition. Because there is to be no needless interference with the advancement of the gospel, wives are told to be conscious of how they present themselves to their husbands. The secret to evangelizing their husbands was not to be found in their words, which would probably be ignored or mocked or resisted; it was to be found in allowing salvation to make their spirits amenable (3:1–2) and attractive (3:3–4).

Quite often the man who uses this passage to relegate his wife to a position of subservience is the very same man who expects his wife to make herself as good-looking as possible for him. If the first half of the passage is given a simplistic, superficial reading, however, the second half must be read in the same way. There is no break in thought, so there can be no change in interpretation. This would mean that wives would be prohibited from enhancing their beauty through the use of braided hair, gold jewelry, or clothing. The Greek text contains no descriptive adjective to qualify the word "clothing" (NIV inserts "fine"), so they would not be able to improve their appearance through the use of any type of clothing.

Such restrictive narrowness was certainly not Peter's intent. He was not trying to subordinate or strip the wife. He was, instead, speaking to the issues of his day, and he must be understood accordingly. Women were being encouraged by secular society to embrace an early version of feminism which was characterized by extreme disregard for men. They were also being encouraged toward bizarre fashion statements which were marked by extravagant investments of time and money. Peter is asking a wife to rise above the world's infatuation with independence and externals and be willing to relate to her husband in a way that reflects her Savior's Spirit and seeks her husband's good.

Similarly, in his words to husbands (3:7), Peter asks them to replace the world's definitions and approaches with some very different definitions and approaches. This is exactly what he asks of citizens and of slaves in the earlier sections, so a consistency is definitely threading through the passage. Being a considerate, respectful husband was simply not the Roman idea of being a husband. If *some* wives had adopted a flaunting of feminism or fashion, basically *all* husbands had adopted a chauvinistic, machismo understanding of manhood. Peter is asking for more of an "about face" by husbands than he is asking for by wives because their wrongdoing was far more culturally and personally entrenched.

He is asking for the husband to be submissive to the wife, to put her before himself by showing her consideration and respect. Peter offers two reasons for his request: the wife's weaker state and the wife's equal spiritual standing. Perhaps the meaning of "weaker partner" or "weaker vessel" cannot be determined with absolute certainty because Peter seems to be coining his own unique expression. Certain possibilities can be eliminated, however. According to the passage, it has nothing to do with spiritual deficiency. The only spiritual standing that a husband has, his wife has as well (3:7). According to the rest of Scripture, there is also no basis for concluding that women are in any way deficient intellectually. What *is* oftentimes recorded by the Bible, however, is the woman's societal disadvantage. From a cultural or legal perspective, she is frequently without honor. This understanding would fit the text in that husbands are being told to honor their wives. It may be that physical weakness is in view as well. Certainly part of the reason men are able to take advantage of women has to do with physical strength. Whichever of these two weaknesses Peter has in view, societal or physical, the husband's right reaction is the focus of attention.

Couched in this code is one other line that requires clarification. Returning to Peter's words to wives, verses 5–6 include a curious statement about Sarah obeying Abraham and calling him her "master" or "lord." Evidently after making the point of wives submitting, which every category of person in the code is being told to do, Peter gives an example of a wife doing so. Some scholars say that he offers the most extreme example possible because, after all, he is asking this submission of women whose husbands are still unconverted. His reference to following Sarah's lead "without fear" (3:6) acknowledges that he is asking a hard thing. Other scholars say that submission is expressed differently from culture to culture and that Peter is simply citing an expression that was culturally appropriate for Sarah. Whatever the case may be, *the universal requirement is submission*. A specific example of submission is then found in Sarah's life.

It is difficult to locate the occasion that Sarah obeyed Abraham. He told her to identify herself to the Egyptians as being his sister which she may have done (Genesis 12:10–20), but this does not seem to be a commendable maneuver on Abraham's part. The only other time Abraham is recorded as telling Sarah to do something, it was to do whatever she wanted to do with her maidservant Hagar (Genesis 16:6). Whatever occasion is being cited by Peter, there are *two* occasions when Abraham obeyed Sarah, one of which was actually ordered by God (Genesis 16:1–2; 21:8–12). If a modern wife is held to obeying her husband on the basis of this Old Testament couple, then a modern husband would have to be held to obeying his wife on the same basis.

Sarah referred to Abraham as her "master" or "lord" in Genesis 18:12. The word that she used was not an expression of servitude, though. It was a common designation of respect such as the English word "sir" and, as some translations indicate in the margin, was a synonym for the word "husband." Somewhat humorous is the fact that Sarah used this expression while she was laughing and muttering to herself, so the image is certainly not one of a wife bowing at her husband's feet with lofty titles flowing from her lips.

If these two references to Old Testament incidents are not fully understood, they are not the only such references found in the New Testament. They do not have to be fully understood, however, because they serve as examples or illustrations rather than as commands. The point is that Sarah was submissive toward Abraham, and Christian wives are to be submissive toward their husbands. This is the command. The fleshing out of the command may indeed differ from culture to culture and even from situation to situation. Every Christian that Peter addresses in his code is to exemplify a submissive spirit, but the details of doing so are frequently culturally and situationally determined.

Additional Guidelines

Other New Testament passages address domestic roles without following the structure of a household code, such as 1 Timothy 5:1–6:2 and Titus 2:1–10. Overall, the instructions found in these portions of Scripture raise no questions regarding women with the possible exception of a few statements.

The 1 Timothy 5 passage opens with instructions about the proper view and treatment of elderly men (5:1) and elderly women (5:2). The word that is used for both of these categories, "presbuteros," is the same word that is translated "elder" or "presbyter" in many locations throughout the New Testament, indicating a specific position of leadership. It is in a masculine form in verse 1 and in a feminine form in verse 2, but it is the same word that is used in such passages as Acts 14:23; Titus 1:5; James 5:14; and 1 Peter 5:1–3. The word is also used throughout the Gospels of the ruling elders of Judaism, again, a clearly recognized level of leadership. The word "presbuteros" can also mean "older" or "elderly," although in New Testament usage this meaning is extremely rare. If the 1 Timothy 5:1–2 reference is to local church leaders, then it is a clear indication of those leaders being both male and female. It seems likely that Paul would maintain one meaning of a term throughout a portion of material, and 1 Timothy 5:17–20 is usually understood to be referring to local spiritual leaders.

1 Timothy 5:14 is sometimes used to lock women into the role of wife-mother, even though such a restrictive view would stand in opposition to other biblical teachings. This faulty interpretation is easily corrected by giving attention to the whole of what Paul is saying. If the best or the only rightful place for a woman were in the home, then older widows would be encouraged to seek remarriage. Instead, provision is made for them to remain as widows and to give themselves to ministry (5:9–10). Paul is simply saying that a younger widow is unlikely to stay with this type of commitment (5:11); so rather than inviting her to make and then abuse or break a pledge to God, it is better to urge her toward replacing her husband and rebuilding a domestic future (5:12–14). (She evidently differs from the singles described in 1 Corinthians 7 in that she has already tasted of marriage.) In this instance, *why* Paul is saying what he is saying is specifically stipulated and must be allowed to qualify his words. This passage is all about widows; it is not all about women. (It should be noted that the Greek text specifies "younger widows" in 5:11. Though 5:14 only says "younger," it is clearly referring back to the subject of 5:11–13 in an abbreviated fashion. Thus, KJV wrongly inserts "women" into 5:14.)

An interesting word is used in the 1 Timothy 5:14 statement. Paul refers to a younger widow remarrying and "managing" or "ruling" her house. The Greek verb that he uses ("oikodespoteo") results from combining "oikos" ("house") and "despotes" ("ruler, master, owner"). It is an even stronger word than is used of elders and deacons managing their households in 1 Timothy 3:4–5,12.[19] The noun version of the word ("oikodespotes") is used throughout the Gospels of the lord or master of a house. In light of the fact that this responsibility is being assigned to a widow who remarries, meaning that a husband is very much present in the home, it is difficult to claim that the husband alone is to be the primary decision-maker and highest-ranking leader of the family. Of course, it cannot be said from this passage that the wife is to be the sole occupant of this position; she simply happens to be the focus of the instructions. The husband and wife hold this position jointly.

Titus 2:1–10 gives specific instructions to five groups of people: elder men (2:1–2), elder women (2:3), young women (2:4–5), young men (2:6), and slaves (2:9–10). Evidently because Titus fits the classification of young men, Paul inserts some instructions for him (2:7–8) immediately following his words to the young men. The Greek words used in the opening verses, "presbutes" for the men and "presbutis" for the women, are in the "presbuteros" (1 Timothy 5:1–2) family but are more likely to refer to age rather than to leadership. It is mentioned that the men are to be "sound in faith" and the women are to "teach what is good" perhaps because the "presbuteros" ("elders") are chosen from this pool of people. Some of the qualities required of each group are similar if not identical to those required of the spiritual leadership discussed in 1 Timothy 3.[20]

Of the five groups being addressed, only two are discussed in a relational way: young women in relationship to their husbands (with Paul accurately assuming that most Cretan women married) and slaves in relationship to their masters. These same two groups are the only ones told to be submissive (the word in the Greek text being the same as is used of all believers in Ephesians 5:21, not "obedient" as KJV indicates). The other three groups are not discussed relationally, so, of course, are not instructed regarding submissiveness. It is noteworthy that only the two groups being handled in this relational way are given a purpose statement. Women are to relate to their husbands in certain "proper" ways "*so that* no one will malign the word of God" (2:5), and slaves are to relate to their masters in certain "proper" ways "*so that* in every way they will make the teaching about God our Savior attractive" (2:10).

Hopefully, no one would use this passage to advocate human subservience via slavery; likewise, it should not be used to advocate human subservience via marriage. Paul is advocating neither. As in the 1 Timothy 5:14 passage, he specifies *why* he says what he says, and this explanation must be given its rightful voice. What is clearly in focus is the reputation of the gospel. The conduct of believers in the arena of daily living is determining the community's perception of Christianity. In an effort to make that perception as positive as possible, young wives and slaves are to be particularly cautious lest they be seen as alarmingly disrespectful and unruly.

Why just young wives and slaves? Of the five groups featured in this portion of material, these two were probably the most likely to be overly eager and harmfully premature in exercising their new-found liberties in Christ. It is also possible that Titus was having the most difficulty with these two groups. Their sections are certainly the lengthiest of the passage. Some of the details that Paul mentions probably reflect specific weaknesses that they were exhibiting. There is no reason to conclude from Titus 2:4–5 that all young women are to limit themselves to wife-mother roles. The only thing Paul says to young men is to be self-controlled (2:6), and this is never interpreted as being their only or their primary function in life.

The New Testament, if read as a whole, offers a liberating, equalizing definition of Christian marriage. It is true that this definition must not be advanced in the midst of a culture that opposes it without exercising extreme caution. Enjoying the personal benefits of the gospel must never threaten the spread of the gospel to others. But this consideration for evangelism does not in any way negate the fact that the New Testament presents marriage as being characterized by absolute equality and mutual submission. This high standard is not being borrowed from the trends of the world, nor is it a result of bending to the demands of the world. This high standard is 2000 years old. It was introduced by Jesus and was adopted and advanced by His apostles. Surely it is time that it be lived for all the world to see.

11

The New Testament View of Personhood

When Jesus began His ministry He made a declaration that told the world what to expect: "The Spirit of the Lord is on me, because he has anointed me to preach good news to the poor. He has sent me to proclaim freedom for the prisoners and recovery of sight for the blind, to release the oppressed, to proclaim the year of the Lord's favor" (Luke 4:18–19). When the Spirit was outpoured and the church was thereby launched into its earthly mission, Peter made a declaration that also told the world what to expect: "'In the last days,' God says, 'I will pour out my Spirit on all people. Your sons and daughters will prophesy, your young men will see visions, your old men will dream dreams. Even on my servants, both men and women, I will pour out my Spirit'" (Acts 2:17–18). Both announcements made particular mention of second-class people. Jesus would eliminate their stigma, the Spirit would engage them into service, and because of these two acts of God they would be second-class no more.

There is a third inaugural declaration found in Scripture that is very much like the first two. It is written by Paul, perhaps the most influential minister to have ever lived, and it is found in what is thought to be his first letter. His apostleship and his message were being called into question, and the gospel itself was being threatened with a contamination that was capable of destroying it. But Paul would continue to be used by God to push the true, full gospel beyond its origins to the very ends of the earth, and he took this occasion to tell *the church* what to expect:

> You are all sons of God through faith in Christ Jesus, for all of you who were baptized into Christ have clothed yourselves with Christ. There is neither Jew nor Greek, slave nor free, male nor female, for you are all one in Christ Jesus. If you belong to Christ, then you are Abraham's seed, and heirs according to the promise. (Galatians 3:26–29)

This is sometimes called the Magna Carta or the Emancipation Proclamation of the New Testament church. Like Jesus and Peter, Paul makes obvious reference to lowly categories of people. Whatever discrimination or oppression they have experienced because of their classification, the gospel is meant to usher them into a community of believers that will treat them as equals.

The Declaration's Roots

Jesus and Peter quoted from Old Testament material in wording their declarations. Paul, too, anchored his announcement in some material that was very familiar to his audience. The prayer that Jewish men recited three times daily gave praise to God for not creating them a Gentile, a slave, or a woman. Similar expressions of thanksgiving were well known in the Gentile world, dating back to ancient philosophers.[1] Even though the designations varied from one version to the next, slaves and women were common entries. There is to be no such spirit of superiority within Christianity. Instead, the focus is to be upon the sameness that results from all being baptized into Christ and all being clothed with Christ (3:27).

Jewish Christians were trying to impose their old elitist ways upon the Galatian Christians. The superiority that enticed a free, male, Jew to place himself above others also tempted him to think that his religious observances could be added to Jesus' work on the cross and, indeed, *should* be added. Consequently, there was much at stake in Paul's declaration. Either the gospel is enough to equalize all people, or it is no gospel at all. This truth was so valued by the Early Church that many scholars believe Paul was actually quoting a confession that was commonly recited at their water baptism ceremonies.

Not only is Paul negating the thanksgiving prayer and perhaps reflecting a baptismal formula, he is making use of some familiar sermon material. The similarity between Galatians 3:28 and Peter's Acts 2 message is not coincidental. A new age began on the Day of Pentecost. Previously, God's Spirit had been poured out upon a select few. Under the new covenant, however, the empowering of God is available to all believers (Acts 2:17). Peter spoke not only of all people, which includes Jews and Gentiles, but specifically of sons and daughters, young and old, and even male and female servants/slaves

(Acts 2:17–18). This disregarding of all human barriers is the mark of God's Spirit and is, therefore, to be the mark of God's people.

The Declaration's Scope

Those who do not wish to see everyone in the church given equal treatment, explain away Galatians 3:28 as referring only to the universal availability of salvation or to a believer's spiritual standing with God. Thus, one of the most uniquely Christian and powerfully life-changing statements in all of Scripture is relegated to a realm of theological abstraction that is denied any practical application. This would mean that everyone can enter the church and be in right standing with God, but some are to continue to receive, even from fellow Christians, the same discriminatory, oppressive treatment that has always accompanied their second-class status. What an obvious misinterpretation and misrepresentation of God's Word.

First, Paul is not dealing with the fact that salvation is equally accessible to everyone. If this was a question or an issue in the Early Church, it was settled with Peter's ministry to the Gentiles as recorded in Acts 10 & 11 and summarized in Acts 11:18, before Paul's ministry even began. What Paul is addressing is the problem that *did* plague the first-century church—*after salvation* what is a person's status? Are Gentile Christians as fully Christian or as "first class" Christian as Jewish Christians? If not, congregations would struggle with inequality and disunity. It is obvious that the Galatians were experiencing these very struggles because Paul's correction emphasizes sameness/equality (3:26–27) and oneness/unity (3:28). Yes, he is dealing with salvation, but he is dealing with it as it impacts relationships within the body of believers.

Second, Paul is not focusing exclusively upon a Christian's spiritual standing with God. The designations of ethnicity, class, and gender that he specifies (3:28) are earthly, not heavenly. They originate and exist in the social realm, not in the spiritual realm. Specifically because they do not affect someone's relationship with God, they are not to affect relationships with others. To limit Paul's words to a purely theological interpretation to the exclusion of any practical application would be to strip them of their full intent. The Galatians were suffering from a two-fold problem. They *believed* the wrong thing about a

Gentile's spiritual standing; consequently, they *behaved* the wrong way toward that Gentile. Paul is correcting both errors, the theological and the practical. He is insisting that spiritual truth must affect everyday conduct. He is insisting that what is true about a person's vertical relationship with God must affect his or her horizontal relationships with others.

The Declaration's Consistency

The Apostle Paul is not a "theory without practice" type of theologian, in fact, a far cry from it. With him there must be consistency and follow-through; a spiritual truth always has application in the practical arenas of life. This would be particularly true of such relational issues as he is addressing in this passage. He insisted upon theology dictating practice when he reprimanded Peter for avoiding fellowship with Gentile Christians (Galatians 2:11–16). In fact, he called this type of inconsistency hypocrisy (2:13) because Peter's beliefs and actions were not in agreement (2:14). He insisted upon theology dictating practice when he told Philemon to free his slave Onesimus (Philemon 15–17) and when he put husbands and wives on equal footing within marriage (1 Corinthians 7).

How can a Christian claim that his relationship with someone of a different ethnicity or class or gender is equal in principle but hierarchical in practice? How can he claim *spiritual* sameness (3:26–27) and *spiritual* oneness (3:28) while exercising inequality and disunity *socially*? How can he denounce ethnic bigotry or class discrimination or gender bias spiritually but engage in these things behaviorally? No, there is absolutely no possibility of such inconsistency and contradiction reflecting a proper interpretation of Galatians 3:28.

Tragically, however, this type of sly, slippery theology defended the institution of human slavery for many centuries. It may be difficult to imagine such injustice being advocated from church pulpits; but, indeed, rather than being indicted as blatant disobedience of Scripture, it was, instead, elevated to noble obedience. Even long after the abolishment of this wrongdoing, leftover ethnic and class prejudice can still be found in the church. Rather than "spiritualize away" the forceful teaching of Galatians 3:28,[2] Christians must hear their Savior's words of warning: "You have a fine way of setting aside the commands of God in order to observe your own traditions!"

(Mark 7:8) A Jew and a Gentile, a white person and a black person, a high-class individual and a low-class individual must have equal access to *all* of the privileges and responsibilities of local church life; otherwise, the congregation or denomination is following its own traditions rather than the commands of God.

There is at least one other classification that must have no bearing on whether a person is invited to enjoy the opportunities and obligations of the church. The Galatians 3:28 proclamation lists women alongside slaves and Gentiles. In so doing, Paul is denouncing all discrimination against them as well, be it spiritual or social or any other type. Just as it is wrong to shut doors of fellowship or leadership in the faces of people because of ethnicity or class status, it is just as wrong to do so on the basis of gender. Very likely, this call to equality and unity applies to every social designation that a culture could devise or recognize, but there can be no question about its application to gender because the text specifies it. Unless Christians are ready to deny ministerial opportunities to the other two groups listed in Galatians 3:28, no consistent interpretation of this passage allows them to deny access to women.

The Declaration's Theology

There is a call being heard throughout the evangelical community that beckons believers to move toward biblically-based sexual equality and gender unity, but it is oftentimes met with a most unfair accusation. Proponents are said to be bowing to the values and demands of contemporary society. This was not what Paul was doing, though, when he penned the words, "There is neither Jew nor Greek, slave nor free, male nor female." He based the equality and unity that he commanded in Galatians 3:28 upon sound theology, in fact, upon *salvation* theology.

In designating Gentiles, slaves, and women as "sons" (3:26) and "heirs" (3:29), Paul is using the language of ancient culture to communicate the gospel's reversal of ancient culture. Within Israel, the free, male, Jew was thought to be the true son of God. There was provision for others to be a part of God's people, but they were looked upon as being included by attachment or by extension rather than by birthright. Even in the natural realm, it was typically the son who was the heir to his family's inheritance, not an outsider or a slave or a daughter. Paul brackets the Galatians 3:28 declaration with son-heir imagery on either side (3:26,29) because he wants to make it very clear that the three categories of people who were thought to be second-class because of their non-son, non-heir status, instead, enjoy the highest possible standing within the new covenant. Their relationship to God (son) is no different from anyone else's, and their privileges in God (heir) are no different from anyone else's.

Next he explains how this can be. All believers have "son status" and "heir status" because all "were baptized into Christ" and all "have clothed yourselves with Christ" (3:27). Here Paul is evidently using a familiar illustration from each world, Jewish and Gentile. Jews knew that circumcision, obviously not available to everyone, was nonetheless the old covenant's outward sign of entering into relationship with God. The new covenant replaces circumcision with an outward sign that is available to everyone, water baptism. Gentiles of the first century were well aware of the toga, the special garment that was given by a father to a son who came of age in order to mark his high standing as a Roman citizen.[3] This status symbol, as well, was unavailable to many; however, *every* believer is able to mark his new citizenship by being clothed with Christ.

Critics of equality complain that Galatians 3:28 says, "you are all *one*" rather than "you are all *equal*." However, the Greek word that is translated "one" ("heis") can mean "one and the same" as much as it can mean "one." If this meaning is Paul's intent, then the ideas of equality and unity are being combined into one very strong expression. Nevertheless, Paul establishes sameness quite solidly in the opening verses of this section (3:26–27), and there is no stronger version of equality than sameness.

Critics of equality for women, in particular, complain that Paul does not campaign for women's equal standing with men as he campaigns for Gentiles' equal standing with Jews; therefore, they conclude that Gentiles and Jews have a different type or degree of equality than do men and women. It is true that Paul's writings are saturated with the Jew-Gentile issue. The presence of this topic far exceeds the presence of material relating to male-female concerns. To conclude from this, however, that male-female equality is to be less than or different from Jew-Gentile equality is faulty thinking.

First, it is difficult to conceive of different types or degrees of equality, especially since it is clear that this Galatians passage (3:26–29) is addressing not just "spiritual standing" but also believer-to-believer attitudes and behaviors that are to result from everyone's spiritual standing being the same. Second, if this line of logic is applied to the third classification that Paul mentions in Galatians 3:28, slave versus free, the results would be alarming. His writings contain even less about liberating and equalizing slaves than women. Does this lack of coverage and emphasis mean that within a body of believers low-class and high-class people are to be put on uneven footing and treated differently from each other? No, of course not, and neither can such a conclusion be drawn regarding men and women.

The Jew-Gentile issue of the first century was different from the male-female and slave-free issues in two ways. First, it was threatening the theology of the gospel; whereas, the other two were not. Jewish Christians were pressing for a Jewish version of the gospel that left room for their old legalistic ways to help attain salvation. This compromised such a core tenet of the gospel, salvation by grace through faith, that it could not be tolerated. Paul had to take every opportunity to address and refute all tendencies in this direction or the gospel would soon be extinct. Of course, no one was suggesting that Christians had to become male or free to be fully right with God, so these two issues were not posing the doctrinal threat that the Jew-Gentile issue was posing.[4]

Second, though Christians were to be careful to avoid needlessly offending all non-Christians, including Jews, the explosive issues of Paul's day had to do with maintaining social and economic stability. The Roman Empire had tolerated and/or absorbed many religions and ethnic groups. A new religion, in and of itself, was not perceived as a problem, certainly not a religion that promoted the compatibility of ethnic groups. A new religion, however, that might upset the comfortable, traditional lifestyle of the elite was very much a problem, a problem that could invite the wrath of the entire empire. It was imperative that the liberating and equalizing of women and slaves be pursued slowly and cautiously.

It is obvious that a doctrinal threat such as the Jew-Gentile issue had to be handled aggressively; whereas, a cultural threat such as the male-female or slave-free issue had to be handled in just the opposite way, rather gingerly. There could be places in the world still today where this differentiation between the nature of issues would cause matters of equality to be handled differently from each other. If, however, a society is ready to be challenged to dispense with class or gender discrimination, the church should not sit silent or, worse yet, oppose the movement and represent God as desiring the discrimination. It is not the newspaper but the Bible that is being quoted when the words go forth, "There is neither Jew nor Greek, slave nor free, male nor female, for you are all one in Christ Jesus."

If there is any doubt as to how far Paul meant for the issues of equality and unity to be taken, the Jew-Gentile issue should be used as the standard. Upon reading everything he wrote on the matter, any student of Scripture would have to conclude that Jew-Gentile sameness and oneness were to be as total and as practical in their application as possible. There were to be no subtle exceptions; the goal was absolute, unequivocal evenness and togetherness within the body of believers. Unless the spread of the gospel would be threatened by this same treatment of class and gender distinctions, then this same treatment is the biblical treatment for these two concerns as well.

The Declaration's Limitations

First, the purpose of the Galatians 3:28 declaration is not the abolishing of a person's characteristics or classifications. Actually, if this were the case there would be little wonder over the liberating, equalizing, and unifying that occurs because everyone would be perfectly identical. Distinctions will not cease to exist. A Christian will retain racial/ethnic identity, may retain class standing, and will certainly retain gender identity. In particular, gender results from the handiwork of God in creation and is part of what He called "very good." The magnificence of what can happen in the community of the redeemed is that even though individual distinctions remain, they have no influence upon the fellowship or function of believers.

The God of creativity and variety never meant for difference to result in divisiveness and discrimination. These negative reactions to diversity are not reflections of God's nature or plan but are products of human sinfulness. Once this sinfulness is exchanged for godliness, believers are free to relate to each other quite differently than they did before. Physical and societal differences, while present, are transcended and are, consequently, not the basis for determining someone's value or role.[5] Everyone has equal status and equal opportunity to access the privileges and responsibilities available within the church. Participation and placement are not decided by ethnicity or class or gender but by the gifts and callings of God. Among the redeemed, no one classification of people has sole claim to any aspect of ministry.

There is no need to think that gender equality somehow undermines or reverses the principles of creation. It is gender that was instituted at creation, not gender hierarchy. It is marriage that was instituted by God, not marriage hierarchy. God is not reversing creation with redemption; He is marvelously restoring men and women and husbands and wives to His original intent for them, not only personally but also relationally. He is restoring in redemption the equality and unity that were present at creation, before sin and its effects. Sexuality should never be denied or even discounted because it is a work of God that is meant to have its rightful place. However, sexual inequality can be exchanged for sexual equality, and sexual disharmony can be exchanged for sexual harmony without in any way diminishing sexuality.

Second, the purpose of the Galatians 3:28 declaration is not to thrust Christians into the launching of gender revolutions throughout society. Efforts to equalize and unify men and women should begin within the community of believers. Among the redeemed, a new kingdom has burst upon the scene. Its full force and absolute reign may await eternity, but even today its citizens enjoy freedom from the dominion of sin in their personal lives and in their relationships with others. Christians should be engaging in kingdom living which is characterized by liberty, equality, and unity of all believers; and they should be displaying this kingdom living for the world see.

The Declaration's Importance

As will be shown in subsequent chapters, the New Testament passages regarding women that are typically given the most attention are not meant to be used in the way they are frequently used, causing the permanent, universal restriction of all women. Each of these passages has something to say as does every passage of Scripture. But if someone is looking for what scholars call "normative" material on the topic of women, texts that prescribe a standard for all belief and practice, the place to look is not a text that clearly addresses unique, local situations. To turn instructions that target exceptional circumstances into normative passages produces conclusions about women that contradict all of the rest of Scripture.

If someone is looking for a normative passage on the Jew-Gentile issue or the slavery issue, Galatians 3:28 would be the likely choice. It is just as much the best choice for the gender issue. Two or three other passages in the New Testament do deal with the "what is" of first-century reality, but Galatians 3:28 deals with the "what ought to be" challenge of the kingdom of God. Will the church of the twenty-first century promote the problems of the first century or the principles of the kingdom? It is not coincidence that Galatians 3:28 aligns perfectly with one other normative passage, the founding sermon of the New Testament church as recorded in Acts 2. God's Spirit is ready to empower for service sons and daughters, male slaves and female slaves because "there is neither slave nor free, male nor female...you are all one in Christ." Is the church ready to embrace the service of all of those God's Spirit is empowering?

12

Questions Regarding
First Corinthians 11

One of the challenges to understanding certain New Testament passages is that of reconstructing the original setting. If a portion of material was penned by an apostle in direct response to questions or problems being experienced by a local congregation, then, obviously, it would be helpful to know something about the local situation. Otherwise, having an answer without knowing the question or having a solution without knowing the problem could result in a partial or faulty understanding of what was actually being said. Similarly, expecting a brief apostolic comment or correction to serve as the full biblical treatment of an issue fails to recognize that omissions and emphases are present in the brief statement which must be taken into consideration before true conclusions can be drawn.

Of course, a reliable reconstruction of the historical, cultural, and theological contexts of the first century is sometimes difficult because various details have been lost with the passing of centuries of time. This results in the need to acknowledge that certain passages of Scripture perplex the modern reader. Surely it is better to admit such difficulty than to claim complete and certain understanding when, in fact, neither is present. Many scholars concede that 1 Corinthians 11:3–16 is a passage that contains some puzzling elements. Fortunately, however, enough can be understood about these verses to see that they are supportive of women rather than in any way restrictive of them.

Interpreting the Passage According to its Context

The Apostle Paul wrote this letter to a church that he had the privilege of establishing during his second missionary trip (Acts 18:1–17; 1 Corinthians 4:15). The writing of it was prompted by his learning about disunity (1:11–12) and wrongdoing (5:1–3) among the members, by his desire to clarify some aspects of an earlier letter that had been misunderstood (5:9–13), and by his desire to respond to specific inquiries that they had made of him (7:1). The bulk of its contents is directly related to one of these reasons for writing the letter and is best understood if this is kept in mind.

Not only does Paul appeal to the Corinthian Christians to start behaving properly because of their need to reflect redemption (1:2), but he also admonishes them to do so because of their need to serve the good of others and thereby guard and advance the gospel. Throughout the letter there is a constant call to avoid any behavior that would harm a believer or hinder a sinner. This theme is particularly present in chapters 8–10, the material just preceding the passage in question. It is within these chapters that he writes, "Be careful, however, that the exercise of your freedom does not become a stumbling block to the weak" (8:9); "We put up with anything rather than hinder the gospel of Christ" (9:12); "I have not used any of [my] rights" (9:15); "I have become all things to all men so that by all possible means I might save some" (9:22); "Nobody should seek his own good, but the good of others" (10:24); and "Whatever you do, do it all for the glory of God. Do not cause anyone to stumble, whether Jews, Greeks, or the church of God—even as I try to please everybody in every way. For I am not seeking my own good but the good of many, so that they may be saved. Follow my example, as I follow the example of Christ" (10:31–11:1).

Paul built his entire ministry upon this "self-sacrificing, always-serving-others, always-advancing-the-gospel" principle. He moves from encouraging the Corinthians to follow his example to commending them for doing so (11:2) and correcting them for failing to do so (11:17), a structure that clearly links chapters 8–10 with chapter 11. Whereas chapters 8–10 apply the principle to issues of individual behavior, chapter 11 as well as chapters 12–14 apply the principle to aspects of corporate worship. Still challenging the church to consider the good of others and of the gospel rather than their own good, Paul writes in these chapters such things as, "Your meetings do more harm than good" (11:17); "When you come together to eat, wait for each other" (11:33); "To each one the manifestation of the Spirit is given for the common good" (12:7); "There should be no division in the body, but...its parts should have equal concern for each other" (12:25); "If I...have not love, I am nothing" (13:2); and "Since you are eager to have spiritual gifts, try to excel in gifts that build up the church" (14:12).

Evidently certain Corinthians were exercising their personal liberties in Christ without sufficient regard for others who were being confused or offended by their actions. Perhaps this was particularly problematic because of the wide diversity of cultures that was present in Corinth. This asserting or flaunting of individual rights was causing turmoil within the church and threatening to result in the rejection of the gospel outside the church. To avoid such negative effects, Paul calls these Christians to a level of maturity that would thoughtfully sacrifice personal liberties for the sake of the sensitivities of others.

In 1 Corinthians 11:3–16 Paul includes in this call to self-sacrifice the women who were violating first-century expectations regarding the proper attire of wives. He is not mandating a physical appearance requirement for the worship service that has merit in and of itself and, consequently, should be honored by all women. No one could be more adamantly opposed to any such notion than Paul. If there were any room in Christianity for marking one's eligibility for worship with some physical indicator, then circumcision would certainly be that indicator for all Christian men. After all, circumcision has the advantage of having been assigned by God rather than by culture. However, Paul himself says that in Christ circumcision has no inherent meaning or value (1 Corinthians 7:19). It was to be practiced only as a means of accommodating surrounding sensitivities (Acts 16:1–3), never for its own merit (Galatians 5:2–6). The compliance that Paul requests of these women is not because God demands a certain physical appearance but because their culture demands it.

Headship

Some people do not read beyond verse 3 of 1 Corinthians 11: "The head of every man is Christ, and the head of the woman is man, and the head of Christ is God." They assume that the word "head" means "boss, authority" and offer the verse as solid scriptural support for a God-man-woman chain of command. Anything else that Paul is saying about the worship activities of men and women is thought to be immaterial and ignorable, and they typically pride themselves in their careful and consistent handling of Scripture.

As has been made clear in a preceding chapter of this book, the figurative meaning of "head" in the ancient Greek language was probably "source, origin" rather than "boss, authority." Two features of 1 Corinthians 11 affirm this meaning. First, the components of verse 3 would be out of proper descending order if a "boss, authority" hierarchy were being proposed. The three tiers of man under Christ, woman under man, and Christ under God would need to be arranged, instead, as Christ under God, man under Christ, and woman under man in order to reflect a patriarchal chain of command. However, if the three components are understood according to a "source, origin" perspective, then they appear in the correct order chronologically. First Adam's flesh was formed by Christ the agent of creation, then Eve's flesh was formed from Adam, and later the flesh of the incarnate Christ was formed by God. Of course, there are differences in how Adam, Eve, and Christ each came from their respective "sources," but there are differences between the three couplets no matter how they are understood. Second, references to creation (source, origin) continue throughout the passage (11:8,12); but there are absolutely no references to hierarchical arrangements, no references to someone being over someone else. In fact, the only use of the word "authority" (11:10) does not involve anyone but the woman or wife, according to a proper rendering of the Greek text.

The subjection of God the Son to God the Father, then, is not the focus in 1 Corinthians 11:3. The relationship between these two members of the Godhead is so multidimensional that no one verse of Scripture details every aspect. This passage simply focuses upon the "source, origin" facet; whereas, other passages address the subjection issue. It should come as no surprise that 1 Corinthians 11:3 does not parallel the Father-Son "hierarchy" with the male-female or husband-wife hierarchy because the two arrangements are not parallel. The voluntary subjection of one divine person to another divine person for the purpose of together accomplishing redemption is not the same thing as the involuntary subjugation of half of the human race to the other half as a direct result of sin. The divine arrangement does not infer inequality or inferiority, but the sinful arrangement does indeed carry these negative connotations.

Public Ministry

What is sometimes overlooked with a quick reading of 1 Corinthians 11 is that Paul assumes and affirms the very same public, vocal ministry for women that he acknowledges for men. He is giving instructions regarding proper decorum to two groups of people: men who pray or prophesy (v. 4) and women who pray or prophesy (v. 5). The fact that he asks each group to engage in these spiritual activities in a manner that is culturally appropriate for its gender does not diminish the fact that he is endorsing the equal participation of both groups.

Obviously from this passage, women were praying and prophesying in the Corinthian worship services. Paul's casual reference to their doing so suggests that these activities were common occurrences. To interpret the absence of any correction as being the equivalent of condoning these activities is not, in this instance, entirely an argument from silence. Not only was the apostle perfectly comfortable saturating this letter with corrections, ranging from mild to severe, but this specific section of his letter deals entirely with corrections. It is inconceivable that he would have viewed women's public, vocal participation in church services as being as wrong as it is presented by some today and have said nothing to check it. Further, it is ludicrous to think that he would have painstakingly regulated female activities that he adamantly opposed. To the contrary, it can be safely assumed that this type of spiritual contribution was common enough among the Corinthians for Paul to mention it without any special notation and that it was completely acceptable to him. There is nothing wrong with *what* the women were doing; the concern was over *how* both women and men were doing it.

It goes without saying that praying and prophesying are *vocal* activities. This causes a contradiction between 1 Corinthians 11 and the interpretation that some give to 1 Corinthians 14 and 1 Timothy 2. In order to lessen this problem, those who forbid the ministry of women usually claim that Paul is not referring here to being vocal in *public* or *congregational* meetings but in small home gatherings. However, there is nothing in the text or in the practices of first-century churches to support this conclusion, and there is much to refute it.

Chapters 11–14 clearly form a unit of material dealing with Paul's concerns about the corporate worship setting. He moves from praying and prophesying to the Lord's Supper to the exercising of such spiritual gifts as tongues, interpretation, and prophecy. With these particular practices being addressed, there can be no doubt that he has in view the local church worship service. As early as 1 Corinthians was written, it is certain that all of these services were being held in homes. There was no differentiation between formal, official meetings versus some other type of gathering, nor were there public versus private sessions. There was certainly no semblance of modern programming which schedules special meetings for women or for children; in fact, the text itself seems to indicate that men and women were in the same gathering. The local body of believers simply met together for worship, and, according to their Master, the location and size of the group were insignificant (Matthew 18:20).

It is true that prayer occurs both publicly and privately, but the fact that Paul is regulating both prayer *and prophecy* further verifies that his focus is upon the corporate worship setting. In the first century, prophecy was "to utter divine truth, under the immediate prompting of the Spirit, in the midst of the congregation, for the mutual edifying of those gathered together."[1] It did not exist in private; it was for the benefit of an assembly (1 Corinthians 14:3–4,31). Perhaps Paul identifies these two worship activities because together they embrace the full scope of what occurs in the congregational setting.[2] Through prayer the church speaks to God, and through prophecy God speaks to the church. Because of this, Paul may intend his treatment of these two practices to serve as a treatment of corporate worship as a whole.

Even if this is not the case and Paul is regulating nothing but prayer and prophecy, his inclusion of women who prophesy right alongside men who prophesy is striking in itself. Prophecy is not only vocal and public, it is also an exceedingly authoritative ministry. First, it should be noted that the New Testament identifies the act of prophecy with the office of prophet (1 Corinthians 14:29–32).[3] Second, it should be noted what the New Testament says about prophets. They stand second only to apostles in "rank," above teachers, administrators, and all others (1 Corinthians 12:28). They have been responsible for providing the church's foundation (Ephesians 2:20) through revealing divine mysteries (Ephesians 3:4–5). Their ministry is to result in the instruction and exhortation of the entire church (1 Corinthians 14:3–4,31), which must include the men.

According to 1 Corinthians 11, this position of leadership is equally open to men and women. Both must exercise their gifts in ways that reflect cultural sensitivity; but both may participate in the act of prophecy and in the office of prophet. Regardless of one's view of the role of this spiritual gift today, in the first-century church its availability was unaffected by gender. Even if someone wishes to claim that other ministries have replaced that of prophecy, God's "gender-blind" approach to dispensing first-century ministry gifts should reveal how He desires to dispense similar gifts today.

Head Covering

In 1 Corinthians 11:4–6 Paul expresses his request regarding the proper physical appearance of those praying and prophesying in the corporate worship setting. This is the crux of the entire passage. For men he forbids "kata kephales echon" or literally "having down or upon the head." For women the prohibition is against "akatakalupto te kephale" or "uncovered as to the head." The adjective "akatakalupto" ("uncovered") in verse 5 is more specific and clear in its meaning than the preposition "kata" ("down" or "upon") in verse 4. Translators allow the clear phrase to help interpret the unclear phrase since Paul is obviously stipulating two opposite behaviors. Thus, the NIV reads, "Every man who prays or prophesies with his head covered dishonors his head. And every woman who prays or prophesies with her head uncovered dishonors her head."

Even an accurate translation, though, falls short of conveying Paul's meaning with absolute clarity and certainty. Historical evidence does not support the custom of women at this time and in this location wearing veils over their faces, plus it is difficult to understand how the provision of hair on the head (11:15) could replace a veil on the face. The possibility of the meaning involving a veil is further diminished by the fact that the word "veil" does not appear anywhere in this passage in the Greek text. With the idea of a face-veil put aside, scholars are quite divided about two other possibilities. Many say that Paul is requesting that some type of covering be worn on a woman's head to cover her hair. Others, particularly in light of several direct references to hair throughout the passage, say that hair length and/or style was the covering that must be worn appropriately.

If Paul is referring to a covering over the hair, why does he prohibit it for men and require it for women? Corinth was a city in which Greeks, Romans, and Jews resided. Because it is difficult to trace the use of head coverings among each of these cultures and to isolate any special religious significance that might have been recognized among them, scholars differ somewhat in assigning their findings to a specific culture. There is relative agreement, however, that Paul's stipulations reflected the cultural expectations of the day. It seems that a married woman's hair was regarded as such a display of her feminine beauty that it was reserved for her husband's eyes alone. For her to uncover her hair in public was an act of immodesty and a display of disrespect for her husband. Amongst Jews, it was grounds for divorce. An honorable wife would not wish to shame her husband by appearing to be single or promiscuous, so she would be sure to cover her hair properly.

In addition to the meanings associated with the covering of the head for a woman, there may have been cultural reasons for a man to refrain from covering his head. Greek men typically bared their heads in recognition of deity, so for a Christian man to do otherwise might connote a denial and a dishonoring of Christ.[4] Jewish men covered their heads to indicate guilt and shame under the law, so for a Christian man to do so might show disregard for the redeeming work of Christ in his life.[5]

If, instead, Paul is referring to the covering that is provided by the length or style of hair, why does he prohibit this covering for men and require it for women? Again, possible answers can be found in the cultural practices of the day. There is evidence that a woman could be associated with prostitution, temple or otherwise, if she wore her hair too short or if she left it long and loose. For example, priestesses and prophetesses in various first-century cults who typically doubled as temple prostitutes were frequently pictured with shaved or very short hair. At the same time, others were well known for wildly tossing their long loose hair in a frenzy-like display of worship. Non-temple prostitutes, for which Corinth was equally famous, took similar liberties. These "evening companions" sported shaved hair, short hair, and long, loose hair styles. Of course, any honorable woman would want to avoid the look of a prostitute, but a married woman had additional concerns. Because the hair was considered part of the special physical attractiveness that a wife was to share with her husband, for a married woman to wear it overly short was to deny him this prerogative and to wear it loose was to invite the illegitimate gaze of other men.

On the male side of the hair length/style situation, there is evidence that men who served as priests in certain pagan cults and/or served as prostitutes sometimes engaged in sex reversal. They wore what was recognized as female clothing and let their hair grow long. Lifestyle homosexuality, as well, was sometimes marked by long hair on a man. Obviously, any of these images would be undesirable for a Christian man, especially if he were leading the congregation in prayer or were proclaiming a message from God through prophecy.

Whether proposing an interpretation of hair covering or an interpretation of hair length and style, some scholars also suggest the possibility of different cultures or classes in the Corinthian church clashing over the matter. With Greek, Roman, and Jewish people all present in the city and presumably in the congregation, this may have happened. It was not unusual for high-society people to disregard certain customs that were thought by them to be out of date but were seen as still in force by the rest of the "common" population. If culture or class did cause conflicting views and behaviors, it is possible that Paul is proposing a middle ground that would be tolerable for all parties involved, as was done by the apostles in Acts 15.

The question of whether Paul is regulating hair covering or hair itself (length, style) may never be resolved. Part of the difficulty of determining which he is addressing has to do with the fact that, at least with women, the two departures from the norm usually went together. A woman who cut or styled her hair unconventionally was likely to flaunt what she did by refusing to wear any covering over it. Because of this joining of the two behaviors, which behavior Paul prohibits cannot be settled with absolute confidence. Whatever violation of custom he had in view, it was obviously so scandalous that the woman might as well do the most shameful thing that the culture could imagine, namely, totally cut or shave her hair (11:5–6).

Scholars not only debate the exact meaning of the head covering, they also debate who is to wear it. Is Paul instructing women in general or wives in particular? The Greek word "gune" that is used throughout the passage can mean either "woman" or "wife," just as the word "aner" can mean "man" or "husband." Any time either of these words is found in the New Testament, it must be determined which meaning is intended. Of course, most men of the first century were husbands and most women were wives, so Paul could be addressing both men and husbands in verse 4 and both women and wives in verses 5–6. It is also possible that he moves back and forth between meanings as he progresses through the passage, sometimes emphasizing one almost to the exclusion of the other. This possibility is supported by the fact that it is difficult to achieve a satisfactory rendering of every detail of the passage using "man and woman" exclusively or using "husband and wife" exclusively. He definitely interchanges the literal and figurative meanings for "head" throughout the verses, so he may be doing the same thing with "aner" and "gune."

This "gender versus marital status" debate can make a significant difference in drawing certain conclusions from 1 Corinthians 11. For example, some argue that verse 3 proves that men are "over" women. Of course, the definition of "head" that they impose upon the verse is that of "rulership, leadership" which has been shown to be an unlikely meaning for the word in first-century Greek. In line with the more likely meaning of "source, origin," Paul may be referring in this verse to Eve coming from Adam which would align with verses 8 and 12. This being the case, he could be saying that "woman" as a gender comes from "man" as a gender. It is also possible, still using the definition of "source, origin" for "head" in verse 3, that Paul is saying something about marriage rather than about gender. Unlike Adam, who was created with gender but without marital status, Eve was created with both. She was immediately upon creation a woman and a wife. If Paul's use of "head" in the middle phrase of verse 3 assumes a focus upon marriage rather than upon gender, this would align with his only other figurative use of "head" (other than references to Christ) which is confined to the marriage relationship (Ephesians 5:21–31). This being the case, he would be saying in verse 3 that the husband serves as the wife's source.

The "*husband* (not man) being the head of the *wife* (not woman)" interpretation for verse 3 is supported by what the rest of 1 Corinthians 11 says. According to verse 5, this whole issue of head covering is receiving attention in order to avoid dishonoring her head. Although there may be a way in which "head" here refers to the personhood of the woman herself, it primarily refers to the head that was introduced for her in verse 3. If this were not the case, verse 3 would serve no obvious purpose in the passage. First-century women who wore their hair inappropriately did not shame all men; a *wife* who wore her hair inappropriately shamed *her husband*. It was primarily a *married* woman who was culturally forbidden from doing the things with her hair that are forbidden in this passage because her behavior had to reflect a proper regard for her husband's rights and honor. Perhaps women in general followed the customs of married women, but to do otherwise was particularly disgraceful for the married woman.

The "husband being the head of the wife" interpretation for verse 3 is also supported by Paul's use of headship in Ephesians 5:21–31. This passage is clearly focusing upon the marriage relationship and is saying that the *husband* is the head of the *wife*, not that all men are head of all women. Claiming that every man is the head of every woman would mean that the care and love described in Ephesians 5 would have to be assigned to every male-female relationship. If it is not plausible to make all men *fully* head of all women, "fully" meaning according to the Ephesians 5 description, then there is no scriptural basis for making them slightly or partially head.

Is it possible that Paul is mixing references to men (gender) with references to wives (marital status)? Is it possible that "aner" in verse 4 means "man" and "gune" in verses 5–6 means "wife"? The answer to these questions is "yes." Paul oftentimes constructs parallels that are not entirely parallel, with verse 12 being an example. Since the culture dictated things about head covering to *men* in general and dictated other things primarily to *wives* in particular, then one would only expect Paul to follow the same pattern in this passage. Even though most women were wives and even though women may have adopted the practices of wives, any universal principles that are drawn from this passage must differentiate between women and wives. Paul is probably not regulating women because they are women; therefore, caution should be taken in drawing gender conclusions from his comments, at least gender conclusions about females. He is simply requiring that wives reflect their marital status in a respectful manner.

Evidently some of the wives in the Corinthian church were exercising their new-found liberties in Christ without considering the misunderstandings that would result. Even though it does not seem to be the primary thrust of the passage, it is possible that some of the men were violating custom as well. Maybe the wives resented the head coverings that identified them as little more than an inferior extension of their husbands. Maybe both groups were disregarding custom in an effort to proclaim the equality and unity that they enjoyed through redemption. Maybe they were allowing the cults which saturated Corinth to act as their worship model and were imitating their free-spirited, anti-social behaviors.

Whatever the scenario may have been, Paul is insisting upon adherence to societal customs that held meaning *in this location* and *at this time* in order to avoid needlessly confusing or offending others, perhaps both inside and outside the church. If head covering is not in practice or does not hold significant meaning in a location today, there is no need to impose it upon Christians in an effort to demonstrate proper respect for marriage, gender, worship, Scripture, or anything else. Paul was not inventing and imposing a practice, nor was he advocating a practice for its own merit. He was asking for sensitivity toward a cultural custom already in existence because of the problems caused by violating it.

This insistence that the cultural aspects of 1 Corinthians 11 be recognized does not mean that the passage is without universal application. It is just as authoritative and meaningful today as it was in the first century. If Corinthian Christians were to present themselves in a manner becoming of their gender and marital status, then all Christians are to do likewise. If the Corinthians were to avoid appearances that were distinctly associated with paganism, promiscuousness, or homosexuality, then all Christians are to do likewise. If these precautions are particularly binding in the worship setting and upon those who engage in ministry activities in the worship setting, then this is still the case today.

Christianity does not abolish a person's gender or marital identity; these are to be respectfully recognized and fulfilled according to Scripture, not dismissed. Christianity does not advocate questionable identification with sinful ways, not in the name of personal liberty or under any other guise. Certainly Christians are to reverence the worship setting and avoid defiling it with cultural improprieties that threaten their harmony and testimony. The proper decorum that accommodates all of these important principles, however, is defined differently from culture to culture. 1 Corinthians 11 is not applied correctly when first-century customs are forced upon the twentieth or twenty-first century. It is not applied correctly when missionaries transfer customs from one culture to another culture. The unchangeable message of this passage is the call for sensitivity, wisdom, and self-sacrifice in deciding one's personal conduct. If a certain practice is laced with significant cultural meaning, then the Christian may have to engage in it or refrain from it, not because it is inherently right or wrong, but because it is perceived by others as being right or wrong. The good of others is to be held above the exercise of personal rights. To do otherwise would not be the *use* of redemption freedom but the *abuse* of it.

Of course, this does not mean that Christians are bound to comply with every whim of people inside and outside the church. Head covering was obviously a serious matter in Corinth. It had social and religious meanings that could not be ignored. It forced its way into the definition of decent character and proper worship, so it was imperative for Christians to comply with this particular cultural expectation. Even more obvious is the fact that a proper view of compliance does not apply to cultural norms that involve sin. This was not the case with head covering; it was a "spiritual neutral," so compliance was possible. Christians must never conform to cultural demands that violate righteousness.

There is nothing in the instructions of 1 Corinthians 11 that subordinates or restricts women or wives. Head covering had to do with honor, not hierarchy. Men and women in Corinth were praying and prophesying; therefore, men and women were to do so in ways that did not violate cultural norms. Even the maintaining of gender and marital distinctions does not in any way suggest that discrimination should result from these distinctions. Perhaps in the world, differences cause disunity and inequality; but if there is any point Paul is making in chapters 11–14 of this book it is that, in the church, differences are to be embraced with unity and equality.

Reflecting Creation

In verses 7–9 of 1 Corinthians 11 Paul attempts to reinforce the stipulations regarding head covering found in verses 4–6 by appealing to creation. The Greek text uses the word "gar" ("for") in verse 7 (omitted in NIV) and in verse 8. Verses 8 and 9 are linked to each other and put on equal footing by the conjunction "kai" ("and" or "also," translated "neither" in KJV and NIV). So, verses 4–6 are supported by verse 7, and verse 7 is supported by verses 8 and 9. For the modern reader, however, verses 7–9 may further confuse rather than further clarify the whole matter and may prove to be difficult to unravel without loose ends resulting.

The difference in head covering specified in verses 4–6 is said in verse 7 to be because ("for") man is the image and glory of God, but woman/wife is the glory of man/husband. The reference to God's image is probably to make the transition to creation which is the focus of verses 7–9. The fact that the woman/wife is not said here to be in the image of God does not negate the creation account which clearly states that she is in God's image (Genesis 1:27). The designation is probably omitted because her head covering did not depict a divine relationship (as did the man's), just a human relationship. (It should be noted that she is *not* said to be in man's image even though saying so would have made Paul's wording parallel. This obvious omission is because she is not made in man's image but in God's image.) Paul is simply making a quick shift to the point of these verses which is the *difference* in the creation of Adam and Eve. This difference is exemplified in the focus or basis of their *glory*.

The shades of meaning available for "being the glory of" are numerous. The expression can mean "to reflect the other party in a corresponding way." This seems to be what Adam exclaimed when Eve was first brought to him (Genesis 2:23).[6] It can mean "to reveal, manifest, or draw attention to the other party" as in what God the Son did in glorifying God the Father. It can also carry the simple meaning of "honoring and/or praising the other party."[7] It is hard to propose an interpretation for this phrase because anything that can be said about males glorifying God seems to be just as possible and even scripturally obligatory for females. It may be that females, either by virtue of their gender or marital status have an *additional* responsibility that males do not have.

At this point verses 8 and 9 prove helpful. The "for" construction that connects these two verses to verse 7 indicates that they offer reasons or explanations for verse 7. According to the creation account, there was a special way that Eve came from

Adam (Genesis 2:22) and a special way that she was to match and help him (Genesis 2:18). Since these two individuals were the first male and female and the first husband and wife, the more general statements found in verses 8 and 9 can be made as well. The woman/wife has a *creation-based relationship* to the man/husband that should be given its proper glory. Violating the culturally prescribed customs of head covering was somehow shaming this relationship, and the Corinthian Christians were, instead, to honor it.

How all of this played out in the understanding of first-century people may be hard to determine from two thousand years away. The secular feminism of their day, however, was not too different from the radical secular feminism of today. It pervaded certain trendy cults, generated perverse sexual activities, and produced independence from and sometimes contempt for men and marriage. If the Christian women/wives were adopting any of the ways of this movement by throwing off their head covering and thereby proclaiming their personhood *to the exclusion of* their gender and/or marital status, then they were being challenged by the creation account to do differently. They are not to use their "new creation status" (2 Corinthians 5:17) nor the leadership opportunities that it afforded them to bring shame to men/husbands, but they are to recognize a biblically-based relationship to them.

Authority and Angels

If verse 3 of 1 Corinthians 11 is the statement most likely to be given a "read and run" treatment, then verse 10 is the second most likely to be given a sloppy, superficial handling. It is a difficult verse to understand, but it is better to admit this and to propose text-based explanations than to literally rewrite the verse as some scholars and translators have done. These re-writes are easy to understand in that they affirm a straightforward male-over-female or husband-over-wife hierarchy, but they fail to reflect what the original text actually says.

The verse opens with the phrase "because of this" which indicates that Paul's presentation is coming full circle. What he proposes regarding head covering in verses 5–6, he then defends in verses 7–9. Because of the reasons given in verses 7–9 and because of an additional reason that he includes in verse 10, he returns to the original premise that women/wives are to have appropriate head covering. The "authority on her head" of verse 10, then, is referring to the culturally proper head covering which is the focus of this entire passage.

The problem comes with this phrase "authority on her head." Many Bible translations, including the NIV, say, "sign of authority on her head." This opens the possibility of the authority belonging to someone or something else because "sign" conveys the idea of pointing elsewhere. Realizing this, several translations volunteer to whom the sign is pointing by adding references to men. Some will even change the word "authority" to "submission" and say, "sign of submission on her head." All of these renderings are faulty because they result from inserting words that are not present in the Greek text or, worse yet, from changing what the text actually says into the very opposite. The Greek text includes no words except the following: "the woman/ wife ought to have authority on/over the head." No other rendering is possible because no other words are present.

The Greek word "exousia" which stands behind the English word "authority" is a relatively common word that means "authority, right, power." None of its 100-plus New Testament occurrences is translated any other way. Further, nowhere in the New Testament or in any other ancient Greek literature does "to have authority on/over" refer to anyone or anything other than the subject of the sentence possessing the authority.[8] This means that the right or power spoken about in verse 10 *must* belong to the woman; there is no other way to read the phrase in the Greek language. It is the only mention of authority in the passage, and without question it refers to something that the woman/wife possesses. It cannot be assigned to a man, nor can it be totally reversed and turned into "submission." To do either is to blatantly and intentionally misrepresent God's Word.

Verse 10, then, must be explained on the basis of what it actually says, "the woman/wife ought to have authority on/over the head." Evidently if she presents herself properly, then this provides her with adequate authority to do the very things that the Corinthian women were doing, namely, praying and prophesying in public gatherings of believers. Somehow the appropriate head covering gives her the right to participate in spiritual leadership, perhaps because it frees her from questions or accusations about her character or because it demonstrates her willingness to accommodate cultural expectations or because it reflects a biblically-based respect for her gender or marital status. Whatever was the case, again, it must be noted that Paul is not dictating a certain hair dress or hair style for all cultures. Whatever he is requiring was meaningful and therefore needful *in first-century Corinth*.

It has also been suggested that the men may have been pressuring the women to remove their proper head covering in a display of Christian liberty. If so, then in verse 10 Paul is assigning the decision regarding a woman's head to the woman herself rather than allowing it to be dictated by others. Of course, he is also making it quite clear how she is to decide the matter. If this is the proper understanding of the situation, then "for this reason" in the opening of verse 10 bridges Paul's argument and conclusion in a very clear way: because she has her honor and her husband's honor to protect (as detailed in the preceding verses), the decision in this matter of head covering rightfully belongs to the wife.[9]

The additional reason for head covering that Paul mentions in verse 10 is perhaps the most perplexing detail in all of 1 Corinthians 11. After referring back to the reasons already given in verses 8 and 9, he adds, "and because of the angels." Elsewhere in Scripture angels are presented in close association with God's presence, particularly in relationship to the worship of God (Matthew 18:10; 1 Peter 3:22; Revelation 3:5; 5:11; 7:11; 8:1–4). Interestingly, they are also presented as being very aware of earthly activity and, of course, very aware of righteousness in earthly activity (Luke 15:10; 1 Corinthians 4:9; 1 Timothy 3:16; 5:21). They are even said to visit believers without revealing their identity (Hebrews 13:2). If by all of this, angels are to be viewed as guardians of creation order and of worship decorum,[10] it may be that Paul is assuming their attendance at worship gatherings, visibly or invisibly, and is desiring absolute propriety because of the obvious sanctity of the occasion.

A second interpretation is based upon the fact that angels cover themselves while engaging in heavenly worship (Isaiah 6:1–3); consequently, the same thing could have appropriateness in earthly worship. For this and the first interpretation, there would have to be a reason why the woman/wife and not the man is told to respond to the angels' scrutiny or example. The text says that her hair is her glory (11:15), and she, in turn, is the man's glory (11:7). During worship there should not be a consciousness of either the woman/wife or the man, only a consciousness of God.[11] In their culture, handling the hair properly perhaps lessened the likelihood of inappropriate attention being focused upon either participant and ensured a worship environment in which only God's glory was evident. Even exposing the man's head somehow symbolized a focus upon God.

A third suggestion for the phrase "because of the angels" must be discarded though it dates back many years. It has been said that the proper handling of the woman's/wife's hair is required not only to prevent the lustful gazes of men but also of fallen angels. Sometimes a faulty understanding of Genesis 6:4 is offered as proof that this could occur. One would only have to study the powers of angels and fallen angels (demons) to realize that a piece of cloth over the hair or a culturally recognized style/length of hair would be no safeguard against lusting demons, assuming that they lust after women which they probably do not do. The rejection of this interpretation does not mean that the reference is not to fallen angels. A fourth interpretation says that because even angels were able to fall prey to the glory of one magnificent angel, Lucifer, it is imperative that no one else's glory be displayed in the worship setting except God's.

Fortunately, being unsure of the meaning of this one phrase does not preclude an understanding of the passage as a whole. Paul is obviously making the bulk of his case on the basis of other considerations. Even though his other arguments also leave some questions in the modern reader's mind, they are clear enough to establish that cultural concerns are in focus and to eliminate any claim that this passage restricts the participation of women in worship.

Interdependence

Whatever first-century details are hard to discern in much of 1 Corinthians 11, verses 11–12 offer fundamental principles for viewing men and women that are exceedingly clear. How odd that these verses, which are so easy to understand, are oftentimes overshadowed by questionable conclusions drawn from the other verses. This must not be allowed because these two verses actually forbid the very attitudes and actions of hierarchicalism that are erroneously drawn from the other verses of the passage.

Verses 11 and 12 open with the word "however" or "nevertheless," setting their contents in sharp contrast to what has just been said. Up to this point, basically the whole passage has been about acknowledging gender and/or marital distinctions in culturally appropriate ways in the worship service. What Paul does next is attempt to stop these necessary accommodations from being misunderstood and misapplied. Evidently recognizing the potential for this to happen, he puts forth a combination qualification-clarification. It has to do specifically with the community of believers. Whatever wrong views the world may insist upon having, "in the Lord" men and women are to be viewed as mutually dependent. This is the attitude that he advocates elsewhere in his handling of congregational activities, and it is clear that he views interdependence as involving unity and equality (12:4–26). Chapters 11 and 12, then, share something in common. Paul is correcting a problem of some believers being seen as primary while others are seen as secondary, and he is saying that this ought not be the case. Hierarchies were the Corinthians' problem, not Paul's solution.

The actual wording of verse 11 is reflected rather well in the KJV's "without" wording. The Greek text says that neither man nor woman is "without," "apart from," or "without relation to" the other.[12] This not only stands against the attitudes of chauvinism but also the attitudes of radical secular feminism. Neither gender is to so esteem itself and so discredit the other as to lessen its regard or need for the other. There are to be no "we are better than you" attitudes and no "we do not respect or require you" attitudes.

What Paul does next in verse 12 is to take the very foundation of the pro-hierarchy position and deny its validity. It is a fact that Adam preceded Eve in creation order, but according to verse 12 this does not indicate superiority, dominance, or anything else of a hierarchical nature because it is "neutralized" or balanced by a second equally significant creation fact. As much as God designed the way in which Adam would "give forth" Eve, He also designed the way that Eve would then "give forth" all others. As woman is said in verse 9 to be created "dia" ("on account of") man, man is said in verse 12 to be "dia" woman, using the identical Greek word. There is only one who stands over both Adam and Eve, men and women, husbands and wives, and that is God from whom everyone comes forth.

Of course, all of this was obscured by the fall and was replaced by the dominant-subordinate hierarchical arrangement between men and women and husbands and wives. However, the unity, equality, and mutuality that was originally designed into God's plan for humanity has been reestablished "in the Lord," in the community of redemption. Even though the gender and marital distinctions remain and should be honored as gifts from God, Paul is crystal clear in saying that these distinctions do not in any way position one person or one category of persons differently from others.

Concluding Remarks

In verse 13 Paul indicates that his presentation has been convincing enough to invite the Corinthians to make their own decision on the matter of head covering. He is not saying that it is all right for them to ignore everything he has said and do whatever they please. He has made a case for what is appropriate in light of the expectations of their culture, and it is propriety to which he turns their attention in his closing words. Evidently if they judge according to cultural propriety rather than according to personal liberty, then the right decisions will be made.

In verse 14 Paul continues the focus upon custom found in verse 13 with his reference to "nature." It is true that the word can refer to the inherent make-up of things as in something to do with the physical realm, but it can also refer to an outward appearance[13] or preference that results from long-term *habit*.[14] Several scholars concur that the latter meaning is the one being employed. Even though conservatives may wish to use this statement to claim that men possess an innate disposition against growing long hair and women possess the same toward growing long hair, this position is questionable. The combination of short hair on men and long hair on women is, indeed, a common phenomenon. However, exceptions have been found across history, including the many women of African descent whose hair will not grow beyond what most people label "short." There is also the ever-changing nature of descriptive words such as "short" and "long." Whenever possible, hair length probably results more from culturally assigned gender roles than from anything else, with men historically opting for the convenience that fits their work-world and women historically opting for aesthetic advantage.

After opening this presentation in verse 2 with a reference to "paradosis" which is best translated "traditions," Paul closes it in verse 16 by referring to the practice of head covering as a matter of "custom." This is an accurate translation of the word "sunetheia." It can also mean "habit." It is far less imposing than other words that Paul oftentimes uses such as "doctrine" or "commandment." This is further evidence that the actual specifics of this passage deal with changeable, cultural behaviors rather than with practices that are meant to become universal norms. The length, style, and covering of hair are not principles of Scripture; these things are simply first-century customs to which the Corinthian church must sensitively adapt in order to maintain its unity and testimony.

Finally, Paul says that if anyone chooses to be contentious about the matter, "we have no such custom." Perhaps it is only fitting for such a challenging portion of Scripture to end with a little touch of challenge. It is unimaginable that Paul would so tediously discuss a custom only to end by dismissing it out of existence. Thus, the custom that does not exist cannot be the custom of proper head covering. It is more likely that this phrase refers to the "custom" that the contentious crowd would be proposing, namely, that of doing other than what Paul stipulates in verses 4–6.

13

Questions Regarding
First Corinthians 14

Those who wish to restrict the ministerial activities of women will oftentimes leap over everything else the Bible says about the matter and quote a two-verse passage found in 1 Corinthians 14:34–35. It seems to have all of the key words: women, silence, submission, shame, husbands, home. Put them together into what is said to be a clear apostolic command and, supposedly, the issue is settled. However, there are two major problems with this approach. First, such a simplistic, superficial handling of the passage actually overshoots the target because it stops women from saying *anything* in the congregational setting. Viewing this as undesirable, lists of "can" and "cannot" activities are invented and explained into the passage. These provisions allow women the participation that men deem useful while keeping them in their "proper place." The second problem is that neither the "absolute silence" interpretation nor the "proper place" modification rings true with the rest of Scripture. Both arrangements, in fact, stand in direct opposition to teachings and practices found throughout the Bible, providing the clearest possible signal that the verses are being misunderstood.

A correct understanding of 1 Corinthians 14:34–35 must acknowledge the fact that the Word of God affirms the ministerial capacity and calling of women over and over again. In other words, this small *piece* of Scripture must be explained in such a way as to align with the *whole* of Scripture rather than contradict it. If Paul seems to be saying something here that is different from the rest of the Bible, in fact, something different from *his own* teachings and practices, then careful attention must be given to what he is saying and *why* he is saying it. If unique local situations are present and are likely to be triggering an otherwise unexplainable statement, then these special circumstances must be allowed to provide the insight that is otherwise missing. All of this being the case, applying such a passage to future generations requires extreme caution so that an unusual "exception to the rule" situation does not obscure the "rule" itself. The "rule" is generated by the universal principles about women which appear throughout Scripture. It is against these principles that passages such as 1 Corinthians 14:34–35 are properly measured and interpreted.

Unacceptable Explanations

In searching for a biblically consistent understanding of 1 Corinthians 14:34–35, then, two explanations are immediately exposed as unacceptable. The first is that Paul is ordering women to be absolutely silent during the public worship service. As has been noted, this would totally contradict the rest of Scripture, including Paul's own teachings. In this very letter, just three chapters earlier, he makes provision for women to participate in worship activities that are both public and vocal. The second unacceptable explanation is found in any list of man-made restrictions that are read into the passage rather than drawn directly from it and, again, are not reflective of what the Bible repeatedly shows godly women doing.

Those who wish to be restrictive of women are not the only ones who propose unacceptable explanations for these two verses. Those who want to open the ministry to women offer equally questionable ideas. For example, some evangelicals and many non-evangelicals challenge the authenticity of the passage, viewing it as a non-apostolic addition to the manuscript. This approach essentially makes the verses disappear so there is no longer any need to harmonize them with the rest of the Bible, but this solution comes at great cost. Allowing individual scholars to redetermine the scriptural canon opens all of God's Word to being challenged and eliminated.

Three other explanations are commonly offered for the passage: women are forbidden from babbling senselessly, from speaking in tongues, or from evaluating prophecies. For various reasons, however, each of these possibilities falls short of being convincing enough to accept.

The case for babbling hinges on the versatility of the verb "laleo" ("speak") in verse 34. It is an extremely common word that can mean many things, ranging from the uttering of sounds to the speaking of words. Because some first-century cult worship did produce delirious gibberish in people, it is assumed that Paul is forbidding such senseless expressions in genuine worship. One problem with this idea is that it fails to explain why only the women carried the activity into the church since both the women and men of the congregation were converts from heathenism (12:1–2). Further, even though the word "laleo" can mean babbling as well as a wide range of other things, it is unwise to reach into the culture for a meaning that is different from the one specified by the text.

The other two explanations, speaking in tongues and evaluating prophecies, claim to have the weight of the text in their favor because Paul discusses these very activities in the preceding verses. Nonetheless, there are problems with both possibilities. The speaking in tongues that Paul regulates in this chapter is identified as a gift of the Spirit in an earlier chapter (12:1,7–10). Assuming that evaluating prophecy involves or signifies the discerning of spirits, it too is a gift of the Spirit (12:10). So, each of these explanations claims that one spiritual gift is off-limits to women, but there is no biblical or logical basis for such a withholding. Paul is explicit in saying that *each* member of the body partakes of these gifts (12:7, Greek text saying "each" rather than "each man" as in KJV), and he is equally inclusive in encouraging everyone to desire them (14:1). In these and in other comments, there is never the slightest suggestion that one of the gifts is for men only.

If there were to be one gift designated as off-limits to women, it is difficult to understand why it would be a lesser gift such as speaking in tongues or discerning of spirits while the greater gift of prophecy (12:28) is available to them (11:5–6). It is also difficult to explain how the exercising of either of these two gifts by women would constitute a violation of submission (14:34) since the exercising of other gifts such as the gift of teaching by Phoebe and the gift of prophecy by Philip's daughters, *both more authoritative gifts* (12:28), did not constitute a violation.

Those who favor the explanation of women being banned from speaking in tongues usually point out that the word "laleo" ("speak") that is used in verse 34 is used throughout chapter 14 in reference to speaking in tongues (14:2,4,5,6, etc.). This is true, but it is also used in the same chapter in reference to prophesying (14:3,29) which is something women may do (11:5–6). It is used in the preceding chapter in reference to speaking in general (13:11), again, something women may do. It is important to realize that whatever type of speaking Paul discusses in chapter 14, whether tongues or interpretation of tongues or prophecy or evaluating prophecy, he always makes it clear how he is using the word "laleo." It is not necessary or valid to force the earlier "speaking in tongues" meaning upon verse 34.

Those who favor the explanation of women being banned from discerning of spirits (evaluating prophecy) usually claim that this activity was accomplished in the churches through a questioning process, thus explaining verse 35. Not only is there no scriptural evidence to support an "evaluating via questioning" theory,[1] but banning women from it is particularly difficult to understand. How is it that they qualify to prophesy (11:5–6) but do not qualify to evaluate prophecy, which seems to be its complement? (See 12:10 for the two couplets: prophecy and discerning of spirits, speaking in tongues and interpretation of tongues.) Surely if Huldah was qualified to prophesy and evaluate scriptural authenticity, then women are capable of evaluating the integrity of local church prophecies.[2] Those who do this weighing or judging are referred to in chapter 14 as "others" (14:29) which, grammatically, must refer to the pool of prophets or to the body of believers. Women, of course, are members of both groups, so they are as much a part of the "others" as anyone else.

Those who do not accept present-day demonstrations of spiritual gifts oftentimes make a quick leap from claiming that the passage bans women from speaking in tongues or evaluating prophecies to concluding that they should not teach or preach or pastor. They argue that the original ban was against authoritative activities, so it should apply to whatever replaces those activities today, namely, the leadership ministries of teaching, preaching, and/or pastoring. To further bolster their case, some contend that none of the instructions regarding spiritual gifts found in chapters 12–14 of 1 Corinthians were meant to address women. The errors in this line of thinking are serious. First, the passage is made to say something different from what it actually says. Teaching, preaching, and pastoring all three existed in the Early Church, but it is not these activities that Paul identifies. Second, women were very much involved in authoritative ministerial leadership in the first century, so there are no biblical grounds for denying them the same involvement today. Third, if 1 Corinthians 12–14 excludes women, then perhaps women are exempt from many other passages such as the Great Commission.

Assistance from the Passage

Unacceptable explanations of 1 Corinthians 14:34–35, then, are offered both by those favoring and by those forbidding the involvement of women in authoritative ministerial leadership. Rather than embracing any of these proposals, it is far better to let the passage supply the signals as to what Paul is saying. Since he is obviously not mandating the absolute, universal silence of all women or restricting them in any other way that would defy Scripture, he must have in view a specific situation in which silence is in order. After all, in the Old Testament "all of the earth" and "all of humanity" are silenced by God (Habakkuk 2:20; Zechariah 2:13) without the intent being an absolute, permanent silencing.

A conditional silencing is precisely the case in verses 28 and 30 in which the very same verb "sigao" ("be silent, be quiet") is used as is used in verse 34. No one suggests that the earlier two verses forever silence all those who speak in tongues or all those who prophesy, so there is no reason to think that verse 34 forever silences all women. No one assumes something negative of glossolalists or prophets simply because they are told to exercise silence for the sake of maintaining an orderly church service, so there is no reason to view verse 34 as an indictment against women. All three uses of the word "sigao" in this chapter are conditional. In certain circumstances the glossolalist, the prophet, and the woman are to be quiet. The silence does not have to do with their personhood but with the situation in which they find themselves.

For the glossolalist, silence is preferable to speaking in tongues in the absence of an interpreter (14:28). For the prophet, silence is preferable to two prophets fighting for the floor (14:30). What is the third disorderly behavior that Paul identifies, involving women, for which silence is preferable? It is clearly specified in verse 35: "If they want to inquire about something, they should ask their own husbands at home." So, the silence that he stipulates in verse 34 is explained or qualified in verse 35, and because this explanation is found within the text itself, it takes precedence over any and all speculative meanings that anyone proposes. He is not imposing an absolute, universal silence upon half of God's kingdom nor is he barring them from engaging in ministry; he is simply correcting a specific disruptive situation that is evidently present and problematic in the church.

Support from the Context

The fact that Paul is rectifying potentially disorderly behavior in the church worship service in 1 Corinthians 14:34–35 aligns well with his focus throughout chapters 11–14, a span of material that definitely forms a unit. Several of the problems that he addresses in these chapters are so specific they may not even exist in a given congregation today; but the theme of thoughtful, orderly worship is constant and is to apply to all situations in all churches.

His focus is particularly obvious in the verses that "bracket" the chapter 14 material about women. In verse 33 he refers to avoiding disorder and maintaining tranquillity, and in verse 40 his reference is to doing everything properly and orderly. Putting this type of "envelope" around one's words to ensure clarity and emphasis was a common technique in ancient writing. In this instance, it distinguishes verses 34–35 as being all about disrupting the service, not distinguishing the genders.

In fact, if verses 39–40 not only close the material about women but also summarize the entire presentation of chapter 14, then Paul is emphasizing an open access to spiritual gifts (14:39, "brothers" or "brethren" referring to all believers) that is restricted only by the dictates of a mannerly service (14:40). To claim that he is doing the very opposite with half of the congregation violates every indication that is present in the text and its context. If the silencing or restricting of women were one of the universal principles being established in chapter 14, it is surprisingly missing from this summary statement.

Understanding the Disruption

Why are women uniquely targeted with regards to disrupting the worship service? Of course, glossolalists and prophets are singled out and told to quiet themselves in a similar way even though it appears that many other spiritual gifts are in operation in this church. Obviously, Paul is correcting specific problems that exist, and this causes him to address the specific individuals involved. It should be noted that the phrase "as in *all* the congregations of the saints" (14:33) is likely to be part of the statement found in verse 33 rather than part of the section about women beginning in verse 34 (contrary to NIV's paragraphing). Otherwise, saying "in the churches" (14:34) would be redundant since the Greek wording "en tais ekklesiais" ("in the assemblies") is identical in both phrases. So, though Paul may be correcting more than one gathering of believers in Corinth, it is unlikely that verses 34–35 are referencing all of the first-century congregations. There was evidently a problem with the women that was unique to the Corinthian church or churches.

Actually, Paul pinpoints the problem even more specifically. The Greek text of verse 34 inserts "your" alongside its use of "women/wives." This possessive wording could be a way of specifically designating the Corinthians, but with the corollary reference in verse 35 to their "*own*" "men/husbands" "*at home,*" it is more likely the common way of indicating that the word meaning either "women" or "wives" ("gune") is to be understood as meaning "wives." So, Paul is not quieting all Corinthian women; he is quieting only the ones who are causing problems, namely, the married women. Further, he is only quieting the one activity on their part that is causing problems, specifically, asking their husbands questions during the service. He is not restricting them because they are women or because they are wives, just as he is not restricting glossolalists and prophets because they are glossolalists and prophets. He is quieting all of these individuals only because they are speaking in a way that is affecting the services negatively rather than positively.

Asking questions was the primary means of learning in the ancient world, among Jews and Gentiles alike. A "give-and-take" between instructor and student was more common than a monologue by the instructor. It should be noted that Paul refers to the wives' effort to "learn" ("manthano") in verse 35 (obscured by NIV's "inquire" translation). It may be that they were interrupting teaching or preaching sessions with their questions. It is also possible that they were asking questions at appropriate times but were asking terribly ignorant questions. Either of these scenarios could be the natural result of first-century women having little or no schooling. If there were a "challenge" dynamic to the asking of questions, this would be particularly offensive coming from an uneducated person and, worse yet, coming from someone's wife. Of course, if other women were equally without answers, then it would do no good to check with them; and, culturally, the only man that could be addressed by a woman would be her husband. It is not known whether believers sat in house meetings in family units or in gender groups, so it is not known whether the questions were being whispered or shouted, but something about their asking of questions was disruptive. Wrong as it may have been for a man to behave improperly in a public setting, it was far worse for a man's wife to do so.[3]

It is possible that these women who had long been denied reasonable learning opportunities, who had gone from the rule of their fathers to the rule of their husbands, were overly boisterous and assertive in exercising their new-found equality and liberty in Christ. Wide-open participation had only been available to them in the fertility cults which were well known for bizarre worship behavior. To transfer this mania into genuine worship or to be misidentified with heathenism because of engaging in its practices would have been extremely detrimental to Christianity. Consequently, Paul is stipulating the same self-restraint for wives that he sets for glossolalists and prophets. His sole intent is to ensure an orderly, effective service that is free from excess and chaos.

Obviously, every detail behind the problem that Paul is correcting cannot be known with complete certainty. Of course, the Corinthians knew what he was forbidding and precisely *why* he was forbidding it; but even without this much clarity, the modern reader can see that he is not restricting women's use of spiritual gifts or their entry into ministerial activities. This is made evident by the fact that he is not placing their silence in contrast to teaching or preaching or leading but in contrast to asking disruptive questions.[4] So the issue is not that they are engaging in *ministry* in a way that is disallowed; the issue is that they are engaging in *learning* in a way that is *disorderly*.[5] To jump from Paul's obvious intent to someone's hidden agenda is inexcusable. The only universal truth that can be drawn from 1 Corinthians 14:34–35 has to do with the safeguarding of orderly worship, not with the straight jacketing of all women.

Upon seeing the word "submission" in verse 34, it is easy to jump to the conclusion that a husband is being put in authority over his wife, especially since the passage seems to be addressing married women. (KJV incorrectly uses the word "obedience.") Since, however, the issue at hand has to do with church order rather than sexual or marital hierarchy, this is probably not the case. The very same Greek word is found in verse 32 regarding the prophets without any connotation of gender or marriage. Because it is the church service that is being disrupted by the disorderly questions, then it must be the body of believers or the "principles of order and decorum in worship" that deserve the submissive spirit.[6] Again, it should be noted that according to verse 35, the women are needing and wanting to *learn*. The attitude that was to be displayed by a learner in first-century culture was that of utmost humility and submissiveness.

It is possible that the shame or disgrace mentioned in verse 35 is a result of cultural reactions to the behavior being corrected. It is the same word that is used in 1 Corinthians 11:6 regarding the cutting or shaving of hair. As has been established, the stigma in this earlier passage is culture-based rather than creation-based, so the same may be the case here. It is very likely that only the married women felt comfortable directing a question to a man, namely, to their husbands; but this was perceived within their culture as something no "decent" married woman would do in public. As in chapter 11, she is being told in chapter 14 to exhibit cultural sensitivity and propriety so that the worship setting is above criticism.

An Alternative Explanation

There is one detail found in 1 Corinthians 14:34–35 that is not adequately addressed by the preceding explanation or by any other explanation. It is Paul's reference in verse 34 to the "law" ("nomos"). To a certain extent, he is basing his instructions on this citation, so it is definitely a significant component of the passage. Serious problems arise, however, when attempts are made to identify what law he is quoting or paraphrasing. If it cannot be identified with any satisfaction, then any explanation of the passage, including the preceding one, that fails to resolve this difficulty becomes questionable.

Basically, there are three possible meanings: a reference to civil law, a reference to mosaic law, and a reference to the "works righteousness" of Judaism that was dependent upon keeping the mosaic law and its accompanying rabbinical tradition.

First, regarding a reference to civil law, though Paul uses the word "law" *many* times in a *variety* of ways (law of faith, of the mind, of sin, of the Spirit, of righteousness, etc.), he *never* uses it in this way; consequently, it is very unlikely that he is doing so here. Second, regarding a reference to mosaic law, though Paul sometimes uses "law" in this way, if he is doing so here, there is no stipulation that can be found in all of the Old Testament that matches his citation. Nowhere does the Old Testament prescribe the submission or silence of women/wives, especially in worship, nor does it associate submission with silence. Of course, the passage that is usually suggested is Genesis 3:16, but Paul understood Scripture too well to confuse a consequence of sin with a command of God.[7] Furthermore, if this passage is cited, then many other Old Testament passages would have to be included in "the law," passages that portray women as dominant rather than subordinate. What mosaic law and Old Testament Scripture *do* say about women in worship describes and encourages an active, vocal involvement in the assembly right alongside men (Exodus 15:20–21; 38:8; Leviticus 10:14; Numbers 18:11,19; Deuteronomy 12:12,17–18; Judges 5:1,12; Ezra 2:65; Psalms 30:4; 33:1; 67:5; 95:1; 96:1; 100:1; 107:22; 150:6).

What about the third possibility, a reference to "law" as understood by first-century Judaism? The legalism and tradition of the rabbis to which Jesus and Paul made frequent reference did contain numerous restrictions against women, including the following regarding their participation in the worship service: "A woman should not read the Torah (mosaic law) out of respect for the congregation" (Babylonian Talmud, Megillah 23a). If this Judaistic "law" is Paul's focus here, then his reference to it cannot be positive. In other words, he cannot be calling upon Christians to obey this code of conduct because he *never* does so. He never sanctions rabbinical legalism or tradition as binding upon the believer. In fact, he does just the opposite; he labels any loyalty to it as devastating to the gospel. Because Paul *always* opposes the infiltration of Judaism into Christianity, his reference here must be read as negative, and this opens the possibility of an altogether different explanation for the entire passage.

A growing number of conservative scholars embrace the idea that Paul is quoting Judaistic Christians in 1 Corinthians 14:34–35 and then rebuking their legalistic restrictions in verses 36–38. This alternative explanation is very plausible because he "recites then refutes" the congregation's erroneous beliefs in other locations; in fact, doing so is characteristic of this letter. Since quotation marks were not used in first-century Greek, they may or may not be present in modern translations. The occurrences must be identified by recognizing locations in which Paul makes a questionable statement and then follows it immediately with opposite or corrective material. Examples include the following (and some scholars recognize several others): I belong to Paul, I belong to Apollos (1:12; 3:4), everything is permissible (6:12; 10:23), food for the stomach and the stomach for food (6:13), it is good for a man not to marry (7:1).[8]

This means that the teaching contained in 1 Corinthians 14:34–35 must be understood as incorrect rather than correct. Such a "dismissal" of these two verses, however, does not mean that any and all verses in 1 Corinthians or elsewhere in Scripture are open to similar treatment. Instances of quoting erroneous teaching in order to oppose and correct it are identifiable by the "recite then refute" structuring of the material as well as by the fact that the erroneous statement is in violation of the rest of biblical teaching, perhaps even in violation of material in close proximity.[9]

In addition to offering the best resolution of Paul's reference to the "law," there are several other reasons to accept this alternative explanation as a likely interpretation of the passage. First, it is also the best resolution of the fact that verses 34–35 stand in contrast to known Old Testament and New Testament practice as well as to Paul's known position. Second, Judaism did surface in many first-century churches and pressured Christians to behave in ways that were absolutely opposite to redemption behavior. Some form of Judaism is probably denounced by Paul more often than any other falsehood. Third, this explanation clarifies why the text shifts abruptly from third person in verses 34–35 to second person in verse 36 and then back again to third person in verses 37–38. Paul identifies their error in verses 34–35, directly rebukes those responsible for it in verse 36 ("you"), and then identifies the arrogance and stubbornness fueling their error in verses 37–38. Fourth, according to this explanation, the role of verses 36–38 is clear; whereas, the relationship between these verses and verses 34–35 is not evident or integral with other explanations. Verse 36 is Paul's indictment against the men who would claim a monopoly on truth to the point of excluding others (women) from learning about it, and his sarcasm serves an obvious purpose. In verse 37 he contrasts the Judaistic "law" that stands behind their position with the "command of the Lord" that stands behind his position. In verse 38 he threatens to exchange their current influence with entire-church rejection if they do not heed his correction.

The fifth compelling feature of this explanation is its acknowledgment of a little word that opens verse 36. Actually, it occurs twice in the verse, once in the opening of the first question and again in the opening of the second question. It is the Greek conjunction "e," frequently translated "or, nor, than, either, neither." Though the first occurrence is left out in many translations ("What?" in KJV, omitted in NIV) both uses of the word are undeniably present *and meaningful* in the Greek text. In the form found in this verse, it serves to distinguish or contrast two things. It is used in all 13 of Paul's letters, but in none as often as in 1 Corinthians. Among its dozens of occurrences in this letter are several instances of the word being used to introduce a correct belief or practice immediately after Paul has just made mention of an error (6:2; 6:9; 6:16; 6:19; 9:6; 9:8b; 9:10; 10:22; 11:14).[10] Though translations may omit or dilute the word in some of these passages, it is nonetheless being used by the apostle each time to accent a difference between wrong and right. The best and perhaps the only correct understanding of the word in 1 Corinthians 14 is that verses 34–35 contain an error that Paul sharply challenges with the two sarcastic questions of verse 36.

In summary, if Paul is actually silencing the women of this congregation in verses 34–35, then he is doing so only in relationship to some very specific behavior on their part, namely, the voicing of disruptive questions during the worship service. This in no way supplies grounds for reversing everything else that is found throughout the Bible regarding the equality of women and their participation in worship and in ministry. Any application of the passage that is made today must align with the original intent of the author, and that intent is not the absolute silencing and subjugating of all women. It is more likely, however, that Paul is *not* establishing a provisional practice for this local church but is denouncing their departure from proper practice. The address "brethren" or "brothers" in his closing words (14:39) is used repeatedly in the New Testament and in this letter to refer to all believers, both male and female. So, in his own summation he encourages *all saints* to prophesy and speak in tongues, obviously vocal activities, and charges the same individuals to do so in an orderly manner (14:40). Whichever one of the two explanations of the passage is correct, neither one prevents a woman from engaging fully in teaching, preaching, leading, or any other ministerial activity of the church.

14

Questions Regarding First Timothy 2

It seems as if many of the major elements of the "women in ministry" issue converge in one brief passage of Scripture, 1 Timothy 2:9–15. The creation and fall are present, submission and authority are mentioned, appropriate silence and inappropriate teaching are addressed, even clothing and children find their way into the picture. One churchman has said, "The passage covers the three things we need to know about women. It opens in verse 9 with their austere appearance, closes in verse 15 with their proper place (childbearing), and mandates their silence and subordination in the verses in between." Regarding the "verses in between," a notable scholar makes an equally alarming statement:

> Generally speaking, women are more relational and nurturing and men are more given to rational analysis and objectivity. Women are less prone than men to see the importance of doctrinal formulations, especially when it comes to the issue of identifying heresy and making a stand for the truth. Appointing women to the teaching office is prohibited because they are less likely to draw a line on doctrinal non-negotiables, and thus deception and false teaching will more easily enter the church.[1]

One can only wonder how he explains the fact that men far outnumber women in any study of the history of heresy. Both of these men are probably hopeful that no aspect of their own spiritual lineage is traceable back to the many early believers who were discipled by Apollos (1 Corinthians 3:6) after he was equipped to do so by Priscilla and Aquila (Acts 18:23–26).

Conclusions such as the ones advocated by these opponents of women in ministry are reminiscent of words spoken by churchmen and scholars in the past. The target was not half of the human race; it was one third of the human race. Blacks were said to have different thinking processes than whites, to be dependent upon whites for their well-being, and to be rightfully positioned beneath whites. These beliefs were presented as biblically based, in fact, were supposedly backed by straightforward, indisputable passages from God's Word.

Rather than expecting a portion of Scripture to align with racism or chauvinism, it should be expected to align with its own Genesis-to-Revelation flow of truth. Rather than expecting God's Word to degrade and suppress one third or one half of His creation, it should be expected to emancipate and incorporate them. Is it possible to understand the teaching of 1 Timothy 2 in such a way as to maintain agreement with everything else the Bible teaches about women? Is it possible to understand these verses in such a way as to maintain the conviction that redemption and everything it entails is equally available to all believers? The answer to these questions is, of course, a resounding yes!

All that is being asked is that 1 Timothy 2:9–15 be interpreted into doctrine in the same way that every other segment of Scripture is handled. For example, as clear as John 3:16 may appear to be, what it actually says is determined by reading the verse against the backdrop of a whole-Bible portrayal of salvation. If this were not done and the passage were, instead, forced to stand alone, then belief may be little more than acknowledging Jesus' existence and believers may be exempt from death. Of course, these notions are totally "off limits" because they cannot withstand the correction of the rest of the Bible serving as the authoritative commentary on John 3:16. Likewise, an authoritative commentary is available for 1 Timothy 2:9–15. Whatever anyone claims the passage means, that meaning must ring true to every other portrayal of women and redemption and ministry found in God's Word.

Pastoral Epistles

A true understanding of 1 Timothy 2 can begin with a clarification of its position within one of the Apostle Paul's three Pastoral Epistles. Evidently Paul was released from his first imprisonment in Rome and afforded one last opportunity for ministerial travel. Some call this his fourth missionary journey. During the trip, he left Timothy in the city of Ephesus and left Titus on the island of Crete, assigning to each one some particularly challenging pastoral responsibilities. As Paul continued his trip, he wrote a letter of counsel to each of these associates, resulting in the books known today as 1 Timothy and Titus. At some point it seems that he was arrested again and taken back to Rome. Whereas his first Roman incarceration was some type of house arrest (Acts 28:30), this arrest put him in chains and threatened his life (2 Timothy 2:9; 4:6–8). It was probably during this imprisonment that 2 Timothy was written, the last document known to have been authored by the apostle.

These three letters are characterized by an intense concern for false teaching. They contain some of the most situation-specific words in all of the New Testament as Paul identifies and corrects doctrinal and behavioral errors that threaten each location. In other words, the letters were written to specific pastors and congregations with some very specific problems and solutions in view. This, of course, does not mean that the material is not relevant today. Oftentimes what Paul does in these letters is apply general principles to first-century circumstances. The general principle is universally applicable and binding, but its appropriate "fitting point" changes as circumstances change. This is only to be expected. Because specific situations generated the letters, then, of necessity, these situations color and even decide the exact meaning of the apostle's words.

This considering of cultural-historical variables is particularly essential for the passages that obviously hinge upon unique conditions of the first-century. It is even more necessary for passages that would contradict the rest of Scripture if read without any understanding of the author's situation-specific intent. For example, most evangelical Christians do not use 1 Timothy 5:23 as grounds for ministers drinking alcoholic beverages but, instead, point out the cultural-historical reasons for reading the verse as reflective of unique first-century conditions. No one would dream of using Titus 1:12 as the basis for assuming that today's residents of Crete are liars, evil brutes, and lazy gluttons. These passages require some cultural-historical explaining in order to understand them in the way they were originally intended to be understood.

However, if there is to be *no* cultural-historical explaining of 1 Timothy 2:11–12, as some critics of women ministers would claim, then consistency requires that there be *absolutely none*. This would leave almost every church in the world in violation of Scripture because almost no congregation *totally* silences women or forbids them from doing *any* teaching whatsoever. Choir lofts and Sunday School classrooms would suddenly empty; special music, congregational singing, children's ministries, and practically everything else would have to be male-only or non-existent. Even more serious, *many* passages of Scripture would be absolutely unexplainable. Obviously, those who oppose women ministers are accusing themselves when they fault others for explaining the meaning of these two verses according to cultural-historical factors. *Both* the advocates and the opponents of women ministers are conditioning the passage with first-century considerations; the question is which group is doing so in alignment with the rest of Scripture and which group is doing so in alignment with personal preference and church convenience?

It must be noted, as well, that verses 9–10 are part of the same unit of material as verses 11–12, so the same hermeneutical handling must be applied to both sets of verses. The churches in which women are not allowed to participate in any form of vocalization or instruction would also have to forbid them from braiding their hair, although every bizarre version of coloring and styling that does not involve braiding would have to be acceptable, and forbid them from the wearing of gold or pearls, although jewelry made from every other material would have to be acceptable. If this interpretation seems ridiculous and even contrary to Scripture (Genesis 24:10,22; Exodus 3:21–22; 12:35–36; 35:4–5,20–22), then it should be clear that an identical handling of verses 11–12 is equally faulty. Either verses 9–10 *and* 11–12 are to be "situationally understood" or *neither* is to be handled in this way, but the third option of treating 9–10 one way and 11–12 in a totally different way is indefensible and, consequently, unacceptable.

Ephesian Heresies

Since the entirety of 1 Timothy 2:9–15 reflects apostolic corrections of specific problems within the church Timothy was pastoring, then, obviously, the better the problems are understood, the better the passage's solutions can be understood. Then and only then can the instructions found in this passage be properly applied rather than blindly and universally misapplied. So, what was first-century Ephesus like? What heresies plagued this city and its church?

Ephesus was unquestionably the most strategic city in all of Asia Minor. It served as a dual-direction gateway, positioned between the western and eastern portions of the Mediterranean world. Trade and travel between Rome and the Orient flowed through Ephesus. It was more accessible both by land and by sea than any other location in the area; consequently, its commercial and political importance far exceeded that of most cities in the Roman Empire. It is no wonder that Paul traveled to Ephesus more than once, assigned its early care to his two noteworthy colleagues Priscilla and Aquila (Acts 18:19–21), assigned its later care to his special assistant Timothy (1 Timothy 1:3), and invested years of his own ministry there (Acts 19:1,8–10; 20:17,31). No city other than Rome could have been more influential in evangelizing the first-century world because whatever saturated Ephesus spread throughout the surrounding area (Acts 19:10).

Culturally and religiously Ephesus was extremely diverse. It was populated by a wide variety of people groups who revered a vast array of deities. One goddess, however, dominated the scene like no other, affecting this great metropolis economically, culturally, and religiously. Artemis was her first-century Greek designation, although she was known at different times and in different locations by many other names. She was identified as the mother of life, embodying and overseeing reproductive power. Her great temple in Ephesus, the Artemisium, was one of the seven wonders of the world. It was four times the size of the Greek Parthenon in Athens. It served as a safe haven for the deposit of enormous amounts of money from all over the Mediterranean region and as a thriving loan agency. Between this enterprise and the lucrative businesses typically associated with heathen temples, such as the sculpting and selling of statues, the worship of Artemis and the economy of Ephesus were intricately interwoven. Daily life in this city could not be separated from the conspicuous, dominant influence of its goddess.

Anything as ancient and as fluctuating as this cult was is difficult to portray today with exactness. Scholars will probably never tire of debating various details. The bulk of scholarship, however, identifies the worship of Artemis as a "mother goddess fertility cult" that was one of many mystery religions of the era.

These mystery religions, oftentimes resulting from a blending of diverse ingredients, were the alternatives to government sanctioned emperor worship. The fertility cults, in particular, were characterized by the prominence of goddess worship which usually featured priestesses and oftentimes involved them in temple prostitution. Oddly enough, a goddess such as Artemis could be portrayed as responsible for giving life and as accepting sexual ritualistic worship while remaining a virgin herself, and a priestess could engage in sexual activities as an expression of worship while maintaining her own personal chastity. Contradictions such as these were common in ancient cults and, actually, served to strengthen them because such elasticity made it easy to absorb challenging ideologies.

Many scholars offer convincing evidence that goddess worship and its correlating priestess roles fostered a theology of female superiority. If this was the case, then Ephesus would have been a stronghold of such views because Artemis was the leading female deity of the day, and Ephesus was literally dedicated to her worship. Of course, whatever "cultic feminism" did exist, its emancipating and elevating effects were primarily restricted to the religious realm. This may explain why women were so highly attracted to the cults. Within them, they enjoyed a level of acceptance and involvement that was unmatched in any other sphere of daily life. Consequently, women were also great promoters of the goddess cults. One first-century native of Asia Minor wrote: "All regard women as the prime movers when it comes to religion."[2]

Even though the Roman Empire was extremely polytheistic, as was Ephesus, there is no question about the widespread popularity of Artemis. Not only have Ephesian coins been found which feature her image, but also similar coinage has been unearthed in numerous other locations. Her statues were transported all over the world. A craftsman whose income was being threatened by Paul's evangelizing of Ephesus referred to Artemis as being worshipped "throughout the province of Asia and the world" (Acts 19:27). In an effort to quiet the city-wide riot that broke out in support of this man's protests, the city clerk stepped onto the scene and mentioned the fact that "all of the world" knew about Ephesus' temple to the great Artemis (Acts 19:35). This cult was an extremely significant force in the ancient world.

In addition to the threat to Christianity posed by the cults of Artemis and other fertility goddesses, there was a second major source of heresy surfacing in Ephesus. Gnosticism, which was present in the second century and prominent by the third century is thought by many scholars to have been in its early stages during the latter half of the first century, especially in locations in which it eventually flourished such as Ephesus. There is considerable evidence in secular and in church writings to support this conclusion as well as numerous references in the apostolic epistles that refute known gnostic teachings.

Basic gnosticism can be explained rather simply and briefly. The physical world is evil, the spiritual world is good, and the two are in constant conflict. The physical world was created by the Old Testament God who is inferior to and opposed to the Supreme God. Emanations of special, secret knowledge about the Supreme God are available and can be ascertained by a few select spiritual individuals who may then mediate the truths to others. This knowledge must be obtained because it is the only hope of salvation. It will enable a person to transcend the deceiving Creator God and relate with the true Supreme God. Christ was a communication from the Supreme God who either only appeared to be human or perhaps entered Jesus' human body at baptism and left before crucifixion, either way avoiding any actual humanness. Because salvation is not tied in any way to faith or behavior and because the physical and spiritual realms do not connect, some gnostics were totally indulgent in their lifestyles while others were extremely restrictive.

This explanation of gnosticism emphasizes the points of agreement in a heresy that embraced numerous ideologies from its inception and evolved into many different forms before declining. Perhaps because of its ideological elasticity, it was so well received in the ancient world, a world of such diverse philosophical and theological persuasions. Some strands of gnosticism taught a "reverse version" of the Old Testament through their fanciful myths and genealogies, especially regarding the creation and fall accounts.[3] Their version depicted the Creator God as withholding knowledge of the spiritual realm from the first couple, whereas the serpent made it available. Eve, existing before Adam and perhaps even instrumental in his creation, proved to be more perceptive than her partner in responding to the serpent's offer of life-giving knowledge. Thus, she was enlightened, not deceived. Because of this she was glorified as the original mediator of spiritual truth and revered as the "mother of all the living" (Genesis 3:20), sometimes even taking on the supernatural qualities associated with a mother goddess. As Eve's offspring, women were credited with being more perceptive mediators of spiritual truth than men and generally superior to men.

It is easy to see how compatible gnosticism was with the fertility cults that were already deeply entrenched in the ancient world. Even Jews were surprisingly susceptible to its charms. It is also obvious how attractive goddess worship and gnosticism would have been to women. Every sphere of life proclaimed their inferiority, and they were deliberately denied the opportunities for education that might have improved such low status. In contrast, the fertility cults and gnosticism recognized and elevated the female gender, placing women into spiritual leadership and allowing them to rely upon mystical and emotional insights rather than requiring them to have rational, educational training.

It must be more than coincidence that Paul makes references in his Pastoral Epistles to teachings and activities based in the fertility cults and developed by the gnostics. These are especially noticeable in the two letters written to Timothy at Ephesus. Of all of the churches Paul planted, Ephesus was particularly plagued with resistance, both from Jews and Gentiles (Acts 19:8–9,23,29), and he warned the early leaders that intense opposition would continue (Acts 20:17,28–31). He described the difficulty that he experienced with this location in unusually strong language (1 Corinthians 15:32) and sent Timothy to the congregation specifically for the purpose of combating the threat and influx of heresy (1 Timothy 1:3).

The situation was definitely serious. This may have been because Ephesus was unusually capable of extinguishing the gospel by absorbing it into its diverse collection of pagan ideologies. Or, perhaps Paul's primary concern had more to do with the city's unique ability to affect the surrounding region, either positively or negatively. Without a doubt, whatever truth or error that captured Ephesus spread through Asia Minor and beyond in very little time.

Whatever his reason for watch-dogging Ephesus so carefully, Paul's references to gnostic teachings and activities are particularly prevalent in 1 Timothy. His closing words are very likely to allude to their special, secret "gnosis" ["knowledge"]: "Turn away from godless chatter and the opposing ideas of what is falsely called knowledge ['gnosis']" (6:20). He refers to the myths and genealogies that so characterized this heresy (1:4; 4:7) and to its equally distinguishing use of argumentation (1:4; 6:3–4). He refutes its ascetic tendencies regarding marriage and diet (4:1–5) and repeatedly rebuts its licentious tendencies (1:9–11; 4:12; 5:24–25; 6:11). Most noteworthy are the possible corrections pervading the very passage that contains instructions regarding women: all people are savable rather than just a select few (2:4), the Creator God and the Supreme God are not two different beings (2:5), earthly mediators are unnecessary for there is only one mediator (2:5–6), reversing or falsifying God's written revelation is not the way to convert Gentiles (2:7), and argumentation is counterproductive to spiritual effectiveness (2:8). Is it possible that the remaining verses were understood by the original audience as temporary, local corrections of gnostic errors rather than as permanent, universal injunctions against women?

It is true that Paul identifies men as the teachers of the heresies Timothy is to combat (1 Timothy 1:20; 2 Timothy 2:17–18; 3:8–9; 4:14–15). Ephesian women, however, are identified as their special target and means of infiltrating the church (2 Timothy 3:6–7). Paul regards the male teachers as responsible and deliberate enough to relegate them to the destiny they deserve. He says of them such things as, "whom I have handed over to Satan" (1 Timothy 1:20) and "the Lord will repay him for what he has done" (2 Timothy 4:14). In contrast, the Ephesian women are described quite differently, as being less than responsible or deliberate (2 Timothy 3:6–7). Is it possible that Paul is making emergency provisions for the protection of these women and their church by stipulating that they first learn (1 Timothy 2:11) before being allowed to teach or lead?

This explanation of the passage would align with what is known about the local Ephesian circumstances while avoiding conclusions that contradict the rest of Scripture. Everyone knows that extreme, temporary measures can be taken in the face of unique, critical situations that are not reflective of the general patterns that would otherwise be followed. Jesus Himself repeatedly ordered the silence of those receiving His ministry (Matthew 8:4; 9:30; 12:16; 17:9; Mark 1:43–44; 3:12; 5:43; 7:36; 9:9; Luke 5:14; 8:56). He even silenced the twelve disciples regarding his identity (Matthew 16:20; Mark 8:30; Luke 9:21).

There were reasons for this restriction, namely, controlling His popularity and timing His death. Once the reasons were removed, the restriction is understood to have been removed.

If there is any initial confusion about the passages from Jesus' ministry, they need only be compared to His overall practice regarding witnessing to be understood as situational accommodations. Likewise, if there is confusion or doubt regarding 1 Timothy 2:11–12, it need only be compared to Paul's overall practice regarding women to be understood as a temporary, local arrangement. Somewhat of a journal of his practice can be found in Romans 16. Here he chronicles a representative sampling of his *ministerial* colleagues over the years. These individuals did not sit silently in sanctuaries; they, like Paul, evangelized and discipled their world through preaching and teaching the gospel. As has been noted earlier, of the 29 people cited by name in this chapter, ten are women, fully one third. Among the ten women is a female apostle. Obviously, Paul and the Early Church did not apply the 1 Timothy 2 restriction universally.[4] How can any congregation or denomination today think it right to do so? What Paul does in 1 Timothy 2:11–12 is propose a long-term solution, women learning, for a short-term problem, women not yet ready to teach or lead. His wisdom is particularly fitting in the Ephesian setting in which cunning, destructive heresy is running rampant and is specifically targeting the untaught, vulnerable women.

Placement of Passage

Paul states his reason for positioning Timothy and for writing to him in 1 Timothy 1:3–4. The young pastor's assignment and the veteran apostle's correspondence are all about combating the heresies that plague the Ephesian church. This is the topic of the entire opening chapter of the book. The motivation for correction is clarified (1:5), multiple identifications and descriptions of the heretics are given (1:6–11,18–20), and, in between, admission of personal error is made (1:12–17).

The "therefore" or "then" that opens verse 1 of chapter 2 ties the two chapters together. The chapter break inserted by translators poses no serious problem, but it should be understood that chapter 2 is clearly a continuation of chapter 1. The topic of heresy that is identified in chapter 1 is further detailed in chapter 2. Timothy is told to fight it in chapter 1 and is told how to do so in chapter 2. What Paul chooses to mention, then, in chapter 2 as well as the solutions he offers for the problems cited must be read as a reflection of the local situation that Timothy is overseeing.

More could be said about praying than is found in verses 1, 2, and 8, but it can be assumed that Paul is correcting the weakness or wrongdoing that is present and is not really attempting to do anything else. The one thing he says regarding men in verse 8 seems rather arbitrary and woefully incomplete if it is taken as the one and only thing all men need to know and practice. Even if it is taken as the one and only instruction men require regarding prayer, it still falls short because men are depicted elsewhere in Scripture as bowing to the ground (Exodus 34:8) and falling on their faces (Numbers 20:6; Joshua 5:14) in prayer, neither of which permits any lifting of the hands. If, however, it is understood as addressing a significant shortcoming found among the Ephesian men, then it becomes very purposeful and adequate *for the target audience*.

The fact that more is said about women than about men means that the women in the Ephesian church were needing more correction than the men. As with the men and prayer, what is said about the women and teaching-leading actually falls far short of representing the complete biblical position on the subject if taken on its own. As it stands, it reflects and corrects the errors of a certain congregation. The rest of Scripture would have to be added to it in order to construct a thorough biblical statement on women and teaching-leading. Of course, the moment this is done, the weight of evidence shifts toward opening these and all other ministries to women who are called and qualified.

Appropriate Appearance

After specifying the proper way in which men are to present themselves in prayer, Paul turns to the Ephesian women in verse 9 with the word "hosautos" ("likewise" or "in the same way"). This construction in the Greek language allows and even invites the idea of praying to be carried from verse 8 into verse 9. Bridging one idea across two statements is not always intended when a Greek writer uses this word in this way, but there are two reasons to think it is Paul's intent here. First, public prayer was something women did in first-century churches

(1 Corinthians 11:5). Second, without the idea of praying applying to both men and women, the connection and parallel between Paul's male-female comments in these verses are virtually lost. Men praying and women dressing are totally mismatched, but men praying properly and women praying properly offers an obvious and sensible match in Paul's presentation, thus, explaining his use of the word "likewise."

So, Paul is correcting male improprieties in public prayer in verse 8, and it is likely that he is doing the same thing as it relates to women in verse 9. This does not mean that the instructions given in these verses are "one-gender-only" in their application any more than Ephesians 6:4 can be understood as "father-only" in its application. It simply means that each gender in the Ephesian church was displaying certain tendencies that required extra, explicit correction to rectify. If someone else displays one of these same wrong tendencies, then its correlating correction applies. Maybe the men used public prayer to further their personal or theological quarrels, and the women used it to draw attention to their wealth or beauty.[5] Whatever the reasons, Paul finds both groups guilty of wrongdoing.

The general principles that are identified in verse 9 are modesty, decency, and propriety, obviously applicable to all cultures and desirable for all Christians. In direct contrast to these characteristics, specifics are then identified as forbidden: braided hair, gold, pearls, and expensive clothing. The only sensible conclusion that can be drawn from this presentation is that the specifics represent, at least in first-century society, obvious and unacceptable violations of the general principles. Every culture would have examples of violations, although perhaps quite different from the four listed here. The general principles of modesty, decency and propriety are universally binding, but the specific examples of attire or behavior that would be in violation of these principles are oftentimes culturally determined and are, therefore, to some degree changeable.

What is known about first-century culture, Jewish and Gentile, confirms this interpretation of the passage. Braiding the hair was considered an extreme style, perhaps because the braids of hair were typically laced with jewels or other expensive materials, thereby associating the style with the extravagance and ostentatiousness of the wealthy. The wearing of gold and pearls seems to have been perceived as equally lavish, and the descriptor "expensive" or "costly" adjoining the reference to clothing is clear. At the very least, then, some of the believing women were violating propriety by flaunting wealth in their physical appearance.

The problem may have been more serious, however. There is ample evidence to indicate that certain extremely showy "high fashions" were not only associated with wealth but also with sensuality. The same features may not convey the same thing in a given culture today, but if a first-century woman knowingly and intentionally presented herself in ways considered sexually suggestive or seductive within her society, then she was wearing her hair, jewelry, or clothing improperly for a godly woman. Evidence also suggests associations with rebelliousness, promiscuity, prostitution, and various forms of pagan worship, any of which would be an undesirable image for a Christian woman to portray. Even the secular literature of the day decried empty displays of wealth through fashion and denounced sexually alluring attire and adornment that disregarded culturally defined respectability. Instead, Paul indicates, a believing, worshipping woman is to be characterized by her good deeds (2:10).

Quietness and Submission

It is rather remarkable that *what* Paul says is to occur in 1 Timothy 2:11 can be so completely obscured by the less significant *how* he says it is to occur. What is even more tragic is that the modern obsession with the "how" manages to misrepresent the way it would have been understood by the original audience, resulting in unwelcome rather than welcome conditions. So, the wrong part of verse 11 is commonly emphasized, and then that part is totally misunderstood. The "what is to occur" is that the Ephesian women are to learn. The "how" is that they are to do this learning quietly and submissively. Neither of these stipulations restricts women; to the contrary, both provisions open privileges to women that were previously the sole domain of men.

The verb "manthano" ("learn") found in verse 11 is used several times throughout the New Testament for various types of learning. In the first century it was commonly used to refer to the learning that occurred in formal rabbinical schools, the very educational experience that was said to be missing in Jesus' background (John 7:15). Paul puts the word in the imperative mood, indicating that he is *commanding* that this learning occur. The KJV "let" is much too soft. Paul is saying that women "should" or "must" be given opportunity to learn. He is ordering that this be done. In fact, even though a command can be given without using the imperative mood, it is the only mood automatically associated with the giving of a command. Interestingly, of everything said about women in this passage, only the provision for their learning is put in the imperative mood.

It was nothing short of revolutionary for Paul to command that women learn. Jewish women were not welcome in the all-important study of the law . Women were equally excluded from meaningful educational pursuits in Greek and Roman circles. Within the Christian community, however, the opportunity for learning is not just allowed or encouraged; *it is ordered*. Paul is not limiting women to some lowly position here; he is lifting them to a lofty position. In a world in which they are not seen as having the ability to learn, he is saying that they have much more than this; they have the *right* to learn. Never before in human history is such a thing known to have been said. Without a doubt when Paul's original audience read what is today 1 Timothy 2:11, it was not the words "quietness" and "submission" that stood out but the words "woman" and "learn."[6]

The modern reader, however, *does* hear the words "quietness" and "submission," and these words were very much present in Paul's letter. The difference is, whereas such stipulations may be perceived today as negatives, this would not have been the case in Paul's day. The first of the two conditions "hesuchia" is better translated "quietness" (NIV) than "silence" (KJV), and it should be noted that the identical word requires proper translation in verse 12. It appears two other times in the New Testament in this noun form (Acts 22:2; 2 Thessalonians 3:12), two times in the adjective form (1 Timothy 2:2; 1 Peter 3:4), and five times in the verb form (Luke 14:4; 23:56; Acts 11:18; 21:14; 1 Thessalonians 4:11). Of these nine other occurrences, three are found in Paul's writings (1 Thessalonians 4:11; 2 Thessalonians 3:12; 1 Timothy 2:2), and all three carry the idea of a tranquil, non-disruptive state of being rather than suggesting any silencing of the tongue per se.

Of the three other Pauline uses of this word in its various forms, two of the three encourage entire churches toward living quiet lives (1 Thessalonians 4:11; 1 Timothy 2:2), including a reference only sentences before the verses regarding women. Obviously, he is not calling whole congregations to lives of absolute silence, either publicly or privately, so there is no reason to conclude this about women. The meaning of the word as he uses it has more to do with one's attitude and spirit than with one's tongue. Paul is describing a disposition that is compliant and harmonious, a life that is without unnecessary, unhealthy self-assertiveness, contentiousness, or commotion.

This demeanor that the female learner is told to display was the demeanor thought appropriate for all learners in first-century education, both Jewish and Gentile. It signified respect for the instructor and attentiveness toward the lesson. It was an admirable quality that made the setting conducive to learning and distinguished a student as receptive. It was not in any way perceived as being restrictive; it was simply associated with a proper approach to learning.

It is possible that the women of Ephesus were in need of this explicit instruction or correction in order to compensate for having little or no experience with the formal learning environment. Worse yet, if their only exposure to public forum came from participation in the mystery cults, then they would have been terribly mis-signaled as to proper decorum since these meetings were characterized by noise and chaos. How easy it would have been for their new-believer exuberance to cause them to be disruptive students. In addition, if several of these women were being misled by false teaching, they may have been approaching the church service with a challenging, wrangling spirit that was not only unbecoming of those needing instruction but detrimental to others.

So, all Paul is asking of women is what was commonly expected of any disciple receiving instruction, specifically, a respectful and receptive approach to learning. The same quality that he desires for everyone in his/her daily life (2:2), he requires of a student in the learning environment. This "quietness" is conducive to peaceful living and to productive learning. It has nothing to do with whether or not someone is talking but has everything to do with *how* he or she is talking. Other passages of Scripture make it quite clear that qualified women did enjoy vocal, public, and authoritative participation in the worship services. This verse does not in any way prevent their doing so.

In addition to learning quietly, women are also to learn submissively (2:11). These two words are probably being used synonymously since both connote a spirit of respect and receptivity. The two together give further clarity and emphasis to what Paul is saying. The word "hupotage" ("submission") is the noun form of the verb "hupotasso" ("submit") found in Ephesians 5:21 and in several other New Testament locations.

Unfortunately, any time "woman" and "submission" are used in the same sentence, many readers assume that the submission is to be rendered to a man or at least to a husband. This stipulation, however, is not found in Paul's statement. Because the focus of his comments is upon approaching learning appropriately, it is more likely that the submission is to be directed toward what is being taught (sound doctrine), who is doing the teaching (local church leadership), and/or where the teaching is occurring (gathering of believers). Rather than being assertive or challenging in any of these directions, the woman who still requires learning is to submissively receive what she needs. It is even possible that no object for the submission is identified because no specific object is intended, the point being that the woman is to simply have a submissive spirit rather than to engage in any specific act of submission.

The one conclusion that is unacceptable is that the use of "submission" in verse 11 establishes a male-female hierarchy in the church. This would mean that women, simply by virtue of their gender, are automatically under the authority of men, and this position does not have the support of Scripture. First, numerous godly women throughout the Bible would render this view invalid. Second, even if someone denies that the Bible teaches mutual submissiveness within marriage and, instead, claims that it teaches a hierarchical arrangement, a husband-over-wife relationship cannot be equated with or transferred into the arena of general male-female relationships. As has been noted repeatedly, doing so would put every woman under every man, an arrangement that few if any husbands would be able to accept.

It should be noted that some scholars do see in verses 11–12 a stipulation that applies only to wives in relation to their husbands rather than to women in general. This is based upon the switch from the plural "men" in verse 8 and the plural "women" in verses 9–10 to the singular language found in verses 11–12. It can even be said that the focus upon marriage is continued in verses 13–14 since Adam and Eve were not only the first man and woman but also the first husband and wife; and, obviously, verse 15 discusses an issue that relates to marriage. However, unless a hierarchical view of marriage is held, it would be difficult to explain why a wife is being told what is contained in verses 11–12. Perhaps Paul is forbidding public behavior that is perceived as culturally unacceptable for a married woman, but this leaves questions as to why he would include a reference to Adam and Eve, a non-cultural reference, in the next two verses. A further difficulty is posed by the fact that reading verses 11–12 as pertaining only to the marriage relationship leaves certain biblical women in violation of the passage.

It is more likely that the Ephesian women in general are the target of verses 9–10 *and* 11–12 rather than any differentiation between women and wives. The rest of Scripture does not support provisions like these being the result of gender or marital status. However, in this very letter Paul refers to church leaders being "able to teach" (3:2) and warns against positioning them prematurely (5:22). The Ephesian women are not yet ready to teach or lead, but they are ready to learn. In a precedent-setting mandate, Paul makes provision for their learning to occur and ensures that it will occur properly.

Paul's Restriction

After establishing in verse 11 that the Ephesian women do qualify for learning, Paul specifies in verse 12 what they do not qualify to do. The two verses are connected with the Greek word "de" ("but") which can serve as a conditioning or contrasting conjunction. The connection between the two verses is further indicated by the fact that verse 11's stipulation "in quietness," which actually appears early in verse 11 in the Greek text immediately after the word "woman," is repeated at the end of verse 12: "but to be in quietness." The word "but" in this latter phrase translates the Greek word "all" which signals a strong contrast with what has just been said. Thus, the bracketing of the restriction with this repeated call for a restful, peaceful spirit along with the structuring of the two verses suggests that whatever these women are not to do is being seen as the opposite of this tranquillity that is appropriate for them and for all believers.

Before investigating what Paul does not allow the women to do, it is necessary to look more closely at his wording "I do not permit." In the Greek language, the present tense, in which the verb "permit" is written, has two "senses" available: one-time or temporary action in the present or continuing action in the present. Even beginner Greek textbooks note these two possibilities. Any time the meaning of a passage is dependent upon determining which of the two senses is intended, the context and perhaps the scriptural canon as a whole must furnish the clues because the Greek language does not differentiate. If Paul has the temporary sense in view, then "I am not presently allowing" would be a clearer English rendering of his point than "I do not allow" which tilts the statement toward the continuing sense.

Two details of the verse are the only clues available from the context as to which sense Paul intends, and neither is decisive. First, he indicates that the restriction is coming from him rather than from God, Scripture, or any type of Early Church practice or policy. Second, the verb "allow" is in the indicative mood rather than the imperative mood. It is true that universal commands can appear in the indicative mood; in fact, examples can be found in verses 1 and 8 of this chapter. However, *the change* from the authoritative wording of verse 11 to the wording of verse 12 may be significant. In verse 12 Paul shifts to "I" while simultaneously shifting out of the commanding imperative mood and into the more stating/informing indicative mood. Verse 11 clearly contains the command (a women must learn) while, in contrast, verse 12 seems to contain the present action that Paul deems prudent in light of current circumstances.[7]

The evidence from the scriptural canon as a whole that verse 12 contains localized, provisional stipulations *is* decisive. Numerous examples can be cited of women in Scripture who taught, who taught men, who exercised authority, who exercised authority over men, and who did "all of the above" with biblical endorsement. There certainly seems to be an "understood latitude" about how the Early Church received the directives found in this verse, indicating that they were known to be situational in nature. If a woman had nothing to do with the cause or the intent of the stipulations, she was exempt from them. After all, Priscilla had ministered in this very city only a few years earlier (Acts 18:19, 24–26), and she would return and be greeted by Paul when he wrote again (2 Timothy 4:19). His second letter to Timothy would be written from Rome, the same city to which he had sent greetings, again, only a few years earlier, to ten female ministerial colleagues (Romans 16). It would not have been possible for them to serve in such capacities without teaching and exercising authority.

This same Paul absolutely forbids circumcision with wording that is much more firm than what is found in this verse about women (Galatians 5:2), but he is the one who had Timothy circumcised (Acts 16:1–3). And, of course, Christians in the western world think nothing of circumcising their baby boys; they certainly do not view it as a serious violation of Scripture. How is it that Paul, Timothy, and millions of believing parents see themselves as exempt from the prohibition of Galatians 5:2? The answer is Paul had in view conditions under which circumcision was wrong and will always be wrong, namely, depending upon it to make a man right with God. Similarly in 1 Timothy 2:12, he had in view conditions under which certain activities by women are wrong. However, if the conditions are not present, then the restriction is not applicable. Of course, latitude like this is not presented or commended in Scripture for many provisions because they are unequivocally universal in nature, but this does not change the fact that some stipulations are just as clearly conditional in nature. To handle one as if it is the other would be to totally mishandle it.

The condition that was present among the Ephesian women and perhaps among women in other first-century locations is indicated by the provision of verse 11. They suffered from an extreme lack of education. Because of this, they were not yet qualified to teach or lead. The Ephesian church was probably comprised of Jews and Gentiles, and among both groups of people, boys went to school and girls did not. This was the case for everyone except a few of the very wealthy who had home tutors for their daughters. These girls, at least, were able to learn how to read and write, skills that most other girls did not acquire. Just as important but just as absent from most girls' backgrounds was the year-after-year training of the mind that schooling made possible. An adult whose mental faculties have had little or no discipline over the life span can be quite handicapped mentally. Thinking processes may not be as analytical and logical as possible. Self-checking skills may not be as thorough and consistent as desirable. Of course, lack of formal education does not necessarily result in any of these weaknesses, but this coupled with a pervading societal image of incompetency would significantly increase the chances of girls growing into womanhood without ever approaching their full intellectual potential.

It is no wonder that women were attracted to the cults which viewed them more positively and gave them generous opportunity for meaningful involvement. It is also no wonder that women were specifically targeted by the heretics who threatened Christianity (2 Timothy 3:6–7). Many of them would have been easy prey for a convincing argument, left so vulnerable by their lack of intellectual training. As the "prime movers when it comes to religion," at least in Gentile circles, their influence upon men and entire households would have been enormous. Any errors accepted and propagated by them would have been rampant through a church and through a community in no time.

If it seems unthinkable that Paul would generalize an entire group of people into one category, the comment that he makes regarding a whole island of people in his letter to Titus is worth noting (Titus 1:12–13). *Generally*, first-century women were not ready to teach or lead. They were too susceptible to error because they were so unlearned. Their need was for training, precisely what Paul prescribes in verse 11. And according to Paul, one of the major reasons someone is given training is to qualify that person to train others (2 Timothy 2:2, with the word being "anthropos" which must be translated "persons" rather than "men"). So, once these women learn properly and adequately, they would be able to join the ranks of the ministering women whom Paul depended upon and commended.[8]

Just as Galatians 5:2–3 must be interpreted "any man *who puts stock in circumcision* must not be circumcised," 1 Timothy 2:12 must be interpreted "any woman *who is unlearned and unqualified* must not teach or lead." Gender caused women to be denied educational opportunities that would have given them an intellectual maturity commensurate with that of men, and it was the resulting intellectual immaturity, *not their gender*, that stood behind the restrictions of verse 12. No one is to be positioned prematurely (5:22). This is the universal principle found in verse 12. But in first-century culture, women comprised an extraordinary proportion of the unlearned, unready believers. What was "wrong" with them was a result of their culture, however, not their gender.

Some scholars do amazing gymnastics with this passage in order to conclude that women may engage in teaching and leading in almost every setting except the main congregational worship service. This position automatically affects the issue of whether they qualify to serve as senior pastors and usually touches the question of whether they qualify for ministerial credentials. These conclusions rest on at least three sizable errors. First, first-century churches did not have the multiplicity and variety of weekly gatherings that characterize the typical local church today. It is difficult to say that women can teach Sunday School and lead children's church if neither existed in the first century. The body of believers simply met and usually did so in someone's home. Second, even if these additional meetings and ministries had existed in the Early Church, it is totally arbitrary and indefensible to claim that part of the congregation sitting in a side room is somehow intrinsically different from the whole congregation sitting in the sanctuary.

Third and perhaps most problematic, this position requires the passage to be read as if it is referring specifically and exclusively to the worship service, thus freeing women to disregard verse 12 in all other settings. Though there are clearly applications of chapters 2 and 3 to the worship service, the focus is more upon the overall functioning of the community of believers, only one phase of which is the sanctuary service. Surely the praying that opens chapter 2 can occur inside and outside the service. The proper demeanor of the men in verse 8 and the proper dress of the women in verses 9–10 also invites application inside and outside the sanctuary. One can only hope that the event referred to in verse 15 will not happen during service! Overseers and deacons (chapter 3) function far more outside the actual church service than they do within its confines. Whatever Paul is saying in verses 11–12 about women, it must be applied to the general functioning of the community of believers, not just to the main congregational worship service. If anyone takes a stand using 1 Timothy 2:11–12, let it be done honestly and consistently.

Teaching and Leading

In considering the specific stipulations found in verse 12, one is immediately challenged to determine whether Paul is forbidding the Ephesian women from engaging in two activities or just one. Is he saying that they are not to do any teaching, and they are also not to do any leading of men? Or, is he saying that they are not to do any version of teaching men that would be the equivalent of leading them? The two items are connected in the text with the Greek conjunction "oude" which has standard translation options of "and not, not even, nor, neither." Scholars are rather split on the use of the word to connect two distinct things versus its role in connecting two related things. A conclusion on the matter does not necessarily affect the "women in ministry" issue because advocates and opponents are found in both camps. Perhaps, then, the whole issue should be set aside and only mentioned as it affects the study of each stipulation.

First, then, Paul uses the infinitive "didasko" (to teach). There is nothing unusual or special about the word; it is the common term for the act of teaching. Obviously, the Ephesian women are not ready to teach until they are given ample opportunity to learn. The evidence that their standing would then change is taken from practically every other reference to women and teaching found in the biblical account of the Early Church. Even if verse 12 is read as referring specifically to authoritative teaching or to authoritative teaching of men, there is impressive evidence that women engaged in these activities with the approval of Paul and of Scripture.

Without repeating the detail that is found earlier, such as in the section entitled "Women as Teachers" (chapter 8), the following represents a summary of New Testament evidence that qualified women did teach in the Early Church. (1) None of the gifts listings indicate any gender restrictions but, instead, emphasize broad availability, even though teaching and leading gifts are included in the lists (Romans 12, 1 Corinthians 12, Ephesians 4). (2) Several references are made to believers teaching fellow believers, again, with the impression being that congregation-wide participation is in view (1 Corinthians 14:26; Colossians 3:16; 2 Timothy 2:2). (3) Specific reference is made to the elder women of Crete teaching others (Titus 2:3). (4) Women are known to have engaged in prophecy (Acts 21:9; 1 Corinthians 11:5), and all believers are encouraged to seek this gift (1 Corinthians 14:1) for it is open to all (1 Corinthians 14:31). One of its purposes is the instruction of the entire congregation (1 Corinthians 14:31). (5) The women who seem to have pastored house churches (Acts 12:12; 16:40; Colossians 4:15) and the two women who are cited as elders (2 John) were pastor-teachers (Ephesians 4:11) and surely engaged in both teaching and leading. (6) The several women identified by Paul as ministerial colleagues (see chapter 8) could not have served in such a capacity without engaging in teaching and leading. (7) Priscilla was the lead member of a husband-wife team whose ministerial involvement was extensive, including teaching the great apostle Apollos (Acts 18:24–26). (8) Timothy, an adult and a minister, is directed by Paul to continue relying upon the teaching given to him by women (2 Timothy 1:5; 3:14–15).

This enormous amount of evidence cannot be set aside with one verse of Scripture that was originally intended for special circumstances in Ephesus. All of it happened because Jesus left a command that all believers are to obey, and the command very much involves authoritative teaching (Matthew 28:19–20). Claims that women taught only women and children do not fit the "all believers" passages or the meeting practices of the Early Church or the activities of Paul's female colleagues. Explanations of prophecy being vertical and therefore "safe" versus teaching being horizontal and therefore "more vulnerable" demonstrate very little knowledge of these two gifts of the Spirit. Notions about it being different for Priscilla to teach one apostle in a home versus several laymen in a sanctuary are without meaning or merit. It is equally futile to argue that verse 12 is referring to the office of teacher-leader, namely, elder or pastor, rather than the acts of teaching and leading. The verse obviously refers to activity; no indication of office is even suggested. Besides, act and office were one-and-the-same in the Early Church. No, the evidence does not "explain away" with any of these efforts. Women did teach in the Early Church; consequently, 1 Timothy 2:12 must represent the exception rather than the rule.

The second infinitive that Paul uses in the verse is "authenteo." Unlike the preceding word for teach, this word appears only here in Scripture. It is not the term normally associated with the use of authority in Scripture or other Greek literature; consequently, its meaning is debated by scholars. If it means something neutral or positive such as "exercise authority," then the Ephesian women are being barred from any leadership roles that would position them over men. If it means something negative such as "wrongfully usurp authority" or "dictatorially domineer," then they are only being forbidden from engaging in this improper approach to leadership.

Just the fact that Paul deliberately chooses to use such an unusual word begins to indicate that he is probably wanting to convey an unusual point, something other than the simple, ordinary "exercise authority." If he has this normal activity in view, it is very likely that he would use the expression "have authority" that he and other biblical writers use repeatedly. This common word for "authority" ("exousia") is found over 100 times in the New Testament, including 28 times in Paul's writings. There was no question in first-century Greek as to what it meant. It meant exactly what opponents of women ministers claim verse 12 means; the only problem is that it is not the word Paul chose to use.

Part of the difficulty of defining "authenteo" results from the fact that its meaning changed considerably over time, from an early meaning of "commit murder" to a late meaning of "exercise authority," with meanings such as "initiate violence," "originate," "instigate," and "dominate" in between. Scholars can pull examples of its use in Greek literature which they offer as proof of the meaning being "exercise authority," but their evidence typically dates from one to several hundred years after the first century. By that time it did carry the meaning they favor (in addition to other meanings), but it evidently did not do so during the first century when Paul's letter was written, received, and circulated.

The little bit of pertinent evidence that is available leans toward a meaning of "dictate, master, dominate, rule heavy-handedly, have absolute power over, take undue control to oneself." It is a strong word, stronger and, consequently, more negative than the simple, common term "exercise authority." Paul is not referring here to regular leadership, and he is certainly not referring to leadership as it is prescribed for the body of believers (Matthew 20:25–28; Mark 10:42–45). If he were, then godly women such as Deborah would stand in violation of this passage, for she was the highest ranking civil and spiritual leader in all of Israel, certainly exercising authority over men, evidently even over her husband. No, Paul is intentionally using a word that carries the idea of forcefully thrusting oneself upon others. This is not to be done by men or by women. The Ephesian women are evidently engaging in this wrongdoing, and Paul forbids it.

Verses 11 and 12 reflect an interesting parallel. The women are in need of learning (v. 11), so, right now, they must not teach (v. 12). Instead of thrusting themselves upon the men who are capable of teaching them (v. 12), they are to learn with spirits that reflect receptivity (v. 11). In doing the right thing (v. 11) and in refraining from doing the wrong thing (v. 12), the over-riding result will be the tranquillity (quietness) that should be present among them. Instead of this scenario, the Ephesian women may have had more zeal than knowledge and were perhaps prematurely and wrongfully pressing themselves forward. They may have been overly aggressive and overly abrasive, maybe even desiring to advance some of the heresies that were especially targeting them. This would, of course, cause them to be characterized by turmoil rather than by tranquillity.

Adam and Eve

Paul follows the provisions of 1 Timothy 2:11–12 with references to Adam and Eve, specifically to their creation and fall. Those who oppose the teaching and leading roles of women contend that Paul is giving two reasons here for silencing and subjugating women, the first being that Adam preceded Eve in creation and the second being that she preceded him in the fall. Those who favor women's entry into ministerial activities see Paul as making one point in verses 13–14, and they have a totally different explanation of the point.

Verses 11 and 12 are linked to verses 13 and 14 with the Greek word "gar." The link is unquestionable, but its meaning is debatable. The word has several uses available, any one of which may be operating in this passage. First, it can be causative, in which case it introduces a reason or cause standing behind what has just been said. A clear English word for this occurrence would be "because." Second, it can be illustrative, in which case it introduces an example or illustration of what has just been said. In these instances, the best English rendering is probably "for instance" or "for example." This is very similar to a third use which has the sense of introducing a confirmation of the previous statement rather than an example per se, and could be represented with the word "indeed." A fourth use simply serves to continue the thought that has just been mentioned, carrying the idea of the conjunction "and."

Obviously, it matters how Paul is using the word "gar" to connect verses 13–14 with verses 11–12. If he means "because," then he proceeds to supply one or more reasons for the restrictions he has just stated. Since what he supplies comes partially from the creation account (as well as from the fall account), people who favor this interpretation conclude that the provisions of the passage are therefore creation-based and universal rather than situation-based and applicable only as appropriate. Of course, no explanation is given for the half of the reason that is fall-based, in other words, Satan-generated rather than God-generated; nor is any explanation given for the fact that head coverings (1 Corinthians 11:3–16) and seventh-day Sabbath observation (Exodus 20:8–11; Hebrews 4:3–4) are also given creation basis in Scripture.

On the other hand, if Paul is using the word "gar" in any one of the other three ways, especially as "for instance, for example," then he is not supplying creation-based reasons that lock his restrictions into universal application. Instead, after warning Timothy about a situation that is present among the Ephesians, he further solidifies his point by citing an illustration of a similar situation with which they are both familiar, noting the tragic results. This type of analogy was popular with first-century Jews like Paul. It supplies a "controlled comparison" for the purpose of likening two things, but it is important to realize that they are alike only on certain points. In fact, Jews oftentimes enjoyed comparing two essentially different things in order for one or more points of similarity to be all the more intriguing and impressive.

There are compelling reasons to reject the "because" option for "gar" along with its accompanying notion that Paul is basing his restrictions upon universal principles that are anchored in Genesis. The two "proofs" that he is supposedly giving in verses 13–14, one from creation and one from the fall, cannot be defended with Scripture, with history, or with reason. First, is the "creation proof" of Adam being formed before Eve. As has been noted earlier (chapter 2), Genesis 1–2 says nothing about Adam's firstness indicating a nature that is better than Eve's or a position that is higher than Eve's. Everything these opening chapters do say indicates just the opposite, an equality of being and an equality of assignment. There is not a word about hierarchy until the sin of Genesis 3 causes it to exist. As has been asked earlier, does the church wish to endorse and promote the other results of sin listed in Genesis 3 or just this one? Paul makes it quite clear in 1 Corinthians 11:11–12 that sexual or marital hierarchy is to be meaningless and nonexistent among believers.

It is, indeed, difficult to understand how the arrival of Adam before Eve thousands of years earlier could cause a first-century Ephesian man to be inherently "more spiritual, more knowledgeable, more qualified" to teach and lead than a first-century Ephesian woman.[9] The biblical examples of women who were more competent than their counterpart men have already been cited (chapter 5). These can be put alongside countless historical and contemporary examples of women who exceed the teaching and leading performances of men. Before anyone can claim that Satan subverted or Eve reversed some divine chain of command, the existence of the chain of command must be proven; and God's repeated violation of it must be explained, neither of which can be done. Obviously, the issue in 1 Timothy 2:11–14 is not chronology or gender but the capacity *of the Ephesian women* to do harm.

The second component of this misinterpretation of verses 13–14 is the "fall proof" of Eve sinning before Adam. Of course, in order for her wrongdoing to have a direct bearing on all subsequent women, there must be a theological connection between Eve and all other women. They have either been imputed her gullibility or her guilt. In other words, they either inherit from Eve a *unique-to-their-gender* gullibility or guilt that renders them disqualified to teach and lead. What a position for the opponents of women ministers to be left trying to support.

Are women uniquely gullible and therefore not qualified to teach and lead? Paul makes it very clear in 2 Corinthians 11:3 that an entire congregation is capable of Eve's gullibility. This includes men as much as women. In this verse he associates *all* of the Corinthians with Eve just as much as he associates *only* the Ephesian women with her in 1 Timothy 2. Just as women are capable of sinning as a result of their own willfulness as Adam did, men are capable of sinning as a result of Satan's deception as Eve did. Neither capacity is in any way unique to a certain gender. And even if it were, how does a propensity for willful sin constitute a better candidate for a teacher and leader? After all, if Eve's tendency toward deception is transferred to all women, then Adam's tendency toward willfulness must be transferred to all men. And all of this would still leave unexplained the fact that men have been responsible for far more theological errors across the centuries than women have been. No, Paul is not saying that women are more prone to be deceived than men. He is simply saying that the Ephesian women are especially susceptible to Satan's deception which causes him to give an example of someone else who fell victim to the same cunning device.

Are women uniquely guilty of the first sin and therefore banned from teaching and leading? If this disqualification is their permanent punishment, one can only wonder why they suffer more than men since Adam's sin was more serious. The verse states quite clearly that Adam was not a victim of the deception that caused Eve to sin. His eyes were wide open to what he was doing, yet he still did it. This must explain why the Bible attributes sin and death to him rather than to Eve or to the couple (Romans 5:12–14; 1 Corinthians 15:21–22). If women deserve or inherit a restriction of their roles because of Eve's sin, then men should be left with an equal or more severe restriction because of Adam's sin. The truth of Scripture is that both sinned, and everyone thereafter has sinned (Romans 3:23).

Paul is not assigning special gullibility or extra guilt to half of the human race. He is simply making provision for the Ephesian women who are being particularly targeted with false teaching. He is trying to protect them from succumbing to it and to prevent them from spreading it. In so doing he makes reference to their "sister" who was also targeted by Satan's trickery. She, unfortunately, also serves as an example of the very scenario that he is trying to avoid among them, a scenario that is probably already occurring, namely, believing the deception and influencing others to do likewise. If they will follow the provisions of verses 11–12, this cycle will stop.

Paul is not making a universal gender statement about women in this passage any more than he is making a universal gender statement about men in 2 Timothy 3:8 when he refers to the men who were targeting the women. In both instances he simply uses an Old Testament illustration to make his point clear. If there is one point being made in 1 Timothy 2:11–14, it is that the women must learn; if there is one reason tucked into Paul's illustration, it is to avoid the ill effects of deception both on the women and on others.

Perhaps Adam did have a slight "advantage" over Eve, mentioned in verse 13. Because he was formed first, he heard the words of God directly, "You must not eat from the tree of the knowledge of good and evil" (Genesis 2:17). Eve evidently heard them indirectly via Adam since she did not yet exist when they were spoken. Likewise, the Ephesian women had lived their entire lives with some direct access disadvantages. When Satan had approached them in the past with the errors of the cults and more recently with new heresies (5:15), they were quick to lunge themselves forward just as Eve had, not realizing their vulnerability. If Ephesus were sent off course by these exuberant, influential women, the effects across the empire and across history would be enormous. The focus of this entire passage is avoiding deception by learning, not assigning blame or prescribing punishments.

One other twist of possibility is worth mentioning in any effort to fully understand verses 13–14. Some scholars see in these two verses a refutation of various first-century heresies. There is evidence that Eve was embraced and revered by certain fertility cults. There is also evidence that a version of gnosticism that used myths to reverse numerous Old Testament accounts put Eve in a similar position of esteem. She was said to have been created before Adam and to have been involved in his creation. Rather than being deceived into error, she was said to have been the mediator through which true knowledge of the spiritual realm entered the world. Because of this she was to be viewed more highly than Adam; and women were said to be suited for acting as men's mediators, teachers, leaders. The two verses do refute these teachings and would have served to humble any female superiority that was creeping into the church. Verse 12 can even be seen in this light with its references to teaching and leading men. Some scholars translate verse 12 as saying "to teach or to instigate violence toward a man," reflecting some of the anti-male stances of first-century feminism. Others translate the verse as saying, "to teach or to represent herself as originator of man."[10] Whether or not any such translation of verse 12 is accepted, the possible refutation of cultic or gnostic errors in verses 13–14 is interesting.

Childbearing

1 Timothy 2:15 is one of the most challenging verses in all of the New Testament to interpret with complete satisfaction. Neither those who oppose women ministers nor those who favor them offer an explanation that is entirely without difficulty. Fortunately, the verse is not the pivotal point of the passage. It can shed light on verses 11–14, and it should connect with them in a very convincing way. However, it may be necessary to walk

away from this overall passage with some minor uncertainties about verse 15.

One of the challenges of the verse is Paul's switch from the singular third person (she), which is wrapped up in the word "saved," to the plural third person (they), which is contained in the word "continue." Does this signal two different subjects? If so, who are they and how do they relate to each other? A second challenge is felt with any attempt to define his use of "saved." Is he referring to spiritual salvation, and if so, how does the physical act of childbearing have any ability to affect the spiritual realm of salvation? If, instead, he is referring to physical salvation, how does one explain the fact that women of faith do die in childbirth?

Since Eve was the focus of attention in the preceding verse, it is most likely that "she" refers to her. However, the focus of the overall passage is the Ephesian women, so Paul may be viewing Eve as representative of them and all other women and be simultaneously referring to them as he prepares to shift back into the plural. In other words, it would not be wrenching his wording to conclude that "she" and "they" refer to the same subject, namely, women in general. It should be noted that he made a shift earlier from the plural (2:9) to the singular (2:11) without necessarily changing subjects. If this explanation is not accepted, it is almost impossible to explain how persons in the present or future ("they") could determine ("*if*") the salvation of Eve ("she").

Assuming, then, that all of verse 15 refers to women in general, including the Ephesian women, the next task is to determine why Paul cites childbearing in such a significant way. The preposition "dia" that precedes the word "childbearing" can carry the idea of "by means of" or "through the midst of," so more than one rendering exists. In fact, at least six major views are available to explain the entire expression "she will be saved by/through childbearing."[11]

First, those who oppose women entering ministry usually say that childbearing represents the proper and ideal role that women should aspire to fulfill. This is, of course, in contrast to the teaching and leading roles that are said to be "off limits" by God's design. Because motherhood is ordained for them, they are to work out their salvation within it. In all fairness to this view, there is no claim that childbearing actually saves a woman because Paul offers the qualification "*if* they continue in faith, love and holiness with propriety." However, this view does emphasize the importance of a woman demonstrating righteousness by accepting her domestic role rather than stubbornly and sinfully resisting it.

Even when presented fairly, this first view has several serious flaws. It seems odd that immediately after mentioning the creation account, Paul would overlook the fact that producing children was a creation assignment given *equally* to both the woman *and the man* (Genesis 1:28). It is also difficult to contend that childbearing is as distinctly righteous as this view requires since far more ungodly women engage in it than godly women, oftentimes as a direct result of fornication or adultery. And, of course, there are obvious exclusions of married women who are childless and of single women who have chosen ministry over marriage which Paul actually calls the better way (1 Corinthians 7:7 with "anthropos" requiring the translation "persons" and 1 Corinthians 7:34). Motherhood is an acceptable role, a wonderful role, and a common role for women. It cannot, however, be depicted as the proper or ideal role for them because this does not align with the rest of Scripture. It certainly cannot be depicted as preventing entry into other roles such as teaching and leading because the Bible presents many godly women as entering these areas.

The second view claims that women are not being relegated to a role that is assigned by God but to a role that is dictated by their culture as proper for them. As a means of guarding the church's outside witness, women are being asked to essentially confine themselves to acceptable behavior rather than enter areas viewed by society as only open to men. This, of course, would require a different explanation of the preceding verses than has been given. It would require a rendering that hinges on a concern for the Ephesians' testimony as it impacts the advancement of the gospel. The problem with this view is that in connecting the culturally determined restrictions of verses 11–12 with a reference to scriptural material in verses 13–14, Paul would be condoning the cultural restrictions and giving them biblical basis, something he would not have done.

A third view focuses upon the presence of the definite article "the" before the word "childbearing" in the Greek text. The expression "the childbearing" is taken to refer to a specific birth, namely, that of the Savior. The idea, then, in moving from verse 14 to verse 15 is that even though Eve carries a unique responsibility for the entry of sin into the world, the immediate response of God's grace was to give her an equally unique opportunity to participate in His provision of salvation (Genesis 3:15). Without overstating her involvement or the involvement of any other woman, including Mary, it can be said that God gave her a special role in His plan to reverse sin. This would fit well with a passage that is all about reversing the consequences of sin by giving women the opportunity to learn, something that male chauvinism had long denied them. If it was necessary for Paul to point out Eve's deception and sin, he intends here to balance the comment and remove any undue sting or stigma from her epitaph.

The fourth view switches the meaning of "she shall be saved" from the spiritual realm to the physical realm and says that women can receive divine protection from one of the most troublesome, threatening consequences of sin, specifically, the pain of childbirth. As is well known, labor pain is only symptomatic of the rigor of birthing a baby, rigor that can put a woman's life at great risk. This was so well known in the ancient world that prayers for safety were common. While it is true that Paul's other uses of "saved" refer to redemption, most of the uses of the verb in Greek literature refer to some type of physical relief or rescue, with several examples appearing in the Gospels and in Acts. So, physical deliverance would have been an optional meaning to an ancient reader, perhaps the more likely meaning in direct reference to an activity such as childbearing.[12] This view is not necessarily weakened by the fact that godly women sometimes die in childbirth any more than the reality of healing is negated by the fact that godly people oftentimes die from illness. What Paul is citing may be a general provision of God's grace that believing women can know about and call upon, rather than feeling as if they are outside of His care in this one area of their lives. Just as He is willing to intervene in the relational consequences of sin by opening male opportunities to women (v. 11), He is willing to intervene in the physical consequences as well.

The fifth view places the meaning back into the spiritual realm. After all, Paul has just referred to Eve as being a sinner, clearly a spiritual designation. According to the theology of Judaism, and there was a large population of Jews in Ephesus, all women carried enormous responsibility for Eve's wrongdoing. The pain of childbirth and its frequent threat of death served as constant, undeniable reminders of their "cursed status." Paul may be saying here that believing women can engage in childbearing, including the pain that so reminds everyone of Eve's sin, and yet still be saved individuals. He may be saying nothing more than that this does not constitute a contradiction. Of course, as with each view, his qualifying phrase "if they continue in faith, love and holiness with propriety" makes it clear that their spiritual standing is dependent upon their walk with God.

The sixth view is similar to the fifth but adds the idea that Paul is specifically refuting Ephesian heresies that oppose marriage (4:3). Even though the fertility cults and gnosticism both featured considerable sexual promiscuity, strong elements within both advocated anti-sex beliefs. Obviously, anti-marriage and anti-sex notions would stand in opposition to childbearing, perhaps seeing it as the predicament of less spiritual women. According to this view Paul is saying something similar to the fifth view, that a woman can be saved and still bear children. If the rest of this passage is specifically corrective of errors and excesses affecting the Ephesian congregation, then there is room to read verse 15 in the same way.

More than one of these views seem to be defensible. What is more important, then, than mounting a case for any one perspective is noticing a non-negotiable truth found in the verse. The closing statement of verse 15 is clearly an attempt to balance or reverse something about the preceding verse or verses. Yes, Eve became a sinner, and all women after her have felt the consequences of her sin. *But*, "women will be saved." Paul is setting this note of hope in contrast to Eve's sin *and its consequences*. God's desire is to remove sin and its consequences, including sexual hierarchy. It is time for His church to join Him in this desire.

If the spiritual result of sin, death, is *destroyed* for the believer (1 Corinthians 15:54–55; 2 Timothy 1:10), is this not sufficient evidence that God wants to destroy the relational result of sin, namely, sexual hierarchy? The Bible says, in salvation, there is "neither...male nor female, for you are all one in Christ Jesus" (Galatians 3:28). Of course a woman does not cease to be a woman, nor does she desire to do so, but would the church be willing to let her cease to *suffer* because she is a woman? Jesus was willing to let women tell men the greatest news of all time, "He lives!" Would the church be willing to let women spread this same news? Would the church be willing to let them go throughout the world teaching and preaching it to everyone?

Endnotes

Chapter 1

[1] Ruth A. Tucker and Walter Liefeld, *Daughters of the Church*, (Grand Rapids: Zondervan Publishing House, 1987), 467.

[2] Ruth A. Tucker, *Women in the Maze*, (Downers Grove, IL: InterVarsity Press, 1992), 33–34.

[3] Gilbert Bilezikian, *Beyond Sex Roles*, 2d ed. (Grand Rapids: Baker Book House, 1985), 60.

[4] Richard N. Longenecker, "Authority, Hierarchy & Leadership Patterns in the Bible," in *Women, Authority & the Bible*, ed. Alvera Mickelsen (Downers Grove, IL: InterVarsity Press, 1986), 82.

Chapter 2

[1] Longenecker, 75–76.

[2] Paul K. Jewett, *MAN as Male and Female*, (Grand Rapids: William B. Eerdmans Publishing Company, 1975), 125.

[3] Mary Hayter, *The New Eve in Christ*, (Grand Rapids: William B. Eerdmans Publishing Company, 1987), 100.

[4] Jewett, 125.

[5] Jewett, 24.

[6] Jewett, 35.

[7] Jewett, 43.

[8] Jewett, 49.

[9] J.I. Packer, "Understanding the Differences," in *Women, Authority & the Bible*, ed. Alvera Mickelsen (Downers Grove, IL: InterVarsity Press, 1986), 297.

[10] Aida Besancon Spencer, *Beyond the Curse*, (Nashville: Thomas Nelson Publishers, 1985), 21.

[11] Spencer, 122; Tucker, 14.

[12] Mary J. Evans, *Woman in the Bible*, (Downers Grove, IL: InterVarsity Press, 1983), 13.

[13] Hayter, 87.

[14] Hayter, 89.

[15] Bilezikian, 24.

[16] Bilezikian, 24.

[17] Sharon Hodgin Gritz, *Paul, Women Teachers, and the Mother Goddess at Ephesus*, (Lanham, MD: University Press of America, 1991), 55.

[18] Bilezikian, 25.

[19] Tucker, 36.

[20] Matthew Henry, *A Commentary on the Holy Bible*, vol. 1, (London: Ward, Lock & Co., Ltd., 1985), 12.

[21] Bilezikian, 256.

[22] Bilezikian 255–256.

[23] Bilezikian, 256.

[24] Charles Trombley, *Who Said Women Can't Teach?*, (South Plainfield, NJ: Bridge Publishing, Inc., 1985), 70.

[25] Bilezikian, 255.

[26] E. Margaret Howe, *Women & Church Leadership*, (Grand Rapids: Zondervan Publishing House, 1982), 50.

[27] Tucker, 38.

[28] Spencer, 27,28.

[29] Jewett, 126.

[30] Marianne Meye Thompson, "Authority, Hierarchy & Leadership Patterns in the Bible—Response," in *Women, Authority & the Bible*, ed. Alvera Mickelsen (Downers Grove, IL: InterVarsity Press, 1986), 96.

[31] Evans, 16.

[32] Katherine C. Bushnell, *God's Word to Women*, (North Collins, NY: Ray B. Munson, n.d.), note 50.

[33] Bushnell, note 46.

Chapter 3

[1] Bilezikian, 56.

[2] Patricia Gundry, *Woman Be Free*, (Grand Rapids: Zondervan Publishing House, 1977), 62.

[3] Spencer, 30–31.

[4] Tucker, 46.

[5] Bilezikian, 268.

[6] Bushnell, note 94.

[7] Bilezikian, 51.

[8] Bilezikian, 51,52.

[9] Bushnell, note 100.

[10] Trombley, 115.

[11] Trombley, 19.

[12] Trombley, 113.

[13] Gundry, 62.

[14] Patricia Gundry, "Why We're Here," in *Women, Authority & the Bible*, ed. Alvera Mickelsen (Downers Grove, IL: InterVarsity Press, 1986), 12.

[15] Bilezikian, 55.

[16] Hayter, 107.

[17] Spencer, 39.

[18] Bilezikian, 55.

[19] Bilezikian, 57.

[20] Spencer, 35.

[21] Bushnell, note 94.

[22] C.S. Cowles, *A Woman's Place?* (Kansas City: Beacon Hill Press, 1993), 76.

Chapter 4

[1] Bushnell, note 595.

[2] Gritz, 60.

[3] Bushnell, note 574.

[4] Bushnell, notes 573 & 575.

[5] Bushnell, note 579.

[6] Clarence J. Vos, *Woman in Old Testament Worship*, (Delft, Netherlands: Judels and Brinkman, 1968), 117–118.

[7] Hayter, 67.

[8] Hayter, 14.

[9] Hayter, 73.

[10] Paul K. Jewett, *The Ordination of Women*, (Grand Rapids: William B. Eerdmans Publishing Company, 1980), 23.

[11] Fannie McDowell Hunter, "Women Preachers," in *Holiness Tracts Defending the Ministry of Women*, ed. Donald W. Dayton (New York: Garland Publishing, Inc., 1985), 17.

[12] Jewett, *The Ordination of Women*, 22.

[13] B.T. Roberts, "Ordaining Women," in *Holiness Tracts Defending the Ministry of Women*, ed. Donald W. Dayton (New York: Garland Publishing, Inc., 1985), 34.

[14] Hayter, 61.

[15] Gritz, 59–60.

[16] Hunter, 16.

Chapter 5

[1] Gritz, 64.

[2] Joseph R. Flower, "Does God Deny Spiritual Manifestations and Ministry Gifts to Women?" (unpublished paper, 1992), 9.

[3] Vos, 187.

[4] Bushnell, note 780.

[5] G.T. Manley, "Judges," in *The New Bible Dictionary*, ed. J.D. Douglas (Grand Rapids: William B. Eerdmans Publishing Company, 1962), 676.

[6] Evans, 23–24.

Chapter 6

[1] Hayter, 38.

[2] Hayter, 53.

[3] Spencer, 22.

[4] Jewett, *The Ordination of Women*, 30.

[5] Jewett, *The Ordination of Women*, 32.

Chapter 7

[1] A. Cohen, *The Minor Tractates of the Talmud*, (London: The Soncino Press, 1971), 288.

[2] Leonard Swidler, *Women in Judaism*, (Metuchen, NJ: The Scarecrow Press, Inc., 1976), 92.

[3] Leonard Swidler, *Biblical Affirmations of Woman*, (Philadelphia: The Westminster Press, 1979),155, 322–323.

[4] Evans, 38.

[5] Tucker and Liefeld, 56–58.

[6] Trombley, 32.

[7] Opal Reddin, "The Importance of the Ministry of Women in Church Renewal and Evangelism," (unpublished paper, n.d.), 8.

[8] Bilezikian, 98.

[9] Tucker and Liefeld, 19.

[10] Fred H. Wight, *Manners and Customs of Bible Lands*, (Chicago: Moody Press, 1953), 111.

[11] Spencer, 41.

[12] Evans, 56.

[13] Cowles, 84.

[14] Longenecker, 83.

[15] Evans, 46.

[16] Swidler, *Biblical Affirmations of Women*, 214.

[17] Tucker and Liefeld, 29.

[18] Jewett, *MAN as Male and Female*, 99.

[19] Spencer, 58.

[20] Swidler, *Biblical Affirmations of Women*, 190.

[21] Evelyn Stagg and Frank Stagg, *Woman in the World of Jesus*, (Philadelphia: The Westminster Press, 1978), 160.

[22] Swidler, *Biblical Affirmations of Women*, 204–205.

[23] Evans, 55.

[25] Bilezikian, 104.

Chapter 8

[1] Ben Witherington III, *Women in the Earliest Churches,* (Cambridge: Cambridge University Press, 1988), 111.

[2] Witherington, 112.

[3] Jewett, *MAN as Male and Female,* 146.

[4] Tucker, 98.

[5] Hayter, 136.

[6] Cowles, 103.

[7] Howe, 80.

[8] Caroline F. Whelan, "Amica Pauli: The Role of Phoebe in the Early Church," *Journal for the Study of the New Testament* 49 (March 1993): 68.

[9] Howe, 78.

[10] Howard George Liddell and Robert Scott, *A Greek-English Lexicon,* (Oxford: Clarendon, 1968), 1526.

[11] Joseph Henry Thayer, *A Greek-English Lexicon of the New Testament,* (New York: American Book Company, 1889), 549.

[12] Wesley J. Perschbacher, editor, *The New Analytical Greek Lexicon,* (Peabody, MA: Hendrickson, 1990), 355.

[13] Spencer, 116.

[14] Howe, 69.

[15] Bilezikian, 300–301.

[16] Liddell and Scott, 1013.

[17] Spencer, 110.

[18] Swidler, *Biblical Affirmations of Women,* 297.

[19] Deborah Menken Gill, "The Biblical Basis for Women in Ministry," (unpublished paper, n.d.), 30.

[20] Bilezikian, 202.

[21] Hunter, 26.

[22] Tucker and Liefeld, 70.

[23] Tucker and Liefeld, 70.

[24] Bilezikian, 281.

[25] Bushnell, note 211.

[26] Tucker and Liefeld, 73.

[27] Gill, 31.

[28] Craig S. Keener, *Paul, Women & Wives,* (Peabody, MA: Hendrickson, 1992), 241–242.

[29] Tucker and Liefeld, 73.

[30] Spencer, 102.

[31] Witherington, 115.

[32] Spencer, 102.

[33] Keener, 242.

[34] Catherine Booth, "Female Ministry: Woman's Right to Preach the Gospel," in *Holiness Tracts Defending the Ministry of Women*, ed. Donald W. Dayton (New York: Garland Publishing, Inc., 1985), 20.

Chapter 9

[1] Stanley Grenz with Denise Muir Kjesbo, *Women in the Church*, (Downers Grove, IL: InterVarsity Press, 1995), 186, 217.

[2] Grenz, 196.

[3] Grenz, 218.

[4] Hunter, 25.

[5] Jewett, *MAN as Male and Female*, 11.

Chapter 10

[1] Bilezikian, 131.

[2] Evans, 72.

[3] Keener, 139–141.

[4] Keener, 211.

[5] Gill, 24.

[6] Keener, 166.

[7] Berkeley & Alvera Mickelsen, "What Does Kephale Mean in the New Testament?" in *Women, Authority & the Bible*, ed. Alvera Mickelsen, (Downers Grove, IL: InterVarsity Press, 1986), 98.

[8] Mickelsen, 103–104.

[9] Bilezikian, 238.

[10] Gordon D. Fee, *The First Epistle to the Corinthians*, (Grand Rapids: William B. Eerdmans Publishing Company, 1987), 503, note 44.

[11] Bilezikian, 238–240.

[12] See Bilezikian, 215–252; Fee, 502–503, note 42; Keener, 34; Mickelsen, 97–132 for extensive analyses of these faulty arguments.

[13] Bilezikian, 157.

[14] Trombley, 154.

[15] Howe, 55.

[16] Don Williams, *The Apostle Paul & Women in the Church*, (Glendale, CA: Regal Books, 1977), 89.

[17] Witherington, 54–55.

[18] Evans, 118.

[19] Tucker & Liefeld, 452.

[20] Fee, 185.

Chapter 11

[1] Klyne R. Snodgrass, "Galatians 3:28: Conundrum or Solution?" in *Women, Authority & the Bible*, ed. Alvera Mickelsen, (Downers, IL: InterVarsity Press, 1986), 168.

[2] Cowles, 115.

[3] Erich H. Kiehl, "Galatians," in *The Complete Biblical Library*, ed. Thoralf Gilbrant (Springfield, MO: The Complete Biblical Library, 1986, 1989), 57.

[4] Snodgrass, 179.

[5] Hayter, #134.

Chapter 12

[1] Jewett, *MAN as Male and Female*, 53.

[2] Fee, 505–506.

[3] Bilezikian, 280, note 17.

[4] Starr, Lee Anna, *The Bible Status of Women*, (New York: Fleming H. Revell Company, 1926), 301.

[5] Trombley, 139–140.

[6] Gritz, 86.

[7] Fee, 516.

[8] Fee, 519.

[9] Starr, 309–310.

[10] Witherington, 88.

[11] Witherington, 89.

[12] Grenz, 113.

[13] Liddell & Scott, 1964.

[14] Thayer, 660.

Chapter 13

[1] Keener, 79.

[2] Gill, 38.

[3] Hayter, 130.

[4] Krister Stendahl, *The Bible and the Role of Women*, (Philadelphia: Fortress Press, 1966), 30.

[5] Hunter, 36.

[6] Witherington, 125.

[7] Jewett, *MAN as Male and Female*, 114.

[8] Bilezikian, 286.

[9] Walter C. Kaiser, Jr., *Toward an Exegetical Theology*, (Grand Rapids: Baker Book House, 1981), 76.

[10] Bilezikian, 286–287.

Chapter 14

[1] Thomas R. Schreiner, "An Interpretation of 1 Timothy 2:9–15: A Dialogue with Scholarship" in *Women in the Church*, ed. Andreas J. Kostenberger, Thomas R. Schreiner, and H. Scott Baldwin (Grand Rapids: Baker Book House, 1995), 145.

[2] Strabo, *Geography*, 7.3.3 as quoted in Richard Clark Kroeger and Catherine Clark Kroeger, *I Suffer Not a Woman*, (Grand Rapids: Baker Book House, 1992), 71.

[3] Kroeger, 117–170.

[4] Manfred T. Brauch, *Hard Sayings of Paul*, (Downers Grove, IL: InterVarsity Press, 1988), 254.

[5] Evans, 101.

[6] Cowles, 143.

[7] Spencer, 85.

[8] Keener, 112.

[9] Bilezikian, 296.

[10] Kroeger, 103.

[11] Gritz, 141–143.

[12] Keener, 118.

Works Cited

Bilezikian, Gilbert. *Beyond Sex Roles*. 2d. ed. Grand Rapids: Baker Book House, 1985.

Booth, Catherine. "Female Ministry: Woman's Right to Preach the Gospel." In *Holiness Tracts Defending the Ministry of Women*, ed. Donald W. Dayton. New York: Garland Publishing, Inc., 1985.

Brauch, Manfred T. *Hard Sayings of Paul*. Downers Grove, IL: InterVarsity Press, 1988.

Bushnell, Katherine C. *God's Word to Women*. North Collins, NY: Ray B. Munson, n.d.

Cohen, A. *The Minor Tractates of the Talmud*. London: The Soncino Press, 1971.

Cowles, C.S. *A Woman's Place?* Kansas City: Beacon Hill Press, 1993.

Evans, Mary J. *Women in the Bible*. Downers Grove, IL: InterVarsity Press, 1983.

Fee, Gordon D. *The First Epistle to the Corinthians*. Grand Rapids: William B. Eerdmans Publishing Company, 1987.

Flower, Joseph R. "Does God Deny Spiritual Manifestations and Ministry Gifts to Women?" Unpublished Paper, 1992.

Gill, Deborah Menken. "The Biblical Basis for Women in Ministry." Unpublished Paper, n.d.

Grenz, Stanley with Denise Muir Kjesbo. *Women in the Church*. Downers Grove, IL: InterVarsity Press, 1995.

Gritz, Sharon Hodgin. *Paul, Women Teachers, and the Mother Goddess at Ephesus*. Lanham, MD: University Press of America, 1991.

Gundry, Patricia. *Woman Be Free*. Grand Rapids: Zondervan, Publishing House, 1977.

_____. "Why We're Here." In *Women, Authority & the Bible*, ed. Alvera Mickelsen. Downers Grove, IL: InterVarsity Press, 1986.

Hayter, Mary. *The New Eve in Christ*. Grand Rapids: William B. Eerdmans Publishing Company, 1987.

Henry, Matthew. *A Commentary on the Holy Bible*. Vol. 1. London: Ward, Lock & Co., Ltd., 1985.

Howe, E. Margaret. *Women & Church Leadership*. Grand Rapids: Zondervan Publishing House, 1982.

Hunter, Fannie McDowell. "Women Preachers." In *Holiness Tracts Defending the Ministry of Women*, ed. Donald W. Dayton. New York: Garland Publishing, Inc., 1985.

Jewett, Paul K. *MAN as Male and Female*. Grand Rapids: William B. Eerdmans Publishing Company, 1975.

_____. *The Ordination of Women*. Grand Rapids: William B. Eerdmans Publishing Company, 1980.

Kaiser, Walter C., Jr. *Toward an Exegetical Theology*. Grand Rapids: Baker Book House, 1981.

Keener, Craig S. *Paul, Women & Wives*. Peabody, MA: Hendrickson, 1992.

Kiehl, Erich H. "Galatians." In *The Complete Biblical Library*, ed. Thoralf Gilbrant. Springfield, MO: The Complete Biblical Library, 1986.

Kroeger, Richard Clark and Catherine Clark Kroeger. *I Suffer Not a Woman*. Grand Rapids: Baker Book House, 1992.

Liddell, Howard George and Robert Scott. *A Greek-English Lexicon*. Oxford: Clarendon, 1968.

Longenecker, Richard N. "Authority, Hierarchy & Leadership Patterns in the Bible." In *Women, Authority & the Bible*, ed. Alvera Mickelsen. Downers Grove, IL: InterVarsity Press, 1986.

Manley, G.T. "Judges." In *The New Bible Dictionary*, ed. J.D. Douglas. Grand Rapids: William B. Eerdmans Publishing Company, 1962.

Mickelsen, Berkeley and Alvera Mickelsen. "What Does Kephale Mean in the New Testament?" In *Women, Authority & the Bible*, ed. Alvera Mickelsen. Downers Grove, IL: InterVarsity Press, 1986.

Packer, J.I. "Understanding the Differences." In *Women, Authority & the Bible*, ed. Alvera Mickelsen. Downers Grove, IL: InterVarsity Press, 1986.

Perschbacher, Wesley J., ed. *The New Analytical Greek Lexicon*. Peabody, MA: Hendrickson, 1990.

Reddin, Opal. "The Importance of the Ministry of Women in Church Renewal and Evangelism." Unpublished Paper, n.d.

Roberts, B.T. "Ordaining Women." In *Holiness Tracts Defending the Ministry of Women*, ed. Donald W. Dayton. New York: Garland Publishing, Inc., 1985.

Snodgrass, Klyne R. "Galatians 3:28: Conundrum or Solution?" In *Women, Authority & the Bible*, ed. Alvera Mickelsen. Downers Grove, IL: InterVarsity Press, 1986.

Spencer, Aida Besancon. *Beyond the Curse*. Nashville: Thomas Nelson Publishers, 1985.

Stagg, Evelyn and Frank Stagg. *Women in the World of Jesus*. Philadelphia: The Westminster Press, 1978.

Starr, Lee Anna. *The Bible Status of Woman*. New York: Fleming H. Revell Company, 1926.

Stendahl, Krister. *The Bible and the Role of Women*. Philadelphia: Fortress Press, 1966.

Swidler, Leonard. *Biblical Affirmations of Woman*. Philadelphia: The Westminster Press, 1979.

_____. *Women in Judaism*. Metuchen, NJ: The Scarecrow Press, Inc., 1976.

Thayer, Joseph Henry. *A Greek-English Lexicon of the New Testament*. New York: American Book Company, 1889.

Thompson, Marianne Meye. "Authority, Hierarchy & Leadership Patterns in the Bible—Response." In *Women, Authority & the Bible*, ed. Alvera Mickelsen. Downers Grove, IL: InterVarsity Press, 1986.

Trombley, Charles. *Who Said Women Can't Teach?* South Plainfield, NJ: Bridge Publishing, Inc., 1985.

Tucker, Ruth A. *Women in the Maze*. Downers Grove, IL: InterVarsity Press, 1992.

Tucker, Ruth A. and Walter Liefeld. *Daughters of the Church*. Grand Rapids: Zondervan Publishing House, 1987.

Vos, Clarence J. *Women in Old Testament Worship*. Delft, Netherlands: Judels and Brinkman, 1968.

Whelan, Caroline F. "Amica Pauli: The Role of Phoebe in the Early Church." *Journal for the Study of the New Testament* 49 (March 1993): 67–85.

Wight, Fred H. *Manners and Customs of Bible Lands*. Chicago: Moody Press, 1953.

Williams, Don. *The Apostle Paul & Women in the Church*. Glendale, CA: Regal Books, 1977.

Witherington, Ben, III. *Women in the Earliest Churches*. Cambridge: Cambridge University Press, 1988.

Scripture Index

Subject Index